GUNDOG TRAINING

GUNDOG TRAINING

Keith Erlandson

Popular Dogs
London Melbourne Sydney Auckland Johannesburg

Popular Dogs Publishing Co. Ltd

An imprint of the Hutchinson Publishing Group
17–21 Conway Street, London W1P 6JD

Hutchinson Publishing Group (Australia) Pty Ltd
16–22 Church Street, Hawthorn, Melbourne, Victoria 3122, Australia

Hutchinson Group (NZ) Ltd
32–34 View Road, PO Box 40-086, Glenfield, Auckland 10

Hutchinson Group (SA) Pty Ltd
PO Box 337, Bergvlei 2012, South Africa

First published by Barrie & Jenkins Ltd 1976
Reprinted 1978, 1980
Reprinted by Popular Dogs 1984
© Keith Erlandson 1976

Set in Century Schoolbook 10 point

Printed in Great Britain by Redwood Burn Limited,
Trowbridge, Wilts. and bound by Anchor Brendon Limited, Tiptree, Essex

ISBN 0 09 161340 X

Contents

To
Walter Rumbelow

Preface

I have been under pressure for several years to write this book from a wide section of the sporting community, including motor industry workers, gamekeepers and a Canon of the Church of England, on the grounds that there has not yet been a book written on gundog training, by a practising professional with a long list of Field Trial successes behind him. This may well be true and is rather sad.

There is a saying that those who can, do, and those who cannot, write about it, no doubt on the assumption that those really competent in their craft are too busy getting on with it to write. This is why this book has not appeared before now as I have for 37 years been fully occupied initially as a gamekeeper, and as gundog trainer for the past 27 of these. During this time I have been mainly occupied with Spaniels and have made up 19 Field Trial champions and several more winners, including two Labradors, father and son.

Gundogs and their training are a very complex subject and people of great experience and success are frequently at complete variance with each other, therefore I do not wish to impose my views upon my readers but merely to give them my opinions for what they may be worth, opinions which are backed by considerable experience and success but which should be accepted or rejected at the discretion of the reader.

I admit I have a certain number of prejudices. If I am prejudiced against a bloodline, an individual (canine or human) or an idea, I leave the subject of my views severely alone for I do not seek to impose my ideas on others. As individuals, I think we must all come to our own conclusions.

The object of this book is to provide a certain amount of amusement for the experienced reader, a good deal of instruction for the novice owner/trainer; I hope that my considerable experience of shooting game over young dogs which are trained but inexperienced may be of benefit to those who shoot but have their dogs trained by others, as it is at this stage that the training of so many good young dogs collapses, owing to lack of handling technique by the owner.

This is tragic, as the owner does not receive the benefit of the considerable amount of money he has spent and the trainer may, quite unjustifiably, be condemned for producing an inferior article.

When a book is produced which is as much an autobiography as a pure book of reference, the writer must reveal a good deal of himself. Although vociferous in argument, I have the inner reserve common to a great many Swedes. This has proved a potent additional factor in causing the delay in my writing this book.

1 How it began

I did not have the advantage of a sporting background. Both my immediate and distant forbears came from Central Sweden. My ancestors did not come to this country to burn and pillage, nor did they invade Russia or colonise the Steppes. They remained quietly behind in Sweden simply being Swedes. One of them even took part in a highly constructive project, the founding of Stockholm. His name was Birger. They decided to make him High Chief of Sweden at a period when Sweden had no kings. If this is not correct, blame Baron Hermelin of English Springer fame, who supplied this information.

The first gundog I ever saw lived on the west coast of Sweden. He was an English Setter called Tel, owned by a famous local hunter and industrialist. The main quarry of this dog was willow grouse and a few pheasants. His owner also hunted elk and roe. I visited his daughter last year after an absence of 36 years and she showed me her father's first modest trophy, the upturned slots of a roe mounted on a plaque, forming a simple but attractive walking-stick rack.

They had a couple of pups at the time I lived there; black and tan, I think they were Gordons. They were called Lippy and Lappy, the latter on account of her alleged resemblance to an old Lapp woman, which I could not myself see. Lapp women remind me of well-washed and rather high-class gypsies. Gordon Setters do not.

Although I have a mathematical blind spot, I was not completely hopeless academically but I had no inclination for further studies so I decided the only possible way for me to live the type of life I wanted, was to enter the gamekeeping profession. The idea met with considerable family opposition but I would not be dissuaded.

When I was 16 I took a job on a lovely downland estate close to Cranborne Chase. About 1,000 acres were enclosed rabbit warren and pheasant coverts and about 850 acres was farm land. At that time there was no headkeeper. I was simply given as many traps and snares as I wanted and told to catch rabbits and kill as much vermin as possible. It was also my job to maintain the eight miles of rabbit fence twice weekly, a losing battle as the warren was grossly overstocked, so much so that the does only produced one litter a year. It was unknown to kill a milky doe for the ferrets and to find a second litter inside her. On the farm, where food was plentiful, rabbits bred as rabbits normally do.

My employer, although then a fairly young man, was a squire of the old school. The youngest son of an elderly Victorian father, he had been very strictly brought up in all matters relating to shooting and this, in turn, was passed on to me. Although he has never taken part in the production of record bags, he proved one of the finest shots in the south of England. He was a brilliant high pheasant shot, would shoot dozens of bolted or walked-up rabbits with scarcely a miss and only seemed defeated by the occasional low pheasant. The question is very frequently asked, 'How high is a high pheasant?' The highest pheasant I was able positively to verify crossed the guns at 180 feet. I flushed it myself at the top of a valley and later checked on a large-scale Ordnance Survey map. Needless to say, it departed unscathed!

This was a wonderful area for wildlife. There were ravens, buzzards, passage peregrines (only one positive kill found, a magpie), roe, sika and fallow deer. A fair number of sparrow-hawks came in from the Chase and I discovered just how damaging the hen bird can be to partridge stocks when paired up in the Spring, invariably taking the hen partridge, who, older keepers assured me, is always the last of a pair to take flight.

Our rabbit warren drew a great deal of vermin as could be expected but the rabbits did act as a buffer between predators and game. Foxes and sparrowhawks would take game but stoats and buzzards concentrated on rabbits, and badgers on the young rabbit nests. I shot the first two grey squirrels ever recorded in the area and caused the housekeeper considerable conster-nation when I asked her to cook them. They were just as good as the Americans would have us believe.

During this period I learned a lot about gamekeeping, shooting manners and how to put high pheasants over the guns, but very little about gundogs. My boss loved dogs (as opposed to bitches, who did dreadful things to his lawn and upset the dogs with their bi-annual nuisance) but he was no handler. He had a Clumber Spaniel which was a really fine example of the breed and had been originally perfectly trained by his vendor. Although formerly rock steady, he was now wild but, on account of the nature of the breed, was never the menace that a Springer or Labrador would have been. He seldom chased a rabbit more than 30 yards–they seldom got further–but in the rare event of a miss, he usually abandoned the chase fairly soon and never rioted ahead looking for fresh game. He was a superb pigeon dog.

We had a small additional shoot that was good for nothing but pigeon flighting. The Clumber would run in to the fall of every bird, his marking being superb. He was surprisingly fast in spite of his short legs and 70 pounds weight. After the pigeon we would stay on for the crows. He was very clever at collecting a wounded crow, holding it so that it could not spike him.

At the end of the season Bill Spinks arrived to take over as headkeeper. He came from the Himley Estate in the Midlands, although originally an East Anglian. He was a first-class man of the old school, terribly vermin conscious and could drive a pheasant just where he wanted it. It had been decided to augment our small wild pheasant stock by rearing a few hundred. Spinks was a very gentle, deliberate man. He fed the wild pheasants right through the Spring and Summer on combined waste. He never let me near his coverts and took great pleasure when his individually known hens appeared on the feed ride with their chicks.

In the Spring, I was detailed to catch some hens on another shoot, a huge conifer forest quite useless from a shooting angle. Spinks showed me how to operate the wire catchers and off I went on a bicycle several miles every day, and twice a day on catching days. Some of his maxims were: always use 2 inch mesh or they will skin their heads; never attempt to move a bird until both legs are firmly held; never put more than three birds in a sack or they may smother; always lift your catcher after a set, whether it has caught or not.

The birds laid and hatched well and were put in open coops among the ant hills. Spinks swore he had never seen birds do better. In addition to the ants and ant eggs, we gave them a simple feed of minced boiled rabbits, soaked flaked maize and barley meal to dry it off. He subsequently reared birds year after year on the same ground with marvellous results. The ant supply never failed. How different from the massive indoor rearing programmes of today. Our birds were sleek, tight feathered and grew evenly. Feather picking and mass exodus from the coverts were unknown as every bird knew its mother hen.

The rest of my gamekeeping career was spent in Lincoln-shire and Norfolk. I was by this time keenly interested in gundogs but so far had been unable to do anything about it. I had read a book before I left school, a paperback, *Gundogs. Modern Methods of Training* by P. R. A. Moxon. Something was mentioned about Field Trial dogs being faster than the ordinary shooting dog. I liked that bit. If I had a dog I would like it to be able really to gallop.

At the time I read this book, a fierce controversy was raging in the sporting press as to whether a dog should be allowed to carry fur in its first season or whether wildfowling dogs should run in or be rock steady. The main combatants were my literary idol, the late Dugald MacIntyre and Peter Moxon, with a trainer, Ronald MacDonald, whipping-in. MacIntyre said 'No' to the first question and 'Yes' to the second, they should be steady. Moxon said 'Yes' and 'No' respectively and Ronnie said all sorts of things. In the light of personal experience, I now hold the view that MacIntyre was wrong on the first point and right on the second.

Now, I decided, I would get myself a dog. I saw an advertise-ment for some Golden Retriever pups, reared, so it read, on unlimited surplus goat's milk; dogs were five guineas, bitches four guineas. The advertiser lived close to the Welsh border, not far from where I now live. I phoned the seller and he agreed to send me a bitch. She duly arrived by train, a small slim bitch, four months old, very gentle but not a nervous trait in her. I trained her according to the book and she was un-believably easy. Her pedigree contained a good deal of Haulston blood. I now owned a trial-bred bitch.

I had my troubles with her. I had her innoculated but the vaccine/virus method currently in use, was, to quote Peter Moxon 'more to be feared than distemper'. She showed an adverse reaction to the vaccine, went completely off colour and would not eat a thing. Eventually she recovered then, at six months, had several attacks of hysteria, at that time quite common among dogs.

I found that when I had her out on my own I could do

anything with her for she was perfectly steady. One of our guns, whom I took into a covert to shoot pigeon, made me a good offer for her when he saw her perform on what he shot. One bird in particular planed down outside the wood into a clover field. We went to the edge of the wood, I put her across the dyke and a hundred yards beyond to collect the bird and thought nothing of it. I had then never seen a field trial handler struggling to collect a bird, nor suffered the same ordeal myself. Dogwork seemed very easy!

I started to take her out on shooting days but things seemed different. I had my beaters to look after and she began to take less notice of me and eventually started running in to the occasional shot bird without my realising it. A bird would get up, there would be a shot and soon after the bitch would push a bird at me. She pulled off some brilliant retrieves and really could get runners. In fact, she became quite a legend as a bag filler and was really good on diving duck. I bred a litter of pups from her by a local dog of unexciting breeding, but a fair proportion of the pups were surprisingly good. I would hang a whole calf or sheep up in the skin for the pups who would soon sort it out. A rough and ready method of puppy rearing but they did well enough on it.

It was during this period that I met my wife. One of the most essential aspects of gundog training, particularly when one has field trials in view, is having the ability to pick the right prospects. However successful I may have been in this sphere, I certainly made no mistake over my wife. If one picks the wrong pup, it can easily be disposed of but pick the wrong woman and the procedure is far more complicated and certainly costly! I happened to go down to the village and tied my pony to a milkstand whilst I made some purchases and sent some skins away. The pony was fresh up from grass, restive and unused to a halter. She pulled the milkstand from its moorings and proceeded to drag it around. It made a horrible grating sound and doors and windows opened all round the village square. The farmer who owned the stand rushed out cursing black, blue and purple but he often shot with us and quickly cooled down. I noticed a girl was taking in the proceedings with an amused look on her face and, I imagined, a little something more than amusement too. We were married 18 months later.

We moved to Norfolk to a purely wild game beat where there

were a lot of rabbits to contend with in terribly rough coverts or 'carrs'. I was, by this time, a particularly good rabbit trapper and had already accounted for thousands but here was very little scope for trapping as burrows were almost non-existent. I did a lot of snaring but the gun became more important in rabbit control.

I decided to breed from my Retriever again. It happened in 1952 that the Golden Retriever Treunair Carla won the Retriever Championship at Six Mile Bottom. To get my bitch to Sussex where Carla lived was quite an undertaking but, thanks to the co-operation of his owner, who met me at a London station, this was effected. She had no pups but I had the transaction tied up that my fee was to be refunded in the event of a non-success. Carla's owner asked me if I would like a six-month-old bitch pup instead of my fee. I jumped at the chance. This bitch was sired by Carla and I had my first taste of a complicated dog. She made a huge, heavy boned bitch with a great, masculine head and a very thick, dark red coat. She was not difficult in early obedience training but her general attitude was rather sullen and she seemed dull compared with my other bitch, who was, I realise now, top class trial material if I had known what to do with her. She retrieved dummies and duck naturally but would not handle a pheasant until her second season.

Our flight pond was a fairly large, natural daytime resting place where the duck were flighted in the morning and a bag of a hundred wild duck was by no means exceptional. The guns took to their butts before daylight. Some had dogs and picked their birds as they shot them which was a great help and those East Anglian Retrievers really could find game. More guns, however, were dogless. I used to go to a small marshy piece on my beat to keep duck from settling on it whilst shooting was in progress, then went to the lake to assist with the pick up. The conditions for dogs and handlers were atrocious. There was a wide margin of soft mud around the open water into which dog and man sank at every step. The cover was dreadfully thick, with a flat rush which cut the eye corners and noses of the dogs. Alan Savory once wrote some kind things about the coypu and how they would, by eating the reeds, keep a lot of water open for duck which would otherwise become choked. This situation applied at Raynham Lake. The coypu, with their powerful scent, were certainly 'riot' as far as the dogs were concerned but without them the cover would have been even thicker and they made platforms of cut reeds which were very useful to climb on to, from which to work a dog.

The bitch once brought me a mallard duck, still warm, with great chunks of flesh bitten from the breasts. Whatever had done this must have had its meal whilst shooting was in progress. I would imagine that an otter would have the cheek, as there were some about. Otters are seldom seen, in fact I have only seen two adult otters going about their lawful business, but they can be quite fearless and this particular otter was no doubt accustomed to shooting and knew it spelt no danger for him but an easy meal. Being very intelligent animals, this would not take much working out.

As Raynham was a pure wild bird shoot, we had to be very vermin conscious. The headkeeper was Jack Batten who, like Bill Spinks, was a master at showing his birds but, unlike Spinks who had natural valleys to drive his birds over, Batten had to utilise the slightest undulations in the ground to get his birds well up. I have seen him station beaters with flags in a stand in front of his flushing point, where most people would have stood their guns, their function being to flag the birds as they came over, making them give an extra lift for his guns who stood much further back, some down in an old chalk pit.

We had little fox trouble for this was real stoat and rat country. We kept our tunnel traps going and patrolled our partridge nests daily to ensure no stoat had slipped through the cordon of traps, to molest our sitting birds. This sometimes did happen, then it was all-out vigilance until the particular stoat was located and trapped. A stoat would seldom kill the sitting bird. It would usually snatch a bunch of feathers from the partridge as it escaped, then molest the eggs. Usually the work of a bitch, I did, however, have one old dog stoat that worked a hedge and killed two English partridges and a Frenchman. He ignored the best meat on the breasts and stripped the wings and back, as a sparrowhawk does when it starts on a kill.

I had a large marshy common on one of my boundaries that attracted a good number of carrion crows. Here I used the moorland method, setting my traps under water in the numerous pools and pegging a rabbit or balancing an egg out beyond. If the traps were correctly placed, the crow quickly drowned and did not signal its distress to the local crow population, causing them to become trap shy.

I thought that I had a real prospect in my young golden but I was soon to be disillusioned. She was certainly steady but the first time I took her out was on a boundary day when we were out to kill some outlying pheasants in the beet fields of our main partridge beat. A cock was soon killed, I sent my bitch and she mismarked, then proceeded to hunt all over the place, sending fresh birds in all directions. I had omitted to train her to the stop whistle. If Moxon's early publication had mentioned such a thing, I had certainly overlooked it.

After the shoot, Jack Batten informed me that I was incapable of controlling a dog once it left my heel. He was no mean dog handler himself and certainly pointed out the reality of the situation to me. A day or two later, he brought me word from on high that I was henceforth banned from ever bringing a dog out again on a shooting day, something which I hope will give heart to readers who may have found themselves on the wrong end of a recalcitrant dog in good company. I have, of course, since witnessed some of our top field trial handlers in identical circumstances but this was no comfort to me. Only *my* dogs ever behaved in such a disgraceful way.

My next place was on a large, rambling, heavy land beat in south Lincolnshire. It was rather badly appointed with the best covert right on the boundary. The other woods were lacking in bottom cover and badly placed for driving. Vermin was very plentiful and there was a fox problem, aggravated by the fact that the period was shortly after the initial outbreak of myxomatosis. The estate was bordered on one side for some miles by intermittent thick forestry, quite unkeepered. We had to show foxes but the policy was simple. In the Spring and Summer we killed every fox we could. In the Winter they moved in from the forestry and we never killed a fox during the hunting season. Hounds never drew blank.

After many years close contact with the predator/prey problem, I am quite satisfied that the fox is the greatest potential menace to game on any terrain. At no time of the year are birds completely safe from him, as even, when mature, some birds insist on jugging on the ground. On this estate, one vixen took 14 hen pheasants and two partridges from their nests from one farm lane alone before she was apprehended. This was on a piece of ground not under the jurisdiction of the keepers. Had it been so, I will admit that had the nests been found and some protective measures used, some of this damage could possibly have been prevented. Second only to the fox I would place the stoat and carrion crow. According to local circumstances, other species can be troublesome. Tawny owls are unlikely to take wild game but can be a positive menace to poults in covert; rats, badgers and hedgehogs can all be a nuisance to partridge eggs and buzzards, when rabbits are absent, can knock the stuffing out of pheasant poults. Cats can be deadly but lack the cunning of wild predators.

The open rearing field encouraged a lot of bad habits. Kestrels, sparrowhawks, jackdaws, and once, I recorded, a hobby, have all taken their toll. Weasels are very pretty but were hardly benevolent little beasts on the open field. Merlins will take far more pipits than grouse chicks. Peregrines will kill grouse on a moor but when the peregrine was far stronger in status in North Wales than is now the case, there were far more grouse. A peregrine is quite capable of taking a healthy grouse but will obviously first clean up the pricked birds as they are bound to be the laggards in a covey.

In this post-myxomatosis period I caught one stoat which, as usual, I skinned, then dissected to find out what it was living on. He had in his stomach, the remains of a rat, including the foot. Being a keen biologist, this was not the first stoat I had dissected. Years previously, I had discovered that the stoat carries his heart in a most peculiar location, namely, a full two inches behind his shoulder which, in a small animal like a stoat, means almost in the middle of his body.

A keeper's wage was not particularly good at this period and with three small children, we were very hard up. Our head-keeper was Walter Rumbelow, a Suffolk man who had been on the estate 25 years. I told him of my financial problem and he came up with the suggestion that I trained a few gundogs for clients, as he always did when he himself lived on my beat. Then he came out with a pronouncement which revolutionised the whole problem of gundog training for me. He said, 'If yew call yer dorg, 'n 'ee 'ont storp, dewn yer gun'n git arfter 'im, 'n when yew catch 'un give 'im a fourlettering good 'idin.'

With modifications, depending on the toughness or sensitivity of the subject, this put the whole problem of gundog training firmly within my grasp, as it could do for anyone willing to adopt the broad principle, which is that when a disobedient or rioting dog finds his handler right out there with him where he thinks he is having fun, he will realise that mere coverage of terrain is no insurance against the wrath of his handler.

Jack Batten pointed out what was wrong. Walter Rumbelow showed me how to put it right.

I bred a litter of Retrievers that year. Mazurka of Wynford had won the 1954 Championship so I sent the Carla bitch to him but he would have none of her. She had grown into a huge, heavy creature and I was told that she would charge Zurka and knock him flying with a resulting dampening of his ardour. I was alternatively offered the use of Mastersinger, Zurka's litter brother, a shooting dog who had not competed in trials. He managed to get her in whelp but she only had three very small pups. My wife said, 'Big women have small babies'. Do they? The bitch's maternal instinct appeared to be very limited but she managed to rear them. I sold the smallest bitch, kept the larger which I should have sold and sold the dog which subsequent events proved I should have kept.

Prior to 1955, I had only seen three working Springers. One belonged to Bob Thirsk, keeper on the Burton Constable Estate in East Yorkshire, one to Geoff Nunn, then headkeeper on Stenigot, Lincolnshire and the other to Reg Vernon, head-keeper on the Arbury Estate in Warwickshire. They were all extremely efficient, well trained dogs of Field Trial type, in fact Reg Vernon's was my ideal type. He was a very powerful dog, very fast but with a nose for gamefinding, had abundant stamina and was a good retriever with a mouth to match. I have no idea how he was bred but I would guess that he was sired by a straight O'Vara dog.

Following Walter Rumbelow's suggestion that I should take in a few dogs to train, I placed an advertisement in a shooting paper. The response was very good. One man from Essex, stated that he had bought a 12-month old bitch from a very well-known northern breeder. She was apparently very shy and particularly disliked children, a trait which was to persist for another 16 years. Her name was 'Bee' after her mother, F. T. C. Breckonhill Bee, winner of the first post-war Springer Championship. She was registered as Breckonhill Brando, though why anyone should name a bitch after a male film star remains a mystery although, I must admit, she never spoke very much!

She arrived at our local station and the porter was afraid she had died in the box, as she lay in the bottom without a movement. I assured him she would be all right, pulled her out and walked her on a lead the three miles home. I brought her inside the house, where she promptly disappeared behind a piece of furniture and remained there. I left her a meal of meat greaves and flaked maize and in the morning it had vanished.

I spent about three weeks taking her about with me on a long cord, feeding and watering my 130 pheasants and going round my tunnel traps. Gradually she began to accept me and would retrieve a dummy at top speed but with a hold so light that a thistle would knock it out of her mouth. It was at this point that she took over and proceeded to teach me what a Spaniel really was. I was amazed at her reaction to command, after my headstrong Retrievers and the way in which she would fling herself down to the stop whistle was quite unbelievable. We had a lot of big combined stubbles which held a large number of hares and wild pheasants. It was here that she showed me how a Spaniel should quarter its ground and use the wind, without pulling away on footscents, although even I knew sufficient to insist that she did not line.

The first thing I shot for her was a duck which fell into a small stream. It looked dead enough as it came down but she was unable to find it. Exactly three weeks later I shot a duck skimming in very low to a small pond. It was Bee's duck. A most wonderful piece of natural surgery had taken place. The wing had been broken high up the body, which, in my experience, is the most common cause of a bird falling as though stone dead and then disappearing. Fresh bone tissue had formed around the break and the wing was fully functional again. Despite her originally light mouth, she soon learned to handle a hare very cleverly, taking it by the muscles of the back in such a position as to turn the legs upwards out of the way. I would take her out for a hunt and she might find 20 hares and several pheasants in a short space of time.

Her owner eventually took her home and was delighted with her. The following season he ran her in a trial and won a Reserve at the first attempt. She ran in at the next one and it appeared that as her owner was not used to the breed, she was developing a head of steam. I offered to have her back to straighten her out and run her in a few trials myself.

During the Summer, I had been training my Golden Retriever pup. She was almost absurdly easy and so steady and honest that I never had to lay a finger on her. She lacked drive however, and whereas she was quick out and back with a marked bird, moved slowly when being handled blind. Her brother was also back for training, a big rawboned dog who could equal any Spaniel in brambles and was extraordinarily intelligent. He was the one I should have kept.

I still fondly imagined that a steady dog was all one required to win trials but I was over 20 years out of date. Speaking of the field trials in the thirties, one veteran handler later told me, 'If you had a steady dog, you were in the first four.' I ran her in three trials. She started off well in her first by ignoring a hare which ran under her nose when she was 40 yards out on a retrieve of a dead hare. Later, on being asked to try a bird about sixth dog down, she decided there were too many people clustered about and turned a little crowd shy, refusing to go out. After all, ten months of age was a bit young for an Open Stake! I tried her again in another trial under the four judge system with no more success.

One of the judges was a very fierce little man who, although he never ran a dog, seemed to do an awful lot of judging but now seems to have faded out. He really ruined my concentration, so I hardly knew what I was up to. At one point, some birds had been shot by a forward gun, who had moved away from his stand to allow the judges to use the birds, leaving his cartridge bag and shooting stick at his peg. I was told to collect a bird. I pushed her out and she retrieved his cartridge bag!

My next trial was a novice dog and novice handler stake held at Bartlow, Essex. We had three kind judges—Andrew Wylie, John Kent and Dr. Gann. Being in novice company and having three pleasant judges, had, I think, a beneficial psychological effect upon me. The bitch did some quite good work and was awarded third prize. I could scarcely believe my good fortune. Before I ran her, I had never even been to a trial as a spectator and was now meeting famous field trial personalities in the flesh who had hitherto only been names in the press.

Bee was now back in the kennel with a steadiness problem to be straightened out. This was accomplished one day close on dusk. She was hunting up on my left and began to feather on a bird. I let her line the bird and kept myself parallel to her course. The bird flushed and I killed it as close to her nose as possible. My gun was on the ground almost before the bird was and I scooped her up before she could touch the bird. I was beginning to find out that I had a particularly quick reaction in situations such as this, which has stood me in good stead for many years.

From these early times, in the event of a problem arising with a dog, I would never attempt to suppress the trouble but would encourage the dog, so swift and positive action could be taken. It is no use cautioning and nagging a dog that is not 100 per cent steady. One can never be sure of it. Far better to keep quiet and see that the dog really does wrong, then administer swift retribution. One gains the dog's respect and can be assured that it knows right from wrong.

Our first Spaniel Trial was the Essex. I had trained Bee to cope with any situation which might arise on the estate and it so happened we had no wire fences to negotiate, so I had never thought of teaching her to jump. Our first bird lay in a gully, over a simple rabbit netting fence, but naturally she did not know what the fence was all about. We had our eye wiped by the oddest little Cocker I have even seen. It must have been a good one as it won the Stake. Its first trial, too.

I do not believe in making the same mistakes twice, so jumping lessons were immediately placed on the agenda. I soon taught her to be a competent jumper and, needless to say, was never faced with a bird over a fence in a trial ever again, at least, not with Bee.

Our next trial was held in heavy woodlands in Northamptonshire. Bee always went her best in heavy woodland. It almost seemed as though a canopy of trees over her head brought out something extra from her. It was one of those very rare occasions when everything fell into place. She started off by doing a very good eye wipe right across the wood. She had marked the opposite dog's bird. I knew she could remember a mark almost indefinitely, so I took it from where we stood. She found several birds, picked a woodcock, collected a runner and stayed rock steady 20 yards out when a bird fell almost on top of her and fluttered. She ran a beautiful run off, beating her brace-mate in very convincing fashion and finishing off with a find and retrieve, well out in the most appalling brambles. She won the trial under two of the toughest judges we had in the country.

So, with one Open Stake under my belt and £190 capital, mainly derived from training fees and the sale of two litters of Dachshunds, I decided to become a free-lance professional trainer.

2 In at the deep end

It appears that anyone aspiring to become a gundog trainer at the present time, first finds a suitable property from which to conduct his business, then acquires a friendly bank manager and attempts to convince him that a great deal of money can be made from gundog training and boarding, and any funds advanced by the bank to finance the project could easily be repaid within the stipulated period.

As my accumulated capital was hardly likely to impress even the most benevolent of bank managers, a species I am not at all convinced exists, the idea of buying a place of our own was definitely out.

A few miles away was a large difficult shoot, consisting of huge blocks of forestry, surrounded by arable on two sides, a disused aerodrome on one and a rapacious neighbour on another. For several seasons this shoot had been run by a syndicate who employed a keeper but results were not sufficiently encouraging to justify the continued expense, so the keeper and the syndicate had parted company more or less by mutual consent.

I contacted the head of the syndicate and offered to look after the shoot on a part-time basis in return for the keeper's cottage and facilities to train my dogs. He seemed to think this would be a good arrangement and told me I could shoot all the pheasants on the woodside overlooking the rapacious neighbour.

Somehow or other, quite a few dogs came in for training, although the time was rather late in the Summer. It was good country for dog training. There was always plenty of scent and a good variety of cover. Rabbits were beginning to reappear, so it was not difficult to persuade the Spaniels to dig in and there was plenty to shoot. Walking around the wood and up the rides, I could put out quite a lot of pigeon. This type of work is particularly good for starting young dogs on fieldwork, particularly Retrievers. Some birds drop in the open, others in thick cover.

This was a good area both for training dogs and for business, but my arrangement with the syndicate was not sufficiently watertight for me, so I began to look elsewhere.

I was offered a house and 200 acres to rent in Caernarvonshire with an additional 5,000 acres of mountain, moor and forest. The idea I had in mind was to form a syndicate of my own, to cover rent and expenses and to keeper it myself.

I had previously been just inside Wales to a Spaniel Trial and had been fascinated by the country but never had I seen anything to compare with the rugged grandeur of Snowdonia.

Some time later I was taken to a Trial in the north of England by another competitor. I met Colin Thomson who asked me if I would train some Spaniels for him. Looking back, I can now say that it was Colin's dogs who kept me afloat over the next 12 months and more. Without them I would not have survived.

I had a very poor Trial season that year. Never have I since had a dog more experienced than Bee was that season which proves that when the dice is loaded against you, experience does not help you to win.

The time drew near for our departure from Lincolnshire and an event may be worth recording which happened that season.

There were quite a lot of wild fallow deer in the neighbourhood and I had skinned an old buck who had been shot in a fox drive when I worked on the estate. The keepers were unused to deer and imagined it would weigh like a small bullock. They were staggered when I got it on to my back and carried it out of the covert. This buck had really had a rough time. One antler was spiralled like a corkscrew in such a manner that no injury when in velvet could have caused it. A pellet of AA in a testicle supplied the answer. He had shot of varying sizes in other parts of his anatomy.

Just before we left, I decided to try for a doe. I had a 7mm Mauser with which I had shot several red deer on some high ground in Derbyshire and one evening found a buck and two does feeding outside a covert. The light was fading and as I had only iron sights as opposed to a 'scope, which would have given me better vision, I had a very good stalk over a stubble to get within 80 yards of the beasts. The doe I picked still appeared as a pretty slim target through my sights but I fetched her down with a shoulder shot. She, too, was a fairly old beast and I found at least three different sizes of shot in her.

I found it very sad that these two beasts had both suffered so unnecessarily and I have often wondered since, with the sport of woodland stalking gaining momentum throughout the country, whether these Lincolnshire deer are now getting a better deal.

The dogs were put into temporary accommodation when we arrived in the Gwibernant and I started work almost immediately on kennel construction. I had brought some floors and roofs from our last place, which I originally constructed plank by plank and made some concrete run bases which I mixed by hand. I also managed to puncture our domestic water pipe when digging post holes. I put up a rabbit pen of about a quarter of an acre in a situation which had an old stone wall for shelter and natural bracken cover.

It was far different country from a dog training point of view to any I had ever lived in before. Whereas I had always had plenty of game to work on, here there was just a sprinkling.

I did find one piece of forestry which had several rabbits in it but it was so thick that the only purpose it served was as an area where young Spaniels could be turned loose to give them scent.

I killed a lot of vermin on this ground and prepared my equipment to rear a few pheasants by the broody/movable pen system. Every farm had a few old-fashioned laying hens and I obtained some from a local character who, it was said, combined farming with salmon poaching and sheep stealing.

The pheasants did very well and mostly stayed on the ground when released. When adult, they developed a curious characteristic on account of the terrain, which I have never experienced before or after. Above the house was a huge crag with a fringe of scrub oak along the edge. My pheasants roosted on this crag and when I fed them at the foot of the crag at daybreak, they would launch themselves into the air from their roost and descend vertically in a very tight spiral and with a tremendous roar of pinions, a similar technique to that employed by geese, when they break formation over water and parachute down. The pheasants were, if anything, even more spectacular than geese, as it would be happening all around me.

During the early Spring Joe arrived from Colin Thomson's kennels. Joe was an unforgettable canine character who wrote his own vivid page of history. He arrived by train at Betws-y-Coed station, bold and eager to get out of his box. He was a short legged, long bodied, predominantly white dog with a dark liver head but his eye was his most outstanding feature, dark hazel but flecked around the iris by amber with a most brilliant expression. His intelligence and trainability were phenomenal and he could put class and style into the most simple action.

I would release him from his kennel for a training session; he would walk at heel, tail wagging furiously, spot a thistle 20 yards away and decide to utilise it. He would charge at the thistle, absolutely flat out, then jam his brakes on, lift his leg and look back at me over his shoulder to ensure that I was appreciating the spectacle, but I think the truth of the matter was that unless he was actually hunting or out on a retrieve, he just had to have his eyes on me. He was one of those very rare Spaniels who, as he came across me when quartering, would give me the merest glance, to check his position in relation to his handler. He had such a perfect quartering pattern. I am sure he took as much pride in it as I did. When marking a retrieve, he appeared to have the knack of keeping one eye on the bird and one on me. He was the complete Spaniel, the ultimate.

His great, extrovert, terrifyingly hard-going niece became more famous in Great Britain but Joe was unique. He was easy in the open, tough in the hard stuff, a brilliant marker who loved being handled on a blind retrieve. He was perfect to hunt up game, never needing a command when he flushed or a bird fell close to him. He was completely stable on driven game and would cross the Lledr in flood. He won in this country, then became a Field Trial Champion in America and won a third in the National Championship. He was nearly a thinking dog. You cannot breed dogs of this calibre. Every now and then one just happens.

I was at this time training some pups we bred from Bee. We had used F.T.C. Harpersbrook Sammy who, it turned out, left a good one here and there but was never a dominant sire. The mating in this case was only a partial success and the progeny in some cases were useful but not brilliant. In the meantime, Bee had gone back to her owner, where she pulled a leg muscle. It looked as though her working career was finished, so I was able to acquire her in exchange for a trained daughter of hers. She was already mated when we completed the exchange, to a rather nice little dog I had trained but he was not brilliant and not the sire I would have chosen.

When her pups arrived they looked much the same as any other pups bar one. She was all white, apart from a well coloured head and a liver section at the base of her tail. One of my shooting syndicate members, a local man who lived up the Conway, had just lost his cross-bred Spaniel, so bought her from me, on the understanding that he brought her back for training. She had the most remarkable appearance and such an unusual sheen to her white coat that it appeared silver, particularly in sunlight. I called her Garreg Wynn, which in English simply means White Rock. Anyone who has seen white quartz stones on a hill will understand why. The rest of the litter were all very ordinary but made good shooting dogs.

In those days, I had little knowledge of legal matters and the necessity for getting business arrangements properly tied up in writing. One of the syndicate discovered that the 5,000 acres of shooting 'let' to us, could not be legally sub-let, so our syndicate could not be carried on. My landlord offered me the house and his own 200 acres with a reduction in rent but the proposition was out of my reach as I would have had no income from the shoot. By a stroke of good fortune, a Northern industrialist whom I knew slightly through Spaniel Trials, had just taken over a very good shooting property in the next county and it was suggested to me by another Spaniel owner that I might possibly be able to find facilities on this estate. He did much to bring this situation about.

We were given an old farmhouse and outbuildings near the boundary of the estate, with leave to take as much ground as we required for rabbit-pen and dog runs. There was a detached grouse moor of about 400 acres near the house on which I was to kill the vermin and, downhill from the house, about 200 acres of arable and scrub. The house stood at about 1,400 feet and could be one of the coldest places in Britain.

The white puppy Wynn, came in for training and turned out to be very easy and co-operative. She had fantastic speed and style and as she matured, could be directed anywhere.

I had my first experience that year of the Conygree Simon line. A dog had originally been bred by the late Hal Jackson but, by other channels, had found its way into the hands of a shooting man. It was out of F.T.C. Gwen of Barnacre and, of course, the Simon/Gwen mating was repeated several times and produced some remarkable stock, with a tendency towards hard dogs and easy bitches; this happened to be a dog of very easy temperament. It took me three months to persuade him to retrieve but his attitude towards the rest of his work was fantastic. He had only one speed for everything he did—flat out but he had brakes to match. He had lovely style in the open and would smash any cover apart in a manner I had never seen before. It is one thing for a dog to be good in cover, it is another for it to treat it with utter contempt. He needed hardly any steadying and the first thing I shot for him was a rabbit on an open field. He hit it at top speed and had flung himself down before I could raise my gun.

He turned out a great success with his owner and was one of those rare examples of a dog with super drive but with a temperament kindly enough for an ordinary handler. He was a monorchid, so I never used him but by this time, the idea of Conygree Simon was firmly implanted in my mind.

My pheasants laid well and I reared a nice bunch of poults which I sold to the benefit of our exchequer. Some went to a local Welshman who had a rough shoot close by and who was keen on Labradors. This was the beginning of a peculiar though mutually useful liaison.

A young bitch came in to me with Field Trials in view who was by Rivington Glensaugh Glean and was out of a part O'Vara bitch. It had been said to me previously that Glean and the O'Vara blood did not mix but in this case this was not so, although this mating did pass on some complications.

I had already discovered that direct Glean progeny tended to be good or bad with a lower proportion of mediocre dogs than seem to come from most sires. Always bearing in mind the influence the bitch has on a mating, I think it would be fairly true to say that most really good dogs sire a few pups in their own class, a lot of mediocre ones and a few bad ones.

Glean, on occasions, appeared to be really dominant and stamped his own likeness on his good progeny in a very positive manner. This particular daughter, Micklewood Slip, was a bit of a monkey. She was not difficult to steady but, for a considerable time, her steadiness was liable to break down, fortunately more often out shooting where it could be dealt with than at Trials. She had tremendous class and drive and really could find game. After a shaky start she began to win consistently in Trials, qualifying for the Championship by winning our local Trial in the December and winning the Championship at Shadwell Heath near Thetford.

Running that same season, but hampered through ill-health, had been a brother to Slip, called Markdown Muffin. He was not to come into his own until two seasons later but he was a dog who turned out to have a powerful influence on the breed though, like his father, he could produce certain peculiarities which I will discuss in a later chapter.

A puppy was brought to me after the Championship for Springers was over in whose breeding I had a finger. A client in South-West Wales had acquired a sister of Rivington Joe named Scottie; she was a granddaughter of Glean and I was asked to suggest a dog for her so I nominated a son of Glean, Rivington Sailor. This mating showed me how close one could line breed to Glean and what one could expect. This pup was a result of that mating and showed me that two lines of Glean could produce anything from brilliance to insanity.

I was able to assess this young bitch as a Trial prospect more quickly than any other I have ever had. I had a foul drive back from Norfolk, becoming completely fog bound in the Midlands and had to spend the night in a terrible boarding house, all decent hotels being full. I fed Slip and the pup on fish and chips and resumed my journey the following morning, our triumphant entry into Wales still shrouded in fog. I had by this time decided the pup had the nerves of an old steam cultivator, so had no hesitation in letting her straight out into my yard when I reached home, as I knew she would not abscond. She dashed across the yard, did the quickest turn in her own length that could possibly be done, dashed back to me, almost boiling over and said, 'Right, let's show them what a Spaniel really is'.

I already owned three of her litter and another came in for training. The latter, a big black and white handsome dog made a good one. He could nearly have made a great one but not quite. He could mark a bird 150 yards away over the heather and would not overshoot a 20 yard Fall. He did a lot of coastal work with his owner and could equal a Labrador in water but then, he did have the size.

My pups were a disappointment. One I just did not like and sold, it making a mediocre dog. One would not accept any training at all. I sold him for £5 and he was allowed to do just as he liked. If he could hunt without restraint and chase any rabbit he saw, or run in to anything shot, he was happy. The other, a bitch, was a brilliant natural hunter who would crash through matted rose thorns. She was a complete non-retriever and used to see ghosts. She would run alongside me, tail going, then suddenly look over her shoulder and bolt forward, tail down and terrified. She was too pathetic a case to be allowed to live.

The good bitch was called Rust but was registered as Dinas Dewi Sele. She was a tough character to train, rough and boisterous, good on the whistle but rather unrefined. She would turn sharply but never dropped to whistle, shot or game; she would stand, absolutely steady but never right down. This was just her way and as she was such a character, I accepted her way of doing it. She would take the hardest cover, never checking her pace and had a perfect pattern in the open, with a natural system on a downwind beat. She was basically a 'goer', who had to learn to find game as a secondary part of hunting, whereas some dogs (most) do not develop full power until they have found a lot of game.

The same summer, I had a litter of pups in from one of Bee's daughters from her first litter. She was the best of the litter and was mated to a Garwgarreg dog I had at the time. The best of this litter, however, went elsewhere. He never won much but became famous for his class and natural ability and was known to many as 'The Parson's Dog'; if you find Theydon Style in a pedigree, you will know who he was.

I had an arrangement with Wynn's owner to breed a litter of pups from her that year, so took her to Conygree Simon. The reasons for my choice were manifold: The success of his various progeny out of Gwen of Barnacre, my own personal experience of one of them and certain bloodlines both had in common, in fact Wynn herself was a great granddaughter of Simon and Gwen.

I kept four of the resulting pups and Wynn's owner had three. One achieved some local fame as 'The Professor's Dog' (his owner lectured in psychology). He fiddled about a bit with the pup himself then sent him to me for further education. The two of them eventually made quite an effective team. Some weeks after Wynn was mated, her mother Bee came in season and so we took another trip to see old Simon. A veteran trainer went with me for the ride and expressed a wish to have one of Bee's pups if and when they arrived. This was to be *the* mating. I had decided to keep every bitch pup myself and run them all on, thus ensuring Bee's female line for the future. She had nine dogs! I was staggered and said 'Right, rear the lot then'. Through her failure to produce even one bitch pup, I lost Bee's female line for good. True, there were Wynn's daughters but that is another story. I could have bought something in from her female line at a later date but good blood in other hands can soon become adulterated and weakened. I am firmly convinced that good strong blood must be carried on through good strong individuals and it is my chosen policy to adhere to these principles, even though I am fully aware that there can occasionally be a resurgence from a weakening line, resulting in a spectacular individual from mediocre parents. However, the best to the best is my policy and I would rather lose a line than put up with its poor relations through sentimentality. There are, after all, several good male lines to Bee available.

I now had 13 pups, which were too many for me to run on, so I kept Wynn's four and three of Bee's. One of Bee's was useless and was put down, one was an odd shape and nervous, although he made a good shooting dog and one was really promising. However, it was Wynn's two daughters who interested me. One had the most perfect mature style at eleven weeks old. The other was quite attractive but rather aloof. An American, who owned Rivington Joe happened to be in this country at the time and made the journey from London to Wales. He was immediately taken by the very flashy bitch and would have bought her right away but I told him I would not sell her, so he asked me to send him whatever I thought could do well in America at a later date.

I started to play with Wynn's pups, as opposed to training them and discovered that the most attractive bitch was not a natural retriever. Later on, she would pick a rabbit if I shot one for her but never liked handled game. In the rabbit-pen she would tear round and round the perimeter, chasing any rabbit in sight but seldom bothering to penetrate the gorse.

The quieter sister was a natural retriever and, although slower than her sister, she really hunted, tore the gorse apart and used her nose. She came on very well in training and I could see she was just what I wanted, so what did it matter if Bee had failed to present me with an heiress? I shot a good many rabbits for her both from hard cover and from rushes and heather. She hit rabbits hard although never caught one in the seat.

One evening in a high wind, when she was running really

hot, she punched out a rabbit. I shot the rabbit which went away legged downhill and I put the bitch on the line, which she worked beautifully and found the rabbit 100 yards away. She threw herself on to the rabbit in a manner which made me say, 'Oh hell!' and eventually presented me with a very dead rabbit, its chest completely smashed in. This I could never forgive. Done in hot blood, yes, but a gundog must be able to stand pressure and yet remain basically sound. Shattered were my dreams of a future line. She never did it again but that made no difference. She had signed her own export pedigree. I had been told by an American that the question of hard mouth in America was never taken as seriously as it is here and that provided a dog picked up smartly and retrieved cleanly, nobody even bothered to examine the bird. Only if a dog appears to be 'working on a bird' is the bird examined and the dog discarded if the bird is delivered in a mangled condition. I was told never to hesitate to send a dog with a sub-standard mouth by British standards, provided the dog ran hard and wide, flushed instantly, marked well, retrieved cleanly and watered well. Well, all this was Ginny.

I had a full team of clients' Trial dogs that year but I did run her in two Novice Stakes, winning a third and a reserve. She had a very successful career in America, although not the large leggy type favoured over there. She stood 17 inches at the shoulder and weighed 33 pounds fit, but as I was told by one American, 'She ran like a big dog and looked big running'. Although not good enough to continue my line, she was good enough to win the American National Championship two years running. Her name was Gwibernant Ganol.

I called Bee's pup Gadwaladr. Although fairly well up in the national heroes of Wales, I do not know much about this particular gentleman, except that, according to Pistol in Shakespeare's 'Henry V', he had a lot of goats. We used him on Micklewood Slip when he was eleven months old and the resulting pups were rather odd. There were two tiny bitches, smaller than a normal working Cocker, who were far too small for Trials and two medium sized dogs that were very reluctant to hunt. After they had been with me a few weeks their owner had a look at them and said, 'I would not have believed pups could be as bad. Either put them down or have them as a gift'. I took the latter course and continued training them. They improved slightly and I eventually sold one cheaply to an undertaker in Devon and continued with the slightly better one. He came on sufficiently for me to actually find a pheasant with him one day which I shot and he retrieved.

His sire by that time belonged to an Irish client, who asked me if I had a rough young dog for him to play about with, as I was handling Gadwaladr in Trials, so I suggested this comic pup and actually gave him a month's approval, as I was not fully confident in the dog. After a fortnight he phoned me and said he was keeping the dog, remarking that he was a peculiar character but that he had something about him that appealed. He gave him a lot of work, took him ferreting and sent him after the legged rabbits that made off into the very heavy Ulster cover. He shot snipe over him, picked up a few pheasants and ran him in Trials. He began to look like a winner every time out but never just made it.

No doubt many readers will have read Siegfried Sassoon's 'Memoirs of a Foxhunting Man' and will recall 'The Mister', whom George Sherston described as 'the best bad rider I have ever seen'. I can think of four people who could compete for the title of 'The best bad dog handler', one is Welsh, two are Scottish and then my Irish friend. England can claim no such colourful character.

The dog had a maddening sense of humour, hated being directed, was totally unpredictable but could split cover in a manner that no Spaniel, bar none, has ever been seen to do since and the three Stakes he chose to win were wrapped up in such a spectacular manner that on those occasions the opposition may as well have gone home. He was Willie Snaffles.

As I previously mentioned, a professional colleague expressed a wish to buy one of the Simon/Bee pups, so I took one down to him one day when they were a few weeks old. It was just a random pup. Two had gone to Ulster, one to North Wales, one to a local moor keeper and one I just cannot remember where. It so happened that the pup had a solid chocolate face and a very well marked body. For some reason the new owner could not take to this pup and the next thing I heard was that the pup had been sold to an estate owner for his gardener to handle.

I thought no more of this until the following year when we had Trials in Shropshire. Rust won the Open Stake, which made her a Field Trial Champion and I took Reserve with a

The author's first Spaniel, Breckenhill Brando. C. M. Cooke & Son.

The author with a hill-top gathering.

The late Mr Harold Timms with his two Cockers, Monnow Elizabeth and Monnow Mayfly, handled by the author (right). Barnsleywold, Cirencester.

funny little dark bitch called Micklewood Smock, who was no relation to Slip but was a good one in her own little way, suffering also from Rust's 39 pounds weight sitting squarely on her tail throughout her career. The Novice Stake, held the following day, did not have any brilliant support from this kennel. I ran the abominable Sambo, whose owner had me run him in Trials as a joke and who, on this occasion, must have been particularly abominable as he was only given a certificate.

Two dogs dominated this Trial. One was the Parson's dog and the other was the dark-faced son of Bee. Style was a big dark dog with tremendous drive but the son of Bee, a smaller dog, had a much sharper action. He did not have Style's weight to tear the brambles apart but went through them like a stoat in a woodpile.

Two of the most extraordinary things then happened that I have ever seen. These two dogs had been hunting side by side in the run off, when the line was halted and the senior Judge decided to try Style on a pheasant which had been seen to enter this particular beat, hard hit, about an hour previously. Style did not find it, the line worked on and the cock was picked by hand from a deep depression in the ground, half buried in dead leaves and under frosty conditions. No doubt a completely scentless bird. He was put out of the Stake for failing.

Bee's son then entered a small piece of cover. There happened to be an unshot bird sitting shoulder to shoulder with a runner. The sound bird flushed. The runner ran and the dog simply grabbed it and was put out for retrieving without orders. Now normal practice allows a dog to pick up any wounded game that happens to be on his beat. That is what a Spaniel is for. Pricked birds need adding to the bag and I cannot see that if a dog has to chase any such bird it finds, with a distinct blood scent on it, that it commits a crime, so in this particular Trial, the only two worthwhile dogs were put out, unjustly I feel, leaving rubbish dogs to take the awards.

Bee's son ran in many more Trials; he never won much but I doubt whether any dog in the history of Spaniel Trials has ever attracted more interest. He has been loved, hated, praised, maligned, exaggerated and slandered in such a manner that he must stand as the most controversial Spaniel of all time. One hard indisputable unvarnished fact stands out above all speculation. He sired more Field Trial Champions, both in Britain and America, than any other sire, living or dead. His name is Hales Smut.

By this time, having been professionally training for about six years I decided it was time we had a place of our own. Bank managers still proved to be a sceptical breed, causing us to lose the best bargain in land that anyone could ever find in a lifetime but we eventually bought a place with eight acres of land and I rented a farm shoot close by. I made some excellent indoor kennels and two rabbit-pens of one and two acres each, but the place had certain snags and as there was no ground other than pasture in the vicinity, I had to travel a mile to my shoot to find any cover. We stayed there three years and then, in the middle of a credit squeeze, we attempted to sell our property and buy a more suitable one. This was quite an undertaking, particularly as nobody seemed to have any funds to buy our place, but eventually this came to pass and by the same token, we were able to buy very cheaply.

I now had 16 acres of my own to train on plus another hundred or so of very steep mountainside with ideal cover. I fenced in a hillside to form a rabbit-pen, about 300 yards long by 40 wide, with natural bracken cover and a few bushes. Below me, I had a canal and the Dee for water work.

I have in this chapter, written at some length about various individual Trial dogs which have been through my hands. Some of these dogs have become fairly potent stud forces in the breed and appear in the pedigrees of thousands of present day Springers, many of whom are owned by people who have never seen a Spaniel Trial but who may be interested to know a little of the history of some of their dogs' ancestors. I will now deal with the more general topic of gundogs, their training, and employment in the shooting and Trial fields.

3 The breeds

In this chapter I will deal with the various breeds of gundog, not in the order of my preference but in the order in which I have had experience of them. In some cases I will not have actually trained any specimens of the breed myself, in others my experience may have been limited to only one or two individuals.

THE GOLDEN RETRIEVER

Considering that the golden is of fairly recent origin, its early days are shrouded in mystery and there is a certain diversity of opinion as to how the breed originated. Some say the golden was originally a Caucasian sheepdog and that Lord Tweedmouth, being particularly impressed by the cleverness of a troupe of performing dogs of this breed at a circus in Brighton, purchased the lot and had them trained as gundogs in Scotland. It has been stated that bloodhound was introduced to improve the breed's scenting powers and that this accounts for the very dark red specimens one occasionally encounters, the slightly drooping lower eyelid possessed by some goldens and the really huge specimen the breed occasionally produces. Having seen an enormous red golden, sitting hunched up and staring into a fire, with muzzle drooping, I would say that in profile the resemblance to a bloodhound was remarkable.

The first goldens I trained were remarkably easy, were very good in punishing cover and had great courage and ability in water. I never had one bite a bird, although my first bitch discovered that a quick nip through the heart of a wounded hare made her easier to carry. She would kill rats, catch mallard ducklings in the evenings and help me put them to bed and once pulled down and held a wounded hind. Eyesight and marking were usually phenomenal and noses were first rate. All the goldens I knew were very friendly with human beings but some have a terrible tendency to fight in kennels, a trait which has often been commented on by other experienced retriever men. As one veteran trainer put it, 'He's got such a coat that no other dog can thrash him and he's a better fighter than any dog in the kennel'. A good golden is second to none and at the risk of sounding controversial, I believe a top specimen can actually be superior to the very best Labrador but I will admit that such dogs are very thin on the ground.

Their successes in Field Trials against other breeds have been outstanding and one kennel has been consistent in this sphere for at least 20 years. It is said by some that goldens confuse easily and, whereas I never noticed it in my early dogs, the last one I trained, a very closely line-bred dog, showed this to a degree. I once saw a golden during the Game Fair Tests, on being sent across water for a dummy, snap at a piece of floating orange peel, find it was not what was required and thereafter refuse to be handled beyond mid-stream. I would imagine a really courageous specimen could make an ideal wildfowling dog but I cannot imagine many fowlers relishing the company, in hide or car, of a shaggy golden plus a liberal coating of Humber mud!

Although it is still possible to find goldens which can win on a show bench and yet give a good account of themselves out shooting or in competition, such animals are in the minority and anyone wishing to purchase a working golden would be best advised to obtain one from a breeder known to be primarily concerned with the working side of the breed. I think I am safe in saying that there were more good dual purpose goldens 20 years ago than there are now. Some well known names in a working pedigree could be Noranby (probably off the paper now but in the background of many dogs), Haulston, Yeo, Stubblesdown, Westley, Treunair, Holway, Larkfield, Belway, Palgrave, Claverdon and Greenfoot.

THE LABRADOR

This is without any question, the most numerically strong breed of gundog, either in the shooting field or in non-sporting ownership. I refuse to accept the show Cocker as a gundog breed at all, in case it should be argued that more Cockers are registered per annum than Labradors.

The Labrador comes in three colours, black,˙ yellow (which may vary from off-white to fox red) and chocolate (very rare). Black parents sometimes throw yellow pups but I am told it is impossible for two yellows to throw a black. There have been many good yellows both in the shooting field and competing in Trials but there has been a higher proportion of blacks in the really top Trial dogs.

About 15 years ago there appeared to be three types of Labrador, the top class Trial dog, bred for many years with Trials and shooting in view, the show dog, some of which would work, some not and then the 'common Labrador', who seemed to consist of a hotch-potch of keepers' working dogs, show dogs and the odd Field Trial Champion here and there. I found these promiscuously bred dogs were usually very easy to train, had good natural ability and although not spectacular enough for competition, made very useful gundogs indeed. I have not trained many Labradors of top class Trial breeding but the majority of those I have had in were very pleasing dogs and could do really impressive work.

A Labrador should be capable of tackling any job in a day's shooting with the exception of hunting up and flushing unshot game. That some can and do this particular type of work cannot be denied but I believe the Labrador is truly out of his element when used as a questing dog. He should walk quietly at heel when walking up roots, stubbles or moor and should virtually mark every bird in the line, in case he should be required to retrieve a bird shot by some dogless gun. He should be capable of being handled fairly long distances with a minimum of effort and once in the correct area, should be capable of hunting the fall out for himself. If the handler knows that a bird has fallen approximately $9\frac{3}{4}$ inches to the left of a bit of wild mustard in a root field, he can place the dog on to the bird and such a performance can be invaluable on a bad scenting day or in a case when, as in a Trial, several dogs have tried to locate a specific bird, by which time scent is likely to be at a minimum.

There are many occasions when accurate marking is not possible; for instance at a stand, birds might fall well behind a screen of rhododendrons. The dog is required to get out in the right direction, then, at a command from the handler, to hunt the place upside down. Many Labradors are top class water dogs and, being big and powerful, are ideally suited for work in or over fast flowing rivers and tidal waters. The Labrador is the wildfowler's dog *par excellence* and doubtless more are employed in this work than any other breed. It has been stated by some that the Labrador has steadily declined over the past few years and that hard mouth is a great deal more prevalent now than was formerly the case. I have not trained any Trial bred Labradors for some years now but I can say that the ordinary animal or 'common Labrador' is now a great deal more difficult to train than it was several years ago, some being terribly stubborn, some completely neurotic. If I wanted to buy some Labrador pups now I would have to go into their ancestry very carefully and make sure both parents had been certified free of hereditary defects. In choosing a dog of working pedigree, one should look for names such as Staindrop, Hiwood, Brackenbank, Zelstone, Sendhurst, Sandringham, Glenfarg, Greatford, Harpersbrook, Hedenham Park, Lambdale, Glenmorag, Creedypark, Shavington Holdgate, Galleywood and Staxigoe.

THE FLATCOATED RETRIEVER

Many years ago, the flatcoat and the curly-coat were the common Retrievers found on any shooting field but were gradually superseded by the Labrador. Since the last war the flatcoat has been struggling hard to make a come-back but has only recently gained ground.

The flatcoat is black or occasionally liver with a longish coat. Some dogs grow to a very large size. I have seen some very useful flatcoats in the shooting field but the distinct impression I have of the breed is that they seem less amenable and more self-willed than Labradors and many do not appear to handle very accurately, which perhaps accounts for the decline of the flatcoat and the upsurgence of the Labrador.

I would say that there is a higher proportion of dual purpose flatcoats than there are dual purpose specimens of any other breed. It appears that breeders have managed to stick to more or less one type. I saw champion Claverdon Jorrocks of Lilling win the Retriever Tests at the Game Fair 12 years ago in really fine style and that particular year the tests were very exacting, with 'coveys' of homing pigeons released to confuse the issue. I was very sorry when this dog just failed to become a dual champion, as he finally retired with one Open Stake to his credit, plus his show title. I really loved to see this dog work, although I doubt if his owner realises I ever noticed him.

38

The most prominent names among working flatcoats are Hartshorn, Claverdon and Collyers.

THE ENGLISH SPRINGER SPANIEL

The English Springer is, without any question, the most popular dual purpose dog in the country. Of very mixed ancestry, the Springer has, over the decades, systematically destroyed the opposition of every other Spaniel breed, leaving only the working Cocker in a cliff-hanging position. As the Labrador has largely displaced the flatcoat and curly through sheer efficiency and trainability, it would appear that the Springer has established its position by the same means. The versatility of the Springer is unique. He is at his best where game is scarce and where his handler may shoot ten or a dozen head of game in a day, or less.

A Springer should work *for* scent as well as on scent, in other words, he should be willing to hunt on command whatever the conditions. If the terrain where he is cast off is completely devoid of game or scent, he should not care one iota but hunt on with what has been termed 'the cheerful optimism of the Spaniel', with the idea at the back of his mind that although his nose tells him the ground is bare of game and has been for at least ten years, maybe, just maybe, half a mile away over the ridge there might be a whin bush with a rabbit in it but in the meantime, he had better explore every nook and cranny in case something just happens to be there.

Conversely, he should be capable of working out a root field that is stuffed full of pheasants and reeking of scent. He should be level-headed enough to keep well within shot despite the profusion of footscent and sufficiently discerning to find his game by body scent against a background of counter scent. He should be capable of being worked up the line of a lone cock pheasant but continue to make the ground good on both sides of his handler, unless hedge hunting, in case other game should be squatting in the vicinity. In this respect we differ in this country from the Americans, who allow the dog to take the line, stopping it by whistle each time it approaches the limit of gun range until the bird is flushed or lost. Should the latter be the case and happens in a Trial, the dog is 'out' having failed to 'produce a runner'. At all times we expect our Spaniels to flush the game without catching it and depriving the handler of a shot. An accurate marker saves time and disturbs the minimum of unshot game, as does the dog which can take the line of a rabbit or hare accurately from the seat to the kill, working out for himself any right angle turns the quarry might have made before the shot.

He should retrieve cleanly up to hand, although allowances should be made if the dog has been hunting really hard or the weather is unduly warm. Springers are cool weather dogs and never go better in this country than when they have rain on their coats. A Springer should have a good mouth, although commonsense should be applied when the dog has had a hard struggle in thick cover with a bird. At the present day, the situation regarding the mouths of Springers is very satisfactory provided we do not become too complacent. He should be an adequate water dog, capable of retrieving a bird from the far bank of a river or duck from a flight pond. Some Springers have made useful coastal wildfowling dogs and continual experience in this work doubtless improves performance, although I still believe the wildfowler would be better served by a retriever.

It is my firm belief that a properly trained Spaniel should sit without a movement or murmur in a grouse butt, at a covert side, by a flight pond or a pigeon-roost. I have known several Spaniels, originally professionally trained, which, out rough shooting with their non-Trialing owners, would become a little wild when hunting and run in when a bird was shot over them, yet when seated at a covert side or snipe drive, would remain completely steady without a lead during quite heavy shooting. I even saw the 'Professor's dog', which was pretty hot when hunting, sit by his owner on a bare field and watch him shoot three woodcock at a stand.

I once took three Field Trial Springers to an ordinary covert shoot which had an adequate quota of wild retrievers and shot 40 birds over them in the day. I never had to speak to the dogs when shooting was in progress and the only movement from any was no more than a tail wag. There was not a squeak or a whine and those dogs had not been trained for covert shooting, nor had they been picking up, or ever been shot over in company except at a Trial. They were simply stable, trained dogs and when I said 'hup' when I took my stand, they knew that I meant 'hup' until further orders. In the past, I have picked up a great deal with Spaniels at stands and when I advanced this information in defence of my claim that a Spaniel should be as stable at a drive as a Retriever, the wiseacres would triumphantly exclaim, 'Ha, but if you had to concentrate on shooting, the dogs would realise your attention was off them and misbehave'. It seems beyond the comprehension of some, that a kind, well trained dog can quite happily and voluntarily behave himself when his handler's attention is diverted by shooting. Anyway, this day proved my point and my host, a keen Trial man himself, was delighted to see it proved.

As rough shooting is carried on over such a vast variety of terrain, a Spaniel must be versatile in his approach to various cover. He should be able to split whin bushes, digging his nose in at the base of the bush and burrowing in low like a mole. He should force briars apart, boring with his nose, throwing his weight on to his shoulders and driving hard with his hind-quarters and, as the Irishmen say, 'throwing the cover over his back'. He should be able to quarter rushes, heather, bracken, roots, rough grass or even combined stubble, covering his ground at a brisk pace, head well up, now down, now a little higher again, like a small Setter and at all times moving with characteristic style, tail moving in conjunction with hind-quarters, always held below the level of his spine.

A really top class Springer should, ideally, combine the qualities of the Spanish fighting bull and the Zulu warrior. He should have their blind courage and fury in attack, with the unquestioning obedience for his handler that the Zulu had for his King.

Prior to 1954, the main quarry of the Spaniel was the rabbit, particularly in Field Trials. Besides being judged on hunting (often under severe temptation in those days) and gamefinding, great importance was attached to the ability of a dog to take the line of a shot rabbit. Some of these pre-myxomatosis Spaniels became very clever on the line of a legged rabbit, unerringly taking the blood scent over ground covered in rabbit foil. Handling out to unseen retrieves was seldom required and I doubt if many handlers of the older generation of spaniel men taught their dogs to handle until the advent of myxomatosis.

Then the picture drastically changed. Overnight, the rabbit

virtually vanished. Trials were conducted on pheasants and the pheasant became the main target of the roughshooter. Marking, which had been unimportant in the days of the rabbit, assumed a new significance and even more so did the art of handling a dog out to blind retrieves as one could not guarantee a succession of straightforward marked retrieves for every dog. So was born the 'sheepdogging cult'. Some handlers and judges became quite fanatical over this aspect of Spaniel work and fuel was added to the flame by the upsurgence of working tests in many parts of the country.

It has been argued by the exponents of handling, that a spaniel which is first class in all departments and will handle well, must be a superior animal to one that is top class in its basic qualities but does not handle well. One cannot dispute the logic of this argument but I know perfectly well that in this day and age, I could win far more with a mediocre hunting Spaniel which would handle well than ever I could with a brilliant hunter which might be a little obtuse on handling. I find this rather disturbing and believe that the deterioration of the Springer which we have witnessed over the past few years is directly connected with over-emphasis being placed on handling ability.

It is particularly important to obtain a Springer with a complete absence of show blood in its pedigree for, with the notable exception of the Higham blood, which perhaps gives the dog a plainer action but does not inhibit working qualities or trainability, show blood normally has a very bad effect upon the quality of a working Springer and I cannot ever recollect seeing a Springer go to the top in Trials which had any show blood in it, apart from some dogs with the previously mentioned Higham in their backgrounds.

I once had a Springer in for training from a show strain and it appeared to make quite a useful dog. In heather it would get its head up and really move, with a tidy quartering pattern. However, if it hit scent, instead of speeding up it would slow down and sniff and sniff and sniff. I ran it in a Trial in Cambridgeshire which was held mainly on stubble with a fair amount of scent. The bitch simply walked in her first run but made a couple of good retrieves. She continued walking in her second run, by which time, I had almost fallen asleep on my feet but she did manage to summon sufficient interest, much to my relief to run in, as this did at least add a spark of interest to the proceedings and, to be quite fair, it was a really good run in.

I informed her owner that he was knocking his head against a brick wall in trying to continue running this bitch and to illustrate my point I hunted her across a bare field, then brought out Micklewood Slip and ran her across the same course. My client remarked, 'I'll sell her, how should I set about it?' I replied that he should offer her back to her breeder. This he did and received a good price, the bitch herself being re-sold to Italy.

Some time later I received a bitch to train, bred by the same kennels. She was quite useless and I was asked by her owner to deliver her to her breeder, who had agreed to buy her back. Upon arriving at this rather large kennels, the proprietrix, a rather fierce little lady, screamed at me, 'What are you doing to my dogs?' I asked for an explanation for this extraordinary question and she informed me that several shooting men who had formerly owned dogs of her breed upon becoming acquainted with myself, had very soon gone in for Trial-bred dogs. I informed her that I could not possibly imagine why. She further informed me that the bitch I had returned would be bred from and it was her policy to refund the purchase price of any bitch pup bought from her that failed in training, in return for the now grown pup which, being close to profit, would become another brood bitch.

This information, staggering though it was, did not entirely surprise me, if one considered the general quality of this strain. It certainly explained why this blood had such a disastrous effect when mixed with better blood.

Good strains to look out for when acquiring a Springer pup are O'Vara, Rivington, Downton, Micklewood, Pinehawk, Hillhampton, Conygree, Racedale, Stranwood, Ardoon, Harwes, Markdown, Saighton's, Pinewarren, Harpersbrook, Breckonhill, Criffel, Chrishall, Staxigoe, Burnhatch, Crowhill, Barnacre, Drumbo, Hales and Gwibernant.

THE CLUMBER SPANIEL

My experience of Clumber spaniels is very limited, owing to the scarcity of the breed in working hands. I have already mentioned in my first chapter, the very good Clumber owned by my first employer in Wiltshire and I have never since seen one of equal quality. I had one sent to me when I lived in the Gwibernant which had been purchased from a breeder in Manchester, by a Colonel from the Isle of Mull, yet the pup was at the time living in a houseboat on the Thames!

He really was a most odd little character. Far too small for an orthodox specimen, he was not exactly nervous but aloof and suspicious: in fact he gave me the impression that he was too stupid to know real fear! The owner informed me that I could expect a Clumber to develop far more slowly than a Springer and begged me to take plenty of time with him and not discard him if he appeared difficult.

Well he did appear difficult, very difficult. He started off by flatly refusing to retrieve and it took me three months to persuade him. I finally accomplished this by giving him rather smelly little rabbits, which he would proceed to chew, then gradually edging away from him, whereupon he would sometimes stop chewing and follow me, the rabbit dangling from his mouth and as he came level with me, I would quietly disengage the rabbit.

We progressed from this point until he one day decided that he actually liked retrieving and would pick a dummy with no hesitation and retrieve right to hand. Several times in my career this situation has repeated itself. A dog has flatly refused to pick a dummy and has been stimulated into retrieving by the real thing and even once by half a very stale loaf. In theory, a dog thus started should continue to refuse dummies and only handle game but this seldom seems to apply and I have found that once the pupil's interest has been fully aroused, it will usually go back quite happily to dummies. There is, of course, the very rare exception which has to have its entire training on the real thing which, in the middle of the Summer, can make life difficult!

This Clumber had two other peculiarities. When a shot was fired and a dummy thrown I would, of course, keep him on the drop for a time. After a few seconds he would start to lean over on one side and would finish up at an angle of 45 degrees. On being ordered to retrieve, he would straighten up in a flash and get out to his dummy. I have never seen another dog behave in such a manner since.

His other peculiarity was his short-sightedness. He was absolutely incapable of marking a fall beyond 25 yards and

44

anything further, he dealt with by quartering out to it beyond the limit of his vision. He was a surprisingly good hunter with a brisk, rather cockery action and he was very steady. I was quite happy about him when I sent him away to Mull and even happier when his owner informed me what a success the pup was. He described him as being dopey for a few days, then the Mull woodcock arrived and the dog was transformed. Apparently he was brilliant at flushing woodcock and appeared to have a sixth sense as to their whereabouts long before he actually winded them. By his actions, the Colonel swore he could tell when a woodcock was in the vicinity. I have come across this trait before. I once trained a very difficult Springer which was a very reluctant hunter. At one period of its training it was useless to order it to hunt as it just would not 'go' but if I walked along and said nothing, it would occasionally work on its own when the spirit moved it and would hunt for a while, then come back to heel.

After its rabbit-pen training (it would always 'go' in the pen) on several occasions it would be skulking along at heel, then it would start to hunt and would find a rabbit which, if shot, it would retrieve well, then continue at heel. On some of these occasions the wind from the rabbit was definitely not in the dog's favour yet, somehow, he knew exactly where it was.

The training of the Clumber was for me, a very satisfying episode. It is one thing for a trainer to have a really brilliant piece of raw material which, if handled with skill, never takes a retrograde step in its training and goes right to the top in Trials. It is quite another thing to take a most unpromising puppy that one does not even like and by infinite patience, persistence and hard work, make a good shooting dog of it to provide the owner with endless pleasure. This is really what professional training is all about.

My only other connection with the breed was in the form of a Cocker/Clumber hybrid, which made a ponderous, steady worker. He was also shortsighted but was excellent in water. His mouth was a little more than questionable and I happened to meet his breeder after I had trained the dog, who asked me what his mouth was like. Upon being told it was rather suspect, the gentleman gave a happy laugh, pointed to a large Clumber in his Land-Rover and said, 'That's his mother, she's got a mouth like a rat trap'.

THE CURLY-COATED RETRIEVER

These peculiar looking black or liver woolly coated dogs belong to the glories of the past. Tales of their prowess are legion, of how one once chased a wounded mallard for a mile across a sea loch and of how another would chase a poacher up a tree and wait there on guard until his master fetched the Law. The curly is a breed which has been 'got at' by the show people and the very few I have seen have been nowhere up to the standard of a good Labrador or golden.

I trained one some years ago and at that time it was my practice to chase the ewes and lambs from my exercising area before letting the dogs out before breakfast for free-running exercise. I did this one morning but the curly hit some sheep scent and disappeared over the brow of the hill. He soon appeared over the rise, a very large lamb balanced perfectly across his jaw, quite unharmed.

His particular peculiarity was, when a shot was fired and a dummy thrown, to lie down on his side, dig his front claws into the ground and pull himself round in a circle. I thought him a pretty ghastly dog but his owner appeared very pleased with him. If a man who shoots, feels he wants a dog that is 'different', there is no earthly reason why he should not own a curly, even though he may be far better served by one of the more common breeds. A subsequent curly I trained proved to be quite a pleasant animal about the place, was quite trainable but had poor ground treatment when searching for its retrieves and did not use the wind to full advantage. Its mouth was not good and nothing would induce it to swim, even when I went in with it myself. They are not among my favourites.

THE COCKER SPANIEL

It is, of course, a well known fact that the old gentleman from the Nether regions is a keen shooting man and when he shoots, he shoots over a pack of Cockers . . . black Cockers, with live embers for eyes! Each one runs in and gives tongue and all bite their birds like fury. Every now and then their owner sends his worst stud dog to earth, to mate a few bitches, thus ensuring that his chosen qualities are not lost.

On a more serious note, the origin of the Cocker would appear to be bound up with that of the Springer as in the early days of Spaniel Trials, the term Cocker appeared to be regarded more as a weight, than a breed classification, as litter brothers could run as Cockers or Springers, depending on whether they weighed under 25 pounds, I think, or over. However, the small dogs must eventually have been bred as a separate breed known as Cockers and the larger ones became known as Springers. H. W. Carlton, in his book *Spaniels for Sport* certainly classes them as separate breeds in 1915.

The colours of Cockers usually vary from those of Springers to a very marked degree, as Springer coloration seems to follow a very definite pattern. Black and White Springers can throw black and white puppies but two liver and whites do not appear to throw a black and white. I have known three instances where this has happened but in each case it was subsequently proved that a Collie or Labrador was involved; Cockers follow no such rules. It appears that any colours can get you any colours. Cockers can be black, liver, liver/white, black/white, lemon and white. I recently mated a liver dog to a lemon and white bitch, which produced three blacks, one black and white and two blue roans.

There is no other gundog breed which has divided so markedly into the show and working strains, as the Cocker. Show and working Springers are as different as chalk and cheese but can still be identified as belonging to the same breed, whereas one could be forgiven for supposing that show and working Cockers are entirely different breeds.

A working Cocker is quite a remarkable little machine. It has ears of very moderate length, a flat wide skull, large, fairly prominent eyes and a very muscular body, particularly in the regions of neck, shoulders, loin and hindquarters. They are enormously strong for their size, much stronger, pound for pound than a Springer or Labrador and one has only to see a Cocker coming back at full gallop with a lively hare to appreciate their unique power.

When writing about a breed one admires it is all too easy to have, to the fore of one's mind, the better specimens one has encountered but in writing a factual account of a breed, one must report on the other side of the coin. When I witnessed my first Cocker Championship, shortly after myxomatosis, there were some very good Cockers running which had been trained before the plague struck and therefore had had the advantage of plenty of rabbits in their training. From this time onwards the working Cocker declined very rapidly, although the odd first class dog still appeared, even though it may have been in the wrong hands to do it full justice. The Springer seemed to overcome the handicap of myxomatosis more readily than the Cocker and adjusted to the new conditions with a greater versatility. Basically, the Cocker needs plenty of game to get it going. The good Springer says, 'Here is a piece of country. Let us smash it apart and shift any game in it'.

The Cocker works the business out in his foul little mind and says, 'Here is a piece of country. Five rabbits fed here last night, two hours ago a pheasant used this track. Those whin bushes look useful, let us investigate. This one smells good. This one smells better, this one better still as a rabbit is hiding in it. What fun it will be to frighten him out and how much more fun if we can catch and kill him before he can escape'. This passage, of course, over-emphasises the potential evil of the Cocker to illustrate the point that the Cocker works best on game, rather than for game and that he is at his best when game is fairly plentiful. He has a terrier-like quality to his hunting, making use of all the little tracks in and out of cover which the game makes and tending to look askance at completely solid cover which is obviously not used by game.

The Cocker hates cover which has been tampered with by man. He is at his worst in a Forestry plantation which has been trimmed out between the rows and the cut cover left in drifts. He hates the cut stubs of brambles and saplings in his feet. He is at his best on a Scottish hillside covered in whin bushes and with a healthy rabbit population.

The good Cocker misses very little game. He is, if anything, more meticulous in his hunting and few Cockers are galloping flat catchers, as are some Springers. He has one distinct advantage over a hard going Springer. All the Cockers I have handled have been far better working on a warm day than most Springers. They appear able to stand the heat better and can still make a clean retrieve at the end of a long hot hunt, when a Springer would be puffing and blowing and fumbling his retrieves.

It has been said that Cockers are harder to train than Springers and are more independent and selfish. I cannot say that I agree with this when considering the Cockers that I have trained from scratch. Nearly all have been very straightforward and not particularly hard although in the early stages

I have found Cockers more difficult to sit and keep down. They are inveterate belly creepers but once this obstacle has been overcome, most have been quite easy.

I have, however, had experience of two Cockers which had been trained elsewhere and had developed a head of steam. These were incorrigible. One was perfect if one shot over him when he was hupped. I shot pigeon all round him one day and he was absolutely steady, even when one runner came towards us and ran within a yard of his nose, but set him off hunting and once he was in motion and a bird was shot, he would run in even if he was only a yard from me. The other was even worse. He is the only dog which has ever run in on me when seated at a stand. Later that day he even broke heel and chased a pair of grouse. His potential was fantastic, his mouth variable and his owner confirmed that he only understood the most brutal handling, which neither of us were prepared to give. Truly, he was sired by one of the Cockers from down below, as his dam later had pups by another sire which we both found were as honest and easy as Spaniels could ever be.

Most Cockers do not mark as well as Springers. This has nothing to do with vision but rather with attitude. A Cocker will often flush a bird, then turn his head sideways, instead of marking the fall. Some will mark the fall, then take their eyes off it. They have, however, remarkable gun sense and can often pick a bird under these circumstances as quickly as though they had marked it, although, of course, there is always more danger of their bumping into fresh game when working the ground out to a retrieve than if they had taken a direct line.

Very few Cockers are as good as most Springers at taking direction on blind retrieves and the sight of a Cocker making an ass of himself on a simple pheasant, coupled with the fact that we have seen a good many weak hunters in the breed over the last 15 years, has tended to bring the Cocker in to a state of disrepute. The attitude of some Cocker owners has not helped the situation for, instead of acknowledging the weaknesses of their breed, they have stuck their heads firmly in the sand and avowed that their Cockers were not only as good as but better than Springers. It is quite impossible to form an accurate picture of the Cocker until one has shot over several specimens of the breed, preferably in conjunction with Springers. One cannot assess Cockers by purely spectating or even judging them at Trials. Of all gundog breeds, I would say

Cockers are the least suited temperamentally to competitive work. They hate waiting their turn on the lead and performance suffers. Sometimes at a Cocker Trial rot seems to set in and dog after dog goes wrong, yet many of us know that several of these dogs that have gone wrong have previously done sterling work and, at home, are excellent shooting dogs.

As one of my female colleagues has remarked: 'The little *******s are full of character and it is not all good'.

Most working Cockers are entirely working bred with one very famous exception but more of her anon. Some successful names are Elan, Carswell, Cromlix, Staxigoe, Lanegate, Templebar, Merlin, Glennewton, Henhamlodge, Exton, Monnow, Headland, Chrishall, Breckonhill, Jordieland, Debdenhall, Greatford, Brookville, Shaffylde, Ardoon, Deewood and Gwibernant.

THE POINTING BREEDS

For the purposes of this section, Pointers and Setters can be bracketed together. This is not to suggest for one moment that the breeds are alike but they do perform the same function, in ranging far and wide over open terrain where game is not plentiful, finding birds and remaining staunchly on point until the gun or guns come up with the dog (or dogs) and work out the point. Pointing dogs are not normally expected to retrieve in this country, although they sometimes do abroad. I have trained some pointing dogs and my experience of Spaniels has taught me sufficient to know when a pointing dog is doing right or wrong. As one who attaches the greatest importance to ground treatment and use of wind in a Spaniel, I can appreciate a good going pointing dog. I am particularly impressed by the manner in which a fit Pointer can range long and hard in hot weather. I can appreciate the terrific speed and style of an English Setter but am not over enamoured with many of the breeds' representatives which are sticky on point, that is, they are reluctant to move forward into comfortable gun range on getting the first whiff of scent.

I find it annoying when any of them false point, as I equate this with the maddening Spaniel which is always poking into stale rabbit seats, or feathering madly on birds' jugging places. I do not enjoy the spectacle of a pointing dog boring out into the wind in a straight line any more than I love a boring

Spaniel and if a big Gordon Setter fidgets about on his point and causes birds to become restless and flush, I class him with a Spaniel which flushes game out of gunshot.

It is generally conceded in many parts of the world, that the Pointer is the most efficient of all the various breeds. Pointers have dominated the American National Championship for a great many years, so much so that it was considered a major happening, some four or five years ago when a 56 lb. English Setter took the title.

The American National takes about three weeks to run. Dogs run flat out for three hours and, naturally, in the U.S.A., dogs must run harder, wider and faster than anywhere else, the field charging after them on horse-back. Dogs are not expected to be steady to deer and provided a dog does not give tongue and comes into view within a certain time limit, he can win the Stake.

In English Setters, I can see a few of the less desirable qualities we already have in some of our Springers, as there is more than a hint of Setter way back in some bloodlines. I do not consider the Gordon a very attractive dog when working against a background of deep old heather; he is almost invisible. I have seen some top class Irish Setters of real Irish working stock. They can be inconsistent but on a good day they can be really spectacular and show real flair. I am told that to see them at their best they must have rain. This I can understand as the Springer works best in a stiff breeze with moderate drizzle. The dog appears able to keep cool and with his breathing apparatus well moistened he will go on for ever.

THE IRISH WATER SPANIEL

The Irish Water Spaniel is a most bizarre looking animal with his tightly curled liver coat, shaggy trousers, whippy tail and his bare, baboon-like face. My experience of them is limited to two specimens only. One was of Irish stock and I was told her parents had both won Trials in Ireland. She was surprisingly trainable and was a good retriever with a gentle mouth. Her hunting was peculiar, with a most un-Spaniel like action and she was very easy to steady and appeared to regard moving rabbits as a very solemn undertaking, never getting 'hot'.

She was a shocking wood chewer and would fight quite a lot

but on the whole was quite a likeable bitch. That same season I saw one of this breed actually competing in a Trial, where it gave a good account of itself and got as far as the run-off. Not surprisingly, the superior style of the English Springers beat it for the placings but it received a very well deserved Certificate of Merit.

THE POINTER-RETRIEVERS

This group consists of the German short-haired Pointer, the Weimaraner and the Hungarian Viszla. The German Pointer is the most common of the three and has quite a large following in this country. There appears to be a strong prejudice against the Pointer-Retriever by many who own more orthodox breeds. It is said that they are very hard mouthed although the only one I ever trained was unusually soft and would take a long time to pick up a lively hen pheasant. I think the truth is probably that as the dog in its native land is required to kill cats, pull down wounded roe and bay stags and boars, the breed probably has a distinct tendency to 'mouth' which may remain dormant while a dog is well under control but will manifest itself should the dog become wild and therefore over-keen. There are some very efficient workers in the breed and my argument against them is an unusual one–they can be just a little too efficient. One could virtually kill every hen pheasant in a root field with a really good dog but, owing to the dogs' manner of working, a good many cocks would creep away which a hard going Spaniel would get into the air.

CHOICE OF A GUNDOG

Two factors will influence a person's choice of a gundog. His type of shooting and his own preconceived ideas on the breed of dog he fancies. A knowledgeable person may advise another that his type of shooting would be best served by a Springer but his advice may fall on stoney ground if the other cannot bear the sight of a Springer and has always favoured a Labrador. Similarly, if a man favours shooting driven game exclusively over a Cocker, it could be pointless to explain the advantages of a Retriever to him. In fact, the majority of people who ask for advice only seek confirmation of their own preconceived ideas. There is a great deal of truth in what a certain Yorkshireman once said on the subject of advice: 'Wise men dunna need it and foo'ils we'ant tak it'.

For the man who may walk up grouse in August and have driven grouse shooting, followed by covert shooting all winter I would recommend a Retriever of whatever breed he fancies. A Springer could do the job but I feel a good Springer's hunting ability would be wasted under the circumstances. If a man shoots driven pheasants every Saturday and some duck on a flight pond occasionally, plus quite a few pigeon at the end of the season, I would also recommend a Retriever. If he is primarily a rough shooter who gets a few invitations during the season to shoot driven game, I would say a Spaniel, as I would if he does nothing but rough shooting. If he has some rough grouse moor along with marginal ground and he abhors Spaniels, there would be a strong case for one of the Pointer/Retriever breeds. If he has rough shooting in the northern counties or anywhere in Scotland, a Cocker could do his job very well.

If his shooting is in Anglesey where there are a lot of steep-sided ditches and hedges on high banks to scramble up and down plus some very hard cover, I would say a Springer would be not merely desirable but essential and a fairly leggy dog would be an advantage, provided its guts were in the right place. If a man has thousands of acres of rather poor quality grouse moor in Sutherland where birds are few and far between he must have a Pointer or Setter. Here personal idiosyncrasies do not enter into the question. The pointing dog is a 'must', as it is under identical conditions abroad, say in Norway and Sweden.

One may well ask why I previously mentioned the Cocker in connection with Scotland and Northern England. Well it so happens that Cockers never go better than in the North. There are miles and miles of damp bogland, carrying plenty of scent and a good variety of game. Cover is mainly rushes and most of the whins have good runs into them. There is comparatively little bramble cover and Carlton recognised the potential weakness of many Cockers in briars in 1915, mentioning that they lacked leg drive and weight, when compared with Springers, so this is not entirely due to post myxomatosis decline. Cockers can also be very good at picking grouse which have fallen close in to butts, as often happens when birds are taken correctly in front. Many Retrievers are very reluctant to hunt close in and love to 'get out'.

There are, however, many people who are not limited to just one dog and, should their shooting demand it, are able to indulge themselves and keep various dogs for their different requirements. I have had a great deal of pleasure shooting over one or two Spaniels and a Retriever, at the times during my career when I have had a Field Trial Labrador in the kennels. The Labrador was trained to such a standard that I would never even see him until I had a job for him. If out with two Spaniels, I would walk one at heel and hunt the other until its pace slackened, then bring it in to heel and work the fresh dog, which is my system of keeping the pace in a Trial Spaniel. The Spaniel or Spaniels would find their game and retrieve it and the Labrador would not put his nose forward. If the Spaniel was working down in a ravine and a difficult bird was shot, unsighted to the Spaniel and likely to run, I would speak the black dog's name and off he would go.

I once worked a Spaniel on the side of a gully from which she flushed a bird which I killed on the far side of the gully. It was a very steep-sided place and difficult for a small bitch to negotiate and when she was on her way out, a cock flushed behind us, which she had actually passed below while working the hen I had just killed. I took a snap shot through the trees and long experience of falling birds immediately warned me that it was a runner, so I sent the black dog. He made a very good job of this runner and had it back before the bitch had negotiated the gully with her hen.

Every now and then we have a controversy in the sporting press—Spaniel versus Retriever or Springer versus Cocker. Really, although they can be good fun, there should be no such controversies. The various breeds should complement and not conflict with each other and the episode I have just described is surely a perfect example.

I have already mentioned that, owing to personal preferences, some shooting men will employ a breed which I would not consider ideal. A perfect example was my Welsh client, whom I have previously mentioned as a potential candidate for the title of best bad dog handler. He had always owned Labradors and always been a rough shooter; he admired Spaniels but insisted that a Spaniel's way of working would give him heart attacks. He used his Labradors for hunting and also ran them with moderate success in Trials. It worked reasonably well but the dogs were always live game minded and did not get quite as high in Trials had they only been worked in an orthodox manner.

We did have a father and son who were remarkably adaptable dogs, and would work well for either of us. In fact the owner won a Second one Saturday and I won a Stake with the same dog the following Thursday. This dog was terribly kind and would put up with quite a bit of nonsense. I remember one day a pricked duck had died a very long way out. I was about a hundred yards away from the dog and his owner and could see the duck. The dog was sent out and when the time was right to stop the dog, I held my hand up and the owner blew the stop whistle. The dog stopped and I gave the relevant hand signal. Between us we handled him out and soon had the duck collected.

I will deal with dogs for wildfowling under a separate heading in a later chapter.

4 Man/dog relationship

There is very strong evidence to suggest that the dog was the first animal to be domesticated by man, yet dog handling does not appear to come naturally to the human race, in the same manner that man can handle the horse. If one studies the history of man, it will be seen that several horse nations have emerged. There were the Mongols, the Tartars, the Cossaks, the Plains Indians and latest of all, the Basutos, who have the distinction of being the only horse people of the Bantu race.

Countless other nations have, of course, used the horse but of the five peoples mentioned specifically, every male member could break and ride a horse, yet I believe it would be quite impossible for every member of any nation to be capable of handling either a gundog or a sheepdog. I believe this to be because a mental rapport between dog and man is so much more essential than it is between man and horse when the horse is simply used for the basic purposes of transport, war and hunting. I am excluding, of course, the highly sophisticated horsemanship required to win competitive events, when a close affinity between horse and rider could mean the difference between success and failure. Under less competitive circumstances so much can be accomplished with a horse by pure physical means. It would require a great deal of physical prowess for an Indian to ride down a buffalo bareback and drive a lance through it, yet hardly a great mental rapport with his pony, who, next day, he might cheerfully ride to death. You cannot dig your knees into a Labrador when he is a hundred yards out in a beet field with half a gale blowing and a live bird under every other leaf, any more than you can with a Pointer 300 yards out and a hare set on a collision course for the dog.

It would appear that some people have natural ability with dogs; some are capable of learning yet others are quite incapable of ever acquiring even the basic principles.

We are told by psychologists and criminologists that human beings are of high, medium or low dominance. Because a person belongs to the high dominance group, it does not necessarily follow that he or she is of a domineering nature, often the reverse is the case. This was clearly illustrated to me in my schooldays. We had members of our staff who could control a class with absolutely no effort or force and others who would scream and rave and who used a good deal of physical violence, yet who could never maintain order and who held the respect of none. So I believe it is with a person who aspires to train and handle a gundog. It would appear that people of high dominance are the most likely to make top trainers, capable of handling really hot dogs, the middle group can very often make a very good job of a dog of kindly disposition but the lowest group are beyond all hope.

An amateur Labrador handler of no mean ability once discussed with me a private professional who is an artist with a Labrador or a Pointer and who could apparently work his Pointer almost without a word. I asked him whether this person knocked the stuffing out of his dogs or did he dominate them mentally? My acquaintance informed me that the dominance was entirely mental and that this handler was a most gentle man with a dog, an opinion I had previously formed.

When approaching a subject as complex as gundog training, where one can have certain types of dog, e.g. hard, kind, oversensitive, bloody-minded, yet still have every individual dog with a different temperament, one requires great flexibility of ideas to cope with every contingency that can arise. I think one could do well to study how hawks are trained and hounds handled and hunted, as what may be applicable in these activities, can occasionally be applied to some gundogs.

I never give edible rewards but just as the whole business of falconry is based on the hawk taking food from its handler first and then the lure, thus associating these objects with something pleasant, so I will 'bait' a difficult dog under some circumstances, such as a dog so nervous that merely pushing him down on his behind causes him to put his ears back and roll his eyes. I will keep him down a few seconds then push a piece of tripe into his mouth, so he comes to trust the hand that makes him sit. Similarly, some dogs having been taught to sit and stay are reluctant to get up and come in to the handler when called. A piece of bait to pull the dog to the handler again builds up a pleasant association with the action of returning to hand. These measures are not normally necessary with a well bred dog but a professional very often has dogs of indifferent breeding and temperament in for training and is obliged to do his best with them. Bait is also useful in treating gun-nervousness but I will go into this more fully later.

Certainly there is knowledge to be gained from hounds. Cub-hunting is a means of educating young hounds and young foxes. The cubs are deliberately headed back into covert and leave a lot of scent in the undergrowth with which the young hounds can familiarise themselves. So I get my young Spaniels hunting rabbits in standing bracken during the Summer. The rabbits hop and double, the young dog hits a line, loses it, finds a rabbit, hunts him through the cover and all the time is learning his trade, just as a young hound learns his.

I think hunting people are more aware of the vagaries of scent than most shooting and gundog folk. I wonder how many realise how scent varies from one part of the country to another and that in Trials, the local dog is at an advantage scent-wise, not merely because his owner attended the sponsoring Society's meeting and managed to obtain judges whom he felt would be sympathetic to his cause!

Our scent is generally good in Wales and my dogs have had a particularly good record of success in Scottish Trials where scent is usually similar to ours, yet I have not done so well in East Anglia. I once took a young Labrador to a Trial in Essex who had been doing wonderful work on the grouse moors, really getting out and using the wind, yet when I placed him in a potato field, I began to doubt if he had ever been trained.

If the Devon and Somerset Staghounds were invited to hunt a buck on the sandy soil of the New Forest, or one of the famous grass country packs of Ireland was to be spirited over to the Essex clay, I doubt whether either pack would give a good account of itself. An appreciation of such factors can only be of help to a gundog person.

5 Choice of a puppy

I will assume that the reader is acquiring a puppy for the first time with a view to training it himself for shooting. Any interest in Field Trials should come later for if a person's first love is shooting, with its attendant dog work, his possible later interest in Trials is likely to be stimulated from a more practical angle than if he simply decided to take up Trials as a sport for its own sake.

If the reader is wise he will have read articles in the sporting Press by recognised authorities on the subject of gundogs and their training. Such authors are not invariably the world's greatest practical trainers themselves but they have a vast insight into the gundog scene and many years of experience of the subject and their advice is not lightly to be dismissed.

In all cases it will be found that writers stress the importance of obtaining a puppy of pure working stock but what exactly does this mean? A litter of pups may have both parents as working gundogs but just how good they are is another matter and a good deal depends on the standard set by their individual owners. It is quite possible for a Springer to have a large amount of show blood in its pedigree and be able to work after a fashion. It might be capable of lumbering through a thorn bush, frightening out any game rather than finding it by nose. It might be capable of making a reasonable retrieve without eating the bird or it may give it a couple of crunches across the back, leaving the breast meat intact and the bird still edible, but is this really good enough? I say it is not and that such an animal, although a worker of sorts, is not fit to breed from.

My ideal shooting dog is a top class Field Trial dog with

stamina for ordinary shooting, a quality Trials can seldom, if ever, test. It may be a Field Trial Champion or it may never have quite managed to win its title. It matters not, so long as the dog is consistent. There have been some very bad and lucky Field Trial Champions and some very good and unlucky Field Trial winners but for the purposes of this book and for simplicity's sake, I will assume the good Trial dog to be the epitome of the best shooting dog, therefore I have no hesitation in recommending that a puppy should come from predominantly Field Trial stock.

There is absolutely no guarantee that such a puppy will turn out satisfactorily. Matings from even top class parents do not always 'nick' and even in successful matings there is usually (but not always) a 'fool of the family'. However, if one adopts as policy the aforementioned advice, the odds against getting a bad one are appreciably diminished. It is a significant but absolutely indisputable fact that no Springer Spaniel with the slightest trace of show blood in it other than the Higham line mentioned earlier, has done any good in Trials over at least the last 20 years and the same nearly but not quite applies to Cockers. I have already mentioned that a certain amount of show blood in Labradors and Golden Retrievers does not always have disastrous effects but if I personally wanted a pup of either of these breeds, I would obtain one of pure Field Trial stock, provided I knew and liked both parents and considered them to be dogs of natural ability and initiative.

Having outlined the type of background I consider a puppy should come from, we now come to the question of source of supply. There are now a vast number of 'backyard breeders' who possess useful working bitches with a background of pure Field Trial blood. Often their owners take them to the nearest or most recently publicised Field Trial Champion, often lacking the knowledge of which bloodlines are likely to be compatible or how much close breeding to one particular 'name' dog is advisable, or if they are, in fact, line breeding to one particular dog which may have had an unreliable mouth. The resulting progeny will therefore be 'chance bred' but the situation is still better than was the case several years ago when, owing to a terrific advertising campaign from a show bred kennel of Springers, practically every shooting man and gamekeeper owned a product of this particular line.

I have trained a good many chance bred Springers and the

results have been very encouraging. Occasionally a really top class article appears so I would not altogether dismiss the backyard breeder as a source of supply. The best method however, is to study Field Trial results and note which owners are consistently successful. It is a good idea for a potential buyer to approach such a person well before he requires a pup and enquire if he might be able to buy a pup from his line some time in the future. Some Field Trial owners are unapproachable, some autocratic, some downright rude but the majority are perfectly reasonable people and although most run a few pups on for themselves, many have pups for sale straight out of the nest.

When such breeders do sell pups at eight weeks, they are unable to pick out the best for themselves so, if they are prepared to sell at this age, the buyer stands a chance of buying the best or the worst of the litter. To advise an aspiring gundog owner to try to acquire a pup from such a source is a counsel of perfection, as the Field Trial contingent could never breed sufficient pups to keep themelves and every shooting man supplied but this is the approach I would certainly advise.

Having found a litter which the buyer considers suitably bred, or which a more knowledgeable person assures him is so, the question now arises which pupply to pick. I would advise anyone, as a matter of policy, to choose a bold, confident puppy and to avoid the one that holds itself aloof. That such pups often overcome such initial nervousness cannot be denied and many have become extremely good dogs, just as many bold pups at eight weeks develop 'nerves' at six to eight months, but I think one must adhere to a chosen policy over such matters, even though the exception sometimes proves the rule.

I do not believe in hand clapping to test a tiny pup for potential gunshyness. Any pup may be startled by a sudden handclap and one that shows no reaction may simply be insensitive at that age but develop gun trouble later. Although, as I have already explained, gun nervousness can be hereditary, in most pups the question is largely one of management over introduction to the gun. If one really wishes to find the boldest pup in the litter at this age, the pups should be individually lifted out of the pen and placed on strange ground. Once away from the rest of the litter, many pups will flatten themselves against the ground and refuse to move. A bold pup, however, will run around and investigate. Having said all this, I still believe that picking pups is like putting one's hand in a bran tub. I have never claimed to be capable of picking pups at eight weeks but I can recognise exceptional quality in a Spaniel in a few seconds when the pup is several months old.

From a purely physical point of view, I love a really round pup but all other things being equal, I would eschew a pot bellied specimen and I would advise anyone to turn down a pup with a navel rupture. Bow-legs are unsightly but many a bow-legged pup straightens out as he matures. Some retain a Dachshund-like quality all their lives, usually coupled with powerful hindquarters, a cylindrical loin (what I term 'otter bodied') and abundant stamina. Nature's compensation for funny looks I imagine. Many good Spaniels have possessed this rather peculiar conformation and in a busy dog this is not too noticeable but a bow-legged, long bodied Labrador looks quite grotesque. This condition in Spaniels is blamed by some knowledgeable breeders on poor rearing of pups during the last war. This may well be so, as the condition is becoming rarer.

⑥ Pre-training management

I think that it is absolutely essential for the pup to be inoculated at the age of eleven weeks against Hardpad, Distemper, Leptospirosis and Hepatitis. If contact with other dogs is unavoidable, I would recommend that the pup is injected right away with one of the special early vaccines. I prefer gundogs to live permanently outside and I think the time to start is as soon as the pup is acquired. It will make an awful noise for a time, as it will miss its litter mates but most pups soon adjust to their new surroundings.

During the next four to six months, the pup should be given no training in the accepted sense of the word. Plenty of human contact is desirable, some children can be good for pups but the little horrors vary in temperament just as much as pups do. Some are kind and gentle with animals, some can be downright vicious, so a child's attitude to a pup must be very carefully assessed. At all times they must be forbidden to throw things for the pup and if discipline cannot be maintained on this matter, then all contact must be completely forbidden.

I have been rather lucky in this respect. My four sons have all owned their own dogs, the eldest, Bruce, training a son of Hales Smut when he was 12 (no mean undertaking considering that the pup was kennelled in the rabbit-pen and spent his early days, eating, chasing rabbits and sleeping) and winning a Trial at 14 years of age which I believe constitutes a record for a handler who has trained his own dog with no assistance. He had a positive, firm approach and a fast reaction when his dog tried to overstep the mark. He was also capable of shooting accurately over his own dog, which should be the ultimate aim of everyone who attempts to train his own dog. My other sons have all behaved well with pups, always requesting permission before going to play with them.

The pup should be given sensible exercise without overtiring it when it is very small. A little controlled retrieving of a small dummy is desirable from time to time and providing this presents no problems and the pup retrieves willingly to hand, unlike some, I see no harm in letting the pup retrieve a cold teal, partridge or baby rabbit. A colleague from the West Country who purchased a Cocker pup from me utilised golden plover, which I imagine would be ideal.

It is a good idea to introduce a Spring born puppy to water before the end of the Summer as I believe that this is easier when the pup is very young than when it has run on land for many months.

If the puppy is a Spaniel, the owner must decide early on whether he intends to allow the puppy to develop its hunting naturally by finding and chasing game, or if he intends to keep it in complete ignorance of the existence of game until it has become thoroughly trained in obedience. If he decides upon the former course, the best method is to walk it round thick cover, such as whin bushes where rabbits live and let it pick up the scent outside the bushes and follow it inside. Before long, a good pup will be penetrating deeply in search of rabbits. He will seldom see one but if he does break cover behind one and give chase he will soon lose it again. A long course across open ground will not help a pup but if such an event occurs, a hare being the usual inducement, it is not going to harm a pup at this stage either. The odd yap of frustration as the pup loses the rabbit in cover should give no cause for alarm at this period as the pup is giving its natural impulses full rein. It will be a different story when the pup finally hunts under its trainer's control, its mental processes by this time having taken a completely different turn.

If the owner decides to teach the pup its hunting, all contact with game should be scrupulously avoided and in this case empty pastures and football pitches make the best exercising ground but one must bear in mind that in hare country, hares can clap down in very open fields. Poultry and sheep should be carefully avoided at all times no matter which hunting method the trainer decides to employ. It is most essential that the pup should neither chase domestic stock nor the owner punish it in the heat of the moment. Steadiness should be brought about under controlled conditions and in its correct sequence in relation to the rest of the training course. If a pup is thrashed for hen catching before its training proper commences, it can be put off retrieving for life at the worst, or be so seriously inhibited at the best, that it refuses to touch feathers or live game for months, thus causing the trainer a great deal of work which could have been avoided had it not been harshly dealt with at an improper time.

Accidents can always happen. Even with careful management the pup can accidentally meet a sheep or chicken and give chase. The owner must run the pup down, catch it and not say a word but be doubly careful in future that there is no repetition of the incident. Pups have a delightful habit of proudly giving their owners the most noxious objects and the prevalence of myxomatosis does not help this situation as, when it occurs, supply of rotting carcases and dead or dying rabbits is constantly available. When an unwelcome object is proudly presented, the owner should grit his teeth, quietly disengage the loathsome thing, cover the pup's eyes with one hand and fling the trophy as far as possible with the other and walk the pup away quickly. At no time must the pup be rated as he cannot distinguish between what is delightful to him and what is noxious to his owner.

Natural retrieving must be fostered at all times and the situation must be appreciated from the pup's point of view. When the pup is fully trained and its retrieving firmly established, it can then be made to 'leave it'. It is generally conceded by experienced trainers that it is most unwise to attempt any training before a puppy is six months old and some authorities, myself included, favour eight rather than six months, the reason being that it is believed that a pup's mental processes are not sufficiently developed before six months of age to absorb training. The story was once quoted of a very eminent and successful Spaniel handler who, being short of a young dog to train one Spring, commenced on a very young puppy which appeared to be unusually precocious. The pup came on extremely well and definitely had all the qualities, but the too early training completely killed its drive and the trainer freely admitted that he effectively ruined this pup.

It is impossible to state the 'ideal' age to start a pup, provided one accepts that a pup should never be started earlier than six months, as they vary to such a great extent that some are better started later than others. Twelve months is not normally too late provided the pup has not been taken out shooting, thoroughly misbehaved and been sent to a trainer as a last resort. I have trained a Springer from scratch as late as two and a half years. She had lived with a sensible client who had given her the odd dummy and plenty of free hunting in heavy rabbity cover.

It must, however, be assumed that the owner/trainer is anxious to make a start, so my advice is to start serious training around eight months. I have heard it stated by one authority that it might assist the novice trainer to commence training at four months, as this would help him to 'get on top of' his puppy more readily. This was in a book written for the 'average trainer with the average dog'. What this combination constitutes would, I feel, be almost impossible to define. I hope this book will assist the novice handler to train the hard, challenging dog, should he find he possesses one. These are, after all, the stallions of their breeds and so much more exciting and efficient than the softies who need continual encouragement. Drive and quality can be curbed, provided the dog has a basically honest temperament and the majority of tough dogs are honest at heart, but drive can never be put into a dog that does not have it. I do not intend to err on the side of caution and assume that my readers will all be incapable of training anything but the mildest specimens. There could well be among my readers, a few Bill Sheldons, who, I understand, never knew he had the ability to train a dog until well into his fifties and who had a glorious but all too brief career, winning every conceivable honour and bringing the fiery Ludlow Gyp and the terribly nervous Micklewood Scud to the top, proving his versatility as a trainer. His exports, Ludbovian Bruce and

The late John and Mrs Forbes in retirement at Cromlix, Perthshire. A successful trainer of all breeds, John remains the doyen of the cocker world, having won the championship six times.

Trehayes Snowflake clears a fence with a strong runner. Howard Pearson.

Scud, won the American National Championships four years in a row. Good horses make good horsemen, good dogs make good handlers, so never be afraid of your dog.

7 Training equipment

I am a fairly simple person who believes in training a gundog with the minimum of commands and equipment. I particularly dislike gadgets and gimmicks.

If a dog has real quality, all I need to train him up to a standard from which he can go on and become a Field Trial Champion, is a slip lead, two skin-covered dummies (or three at the most) two whistles (one to stop, one to turn) something which will make a bang and a bag to carry my dummies in. The article which makes the bang is all important and care should be exercised in its choice. A .410 shotgun is ideal but expensive to use. The .22 cap pistol is not sufficiently effective and some of the .22 long blank pistols are atrocious and can almost deafen me, so it is anyone's guess what effect they have on the hyper-sensitive hearing of a dog. I do possess a .38 blank pistol, which fires black powder cartridges and gives a loud, flat report rather than a sharp crack but it is now expensive to use.

For general purposes I use an old Martini-action carbine, which saw service in the Sudanese campaign, and has been cut down and converted into a dummy launcher, a use I seldom put it to except for advanced water work. It makes a good blank gun as it has several inches of barrel to contain the report.

This brings me to the American dummy launcher, a piece of equipment I do not possess but am thoroughly conversant with. Depending upon the mentality of the handler, it can either become a very useful piece of equipment or a gimmicky toy. It is unrivalled at placing a dummy across a river too wide for throwing or well out to sea (I once had to give a Labrador specific sea training for salt water duck shooting in America), it can teach, or help, a dog to mark and is useful for placing a blind retrieve out into a meadow, so the trainer does not foul the ground by his footscent. It can, injudiciously used, encourage dogs to run in and can make some gun-nervous, which I will go into under the relevant heading.

There are heavy, not quite spherical balls, which are supposed to pursue a zig-zag course downhill and simulate a weaving runner. This is something of a sore point with me as I train in a mountainous region and possess about one quarter of an acre of level ground. Even ordinary dummies are capable of rolling further than I would wish them to at home. There are spring throwers for dummies, which remind me of pieces of disused farming equipment.

Most of the modern training aids are not bad or harmful things in themselves but a point I wish to make is that we are never likely to see better dogs in the future than we have seen in the past; it would be as well to bear in mind that the good dogs of bygone years were all brought to the top without these modern aids, so even though they may be useful, never let us lose sight of the fact that they are no substitute for natural quality in the dog and ability on the part of his trainer.

8 **Training commences**

When training a Retriever, the first lesson I teach it is to walk to heel. This is usually quite an easy lesson as heel keeping appears to come almost naturally to a great many Retrievers. To assist me in this lesson, I would use a woodland ride when I was a gamekeeper and nowadays I use the high banked, narrow mountain road that runs through my land or sometimes a sheep track, as this helps to induce the dog to pursue a straight course at my side. Unlike many, I do not use a choke chain for this lesson but a simple nylon slip lead and a light hazel switch. The dog should be taught to walk on the side of the trainer opposite to the one on which he carries his gun, which in most cases will mean that the dog should be trained to walk on the left of the handler.

A Retriever, being a fairly tall animal should be kept on a fairly short lead and held in the position the trainer wishes the dog to walk in. If the dog digs its front feet into the ground and strains backwards against the lead, the trainer should firmly pull the dog level with him, at the same time giving the command 'heel'. Before long, the dog will discover that it is far more comfortable not to strain backwards. It is more usual for a dog to pull forward than to hang back and this is where the switch comes in. I never jerk the dog backwards but give him the lightest tap across the bridge of the nose accompanied by the command 'heel'. I repeat this every time he puts his nose in front of my knee. The taps are too light to hurt but irritate him, like a fly walking on his nose and he soon learns to keep his nose back out of the way of the switch.

Occasionally he will attempt to cross behind me to my right side, in which case I give him a tap on the right hand side of his neck, drawing on the lead behind my back, accompanied by the relevant command and pulling him back into the correct position. I find that the gentle application of the switch is far better than tugging and jerking at a sensitive puppy who could easily become upset by such treatment and I find I receive a far higher percentage of sensitive pupils than tough ones to train.

The next stage is to teach the dog to heel 'free'. In this case I loop the lead in such a manner that it lies in an S shape down the length of his back. As the loop has not been removed from his neck, he does not get the idea that he has been released and goes rushing off. I walk him along, restraining him with the switch if he deviates from his correct course, then surreptitiously remove the loop from his neck. The chances are that by now the lesson will have been learned and the dog will walk correctly to heel. In other words, he should know what is required and any cunning move on his part should be countered by replacing the lead and this time really giving him a sharp jerk into position with a much sharper command than the one normally used. The change in both tactics and tone will show him he has erred.

With Spaniels my method of heel teaching is similar but is usually the last thing I teach the pup in its training course. In common with many other trainers, I consider that rigorous heel keeping early on could inhibit hunting which is to be avoided at all costs, as hunting is the primary function of a Spaniel. Nevertheless, I feel it is absolutely essential that a Spaniel should be taught to walk to heel before he is shot over. The reasons are manifold. One cannot keep a Spaniel continually hunting as that is completely impractical. When shooting, one has to cross open pasture with no cover to hunt and in the absence of proper ground the Spaniel will start 'scrounging'. It loses its hunting pattern, pulls about in search of cover or slows down and potters. This will be avoided if the dog is brought smartly to heel.

One may decide to walk a stubble for a few partridges or a bit of bog for snipe where the quarry is likely to get up on its own all too soon without the bustle of a questing dog which may cause the game to flush out of shot. One may wish to walk quietly up to a pond or river bank for a chance at duck and in all these cases the place for a Spaniel is at heel. Heeling has an important part to play in the preparation of a Field Trial Spaniel. The dog should be hunted for varying periods of time, according to climatic conditions, then called in to heel as soon as its pace begins to slow down. Ideally, another Spaniel, already at heel, should then be sent out to relieve the first dog which is rested at heel for a period, then sent out to hunt again but this is advanced Spaniel work which will be dealt with later.

As a Spaniel will have spells of hunting and heeling in its shooting career, there is one variation I use in a Spaniel's heeling course–when the dog has become reliable at heel, I send him out to hunt for a period, then call him in to heel. The hunting often excites him to such an extent that he partly forgets his heeling, so if he does not come into heel on command, I 'hup' him, put the lead on and pull him in to heel and walk him for a time, take the lead off, walk him free and send him out to hunt again, repeating the process if I do not achieve the correct response and until he will come in to heel instantly on command after a period of hunting.

9 Dropping to command

Training consists of a series of progressive lessons, each one different from the last and one ultimately has a finished product when all these separate lessons, or loose ends, are tied up to make a complete trained dog. All lessons are important but if I were to be asked which, in my opinion, is the most important of all, I would reply, without hesitation, that to teach a dog to sit and stay is the most vital lesson of all. It is the keystone of the archway, the focal point of training around which the entire structure is built.

From the drop we progress to steadiness to the retrieve, steadiness to the flush in the case of questing dogs, the acceptance of hand signals to direct a dog on its retrieve and the most essential business of sitting still whilst being shot over. Unless a dog is taught to drop properly, it simply cannot be trained at all.

Although I have not seen this in print before, the period of training in which a dog is taught this lesson can teach the trainer more about the dog than any other single factor. This is a lesson which I find intensely interesting as it assists me to make an assessment of the pup's temperament. With a Spaniel in particular, I will already have made an assessment of the pup's basic quality, how he covers the ground, with what speed and style, how he finds game, is he positive in his approach to it and is he so keen that very little more free hunting is either necessary or desirable, is he a natural retriever, does he tend to drop a dummy short of me or does he hang on to it but circle me and refuse to deliver? Can he use the wind when hunting for a dummy and is he bold in his quest for it when it is thrown into cover? A consideration of these factors can tell me if he has basic qualities or otherwise but I have still to find out how willing he will be to allow me to channel these qualities, should he possess them, into the paths that will lead to his becoming a top class dog.

When I get him down on his backside the position begins to clarify. I decide whether I like him. He decides whether he likes me. If I like him in those first few vital lessons, I know I can get him to the top. If I do not like him I have to persevere and work twice as hard and try my best to conceal my dislike so that he will ultimately become a useful shooting dog and I can like him as a finished product a good deal better. Some who aspire to train gundogs professionally seem to think a trainer's life consists of taking a few favourite dogs around the Trial circuits and winning honour and glory; this is not so. A trainer's occupation is to make the best job possible of every dog that comes in to him, so it will become a useful dog for its owner, even though through lack of handling technique, he cannot do it full justice. Some animals inevitably fall by the wayside and have to be discarded but with hard work on the part of the trainer, the bulk of them will get through. Some will cause the trainer headaches and problems but if he is a good man he will usually overcome them. Dogs vary tremendously in their attitude to being taught to drop and it is this variation in attitude which teaches me so much about them.

A Retriever will already have been taught to walk to heel on the lead and free, so he will be thoroughly accustomed to sticking close to me. I will let the dog out of the kennel and allow him to race around for a few seconds if he feels so inclined. I call him in to heel and walk him about a hundred yards then turn and face him, press him down on his haunches and give him the command 'hup'. Upon my releasing the pressure it will almost invariably stand again. Again I push him down and repeat the command. I repeat this procedure and keep on repeating it until he will sit down and stay.

Most Retrievers will learn to sit without the assistance of a lead but if I have any difficulty, such as sidestepping and darting out of the way, standing back and glaring at me with a resentful expression in his eyes, I put the dog back on the lead and carry on with the lessons, dispensing with the lead as soon as he begins to accept the lessons without obvious resentment.

After continuous repetition of pushing down and giving the command 'hup', we reach the stage when he will sit to the command without hand pressure. This is the time to relieve a little of the mental pressure I am exerting, so he will not become repressed by too much repetition. I walk him on and take his mind off sitting then 'hup' him in a different place. The chances are that having learned to sit in one place, he will sit to command in another but occasionally, a dog having learned to obey the command in one spot, fails to register it in another, in which case hand pressure must be applied again until he accepts that 'hup' means 'hup', wherever he happens to be. I keep moving him on at heel, hupping him every now and then, the walk between drops easing the pressure on his nervous system.

With Spaniels my technique is different. A good deal more ingenuity is required as I find Spaniels vary to a greater extent in attitude to the drop than to the majority of Retrievers. If he has free hunted and is therefore more likely to be inquisitive, the chances are that he will be harder to contact than should he have had a more restrained upbringing, as I only free hunt dogs I intend to run in Trials myself or potential shooting dogs who show very little inclination to hunt about naturally.

This is the Spaniel's first lesson, as opposed to the Retriever's second. He has never had a lead on and his normal position is foraging about in front of me as opposed to walking to heel. I let him rummage around for a time then give him the command 'hup' to attract his attention. He does not understand what I mean but having gained his attention I move forward, put my hand on him, push him down with another command 'hup'. That is, if I can catch him! This can be the difficulty with a Spaniel, particularly a mischievous Springer, some of which love to keep just out of reach. In this case I work him into a corner, in the angle of a fence until I can get hold of him.

Cockers seldom move out of reach; as soon as a hand is put anywhere near them, most will fuss all over it and will wriggle and squirm to such an extent that it is impossible to put pressure on the haunches. I have developed a technique of getting the back of my fingers into his flank and with a quick backhanded flick, throwing him onto his haunches with the command 'hup'. A lively Spaniel often reacts well to this method and whichever I use, either hand pressure when possible or throwing him onto his haunches if necessary, I keep moving him around and take particular notice of his tail action between drops. If it goes furiously, I know we are all right. If he drops it or even runs with it stiff out behind him, I know he is a bit soft and must gauge the duration of the lessons accordingly.

Occasionally a Spaniel refuses to come to terms with me at all, consistently keeping out of reach. In this case I must resort to a lead. I simply get him accustomed to being led, without actually teaching him to heel and having accomplished this, teach him to hup on the lead. His earlier reluctance to conform may have been due to nervousness or independence, or, if I am very unlucky, both. If nerves were the problem, there could well be a strong case for 'baiting' him with tripe as described earlier. As I have an excellent supply of tripe, my dogs will seldom take anything less messy from me during training, so I carry pieces of tripe in my dummy bags, which is far better than carrying it in my pockets, particularly during hot weather!

The independent dog can be quite difficult. Once he has been taught to hup on the lead, he will often try to make a bolt for his kennel when the lesson is continued with him free. If I can see this problem arising, I will walk him with myself between him and the kennels and attempt to 'hold' him by placing myself between him and his objective. This may work. On the other hand, I may notice him darting his glance to either side of me, seeking an opportunity to dodge around me. If he continues to give me trouble I will make one of my very rare uses of a cord, which I allow to trail and only use it as a medium for catching him when he bolts for home. Sometimes this works before he quite grasps the point that the cord he is wearing is responsible for his capture. The idea becomes ingrained that he can be caught, so he stays put. If all else fails I take him where he has no kennel to run to. I drive him away from home a few miles and work on him on completely fresh ground. He is 'lost'; so cannot run home. He may run back to the car, in which case I drive it into a field and continue the lessons right by the car. Only once every few years do I find a dog as difficult as this.

10 Sitting and staying

This is a most important extension of the previous lesson and tells me even more about the dog's temperament. Built into it is another lesson, the recall or turn to the whistle. Having by any of the methods already outlined, taught my Retriever or Spaniel to hup instantly to command, I begin to ease myself away from him backwards. He will obviously attempt to follow me, so I give him the command 'hup' with a raised hand, taking a pace towards him to emphasise the command. The lesson simply becomes one of repetition until he will remain seated whilst I move several yards away.

After keeping him down several seconds, I give him two pips on the whistle which I utilise as the turn or recall, giving him vocal encouragement in conjunction with the whistle. Most pups are only too willing to leave the drop and gallop up to the handler so, unwittingly, the pup has obeyed the whistle. When he comes up, I always insist upon his touching my hand with his nose. If he bolts past me, full of exuberance, I am not content until he has turned back to me again and touched me. I cannot say exactly why I insist upon this; it just seems to me to be the right way to increase our contact.

The distances become greater and I take the keenest interest in whether the pup keeps his mind and eyes on me, or whether he gazes around, snaps at flies, chews grass or sniffs around for sheep dung. It is the usual and common action of a pup who does not take kindly to training, to ignore his handler as he retreats backwards. If his attention wanders I give him the command 'hup', sharply, and get his eyes back on me.

This is the lesson which enables me to penetrate the inner being of the dog, to put something of my own personality into him; to hold him down at a distance by sheer willpower establishes the contact between us which will, in the future, enable me to stop him when he is halfway out to a retrieve and a hare jumps up under his nose. Constant repetition of the long drop and recall will improve contact between myself and an animal of low calibre and indifferent response. Sooner or later he will bring his gaze to bear on me and ignore the buzzard floating over the valley or the tuft of grass in front of his nose. Some dogs 'creep' during this lesson, Cockers being the chief offenders. This poses problems for me as the Cockers look so funny pulling themselves along on their bellies with their elbows, hind legs stretched out behind them so that I am liable to start laughing which causes a rift in concentration and the Cocker comes tearing in and leaps all over me. Then I have to pick him up by the scruff and carry him back, dangling like a dead rabbit but with his tail going like mad and as I put him down, none too gently, I give him a slap across his villainous little face, a hup and a good cursing. He does not mind but usually registers, that is, until he decides to do a crawl again! Cocker training is really a subject on its own.

After this lesson has been learnt, it will often be found that the dog has thoroughly absorbed the recall whistle; when the animal is taken out for future training and allowed his several seconds free gallop, he will return to the whistle instantly when his trainer wants to call him to order. This lesson also paves the way to introduction to the gun, as it enables the trainer to put an appreciable distance between himself and the pupil before the gun is fired. However, I teach another two lessons before introducing the pup to the gun.

11 Stopping to the whistle

Once a dog has become thoroughly reliable at sitting and staying, the natural follow on is stopping to the whistle. This is an essential but usually easily taught lesson as it is simply an extension of the verbal 'hup'. The advantages of the stop whistle over the verbal command are that the whistle is far more effective at a distance than the voice and is believed to be less disturbing to game.

Some thought should be given to the pattern of whistle one intends to employ. Some favour the silent type. A Retriever going at full gallop, well out, who gracefully subsides into a sitting position to a note on the silent whistle, is an impressive sight but, owing to the small aperture in the mouthpiece of the silent whistle, it takes a split second longer to get the air into the whistle and the note out. When we consider a hard going dog, bent on mischief, we must realise that we do not have this split second to spare. I have used as a stop whistle, both the Acme Thunderer (the referee's whistle) and the police whistle. To be fully effective, the police whistle must be 'pipped' with the tongue darting quickly in and out of the aperture and not blown, like a guardian of the Law summoning aid. I found some of my clients were unable to master the technique so changed exclusively to the Thunderer. The advantage of the Thunderer lies in its large aperture, easy to find in an emergency and easy to blow into. It is the quickest stop whistle on the market and much favoured by American Spaniel handlers.

To teach the stop whistle I simply give the pup the whistle followed by the command 'hup'; with very little repetition the stop whistle is usually well absorbed. I do a few variations on it, such as using it when the dog is running about free and making sure he obeys it when his mind is on his own business. I also drop him sometimes and walk away, calling him in and stopping halfway with the whistle and raised hand signal but care must be taken not to overdo this lesson. The pup can become so conditioned to coming in to the handler immediately after stopping to the whistle that during advanced training, when the dog is being taught to handle on blind retrieves, it can habitually come in towards the handler after the stop whistle is blown instead of 'getting back' in the opposite direction.

12 Retrieving and steadiness to the dummy

From the period immediately prior to training and in addition to his early obedience lessons, the pup has frequently been tried with a dummy. I use a woollen or cloth dummy, covered with a rabbit or hare skin and containig a core of wood to add weight and rigidity. Pups vary enormously in their attitude to retrieving and these attitudes tend to be hereditary to a very large extent. We all like a natural retriever, the puppy who from its earliest days runs out and picks a knotted handkerchief, progressing to the dummy without a hitch but this desirable state of affairs does not invariably manifest itself later on. As some pups develop mentally they tend to become mischievous and independent and can exhibit every variation of misconduct. The Springers are, I find, generally the biggest culprits in the faulty retrieving field but, strangely enough, I find that the wicked Cockers are usually the best and cleanest retrievers of the lot, although some do have a delightful little habit of burying the retrieve occasionally, a characteristic sometimes retained well beyond puppy days. In fact, there was a certain Cocker, dressed in sober black, who won the Championship and was privately christened 'The Undertaker', for very obvious reasons.

I always allow my pups to run in to the dummy for quite a period. It encourages keenness and marking but, more important, one is able to draw a sharper dividing line between running in and complete steadiness once the latter lessons commence. A pup which is basically a natural retriever will often come in within two or three yards of the trainer, then proceed to do everything bar give him the dummy. Some will come so far in then stop and tear at the dummy. Others will habitually drop the dummy within a few yards of the handler, not, I believe, due to lack of confidence in their trainer but because they just do not want the thing in their mouths any longer. The commonest advice given to overcome these situations is to run away from the pup in the opposite direction, calling his name. I agree with this; but for the persistent circler, a much heavier dummy, used in dense cover such as thick, tall grass or bracken, will often make the business of running around with the dummy much more difficult (and consequently less enjoyable) so he decides to come in to hand.

When the dog consistently delivers short and after an appreciable period there is no improvement, I will force his delivery.* I do not propose to go into this system in detail but the basic principle is to apply a measure of discomfort to the foot, ear or lips of the dog so he opens his mouth in protest, then the trainer puts the dummy in his mouth and removes the discomfort. The dog associates the cessation of pain with the reception of the dummy, so eventually it will take and hold the dummy directly the relevant command is given. Some trainers can by this method make a complete non-retriever pick up and deliver and adopt a rather 'holier than thou attitude' to those who cannot 'force from the floor'. I cannot do this but I find myself in excellent company as some of our top private professional trainers know nothing about this method and opt for the natural retriever every time. If too many complete non-retrievers were forced, brought into the public eye and then bred from, surely the greenest student of gundogs would be able to recognise the danger without my having to spell it out.

I once had a Labrador which completely refused to pick anything. I had trained his sire who was top class but this pup had a blind spot in his make-up. I managed to start him off retrieving half a stale loaf, so hard he could not bite it. I later bound a leather glove to it. I then rolled the glove up on its own and he accepted that. Later still I bound the glove to the dummy which he would retrieve and spit out a couple of yards away. When he became really keen I forced his delivery and the end product was a dog with a perfect delivery.

We can now assume that I have a pup which is either a good natural retriever or which has overcome any initial difficulties by the methods described but runs into the dummy. He has learned to stop instantly to the whistle and it is now time he was steadied. One does not necessarily have to confine oneself to one method only. In the case of a reasonably bold, confident pup, I sit him down in front of me, if possible in the angle of the corner of a sheep fence or other confined space, with myself blocking the exit. I throw the dummy over my shoulder away from the pup, so that it falls behind and to one side of me. The pup, of course, runs in but has to pass close by me in

* For full details on force retrieving see *Spaniel training for modern shooters* by Maurice Hopper (David & Charles).

the attempt. I either use the stop whistle or a verbal 'hup'. If the pup stops, all well and good. I keep him down several seconds, then send him for the dummy. After being stopped for the first time, a pup's approach to finding the dummy is seldom enthusiastic, so I normally teach this lesson on fairly bare ground, so the dummy can be visible and act as an added inducement when the pup is ordered to retrieve. If the pup does not stop on command, I get after him and grab him before he gets to the dummy, or when he overshoots it, as young dogs are apt to do, not yet having weighed the power of their own momentum. I carry him back to the spot where he failed to stop, not saying a word until I arrive there then sit him down with a sharp 'hup'. I walk out and pick the dummy myself, repeating the exercise until he will watch the fall of the dummy and only retrieve it when ordered to.

An alternative method which is useful with a more sensitive pup, which might not relish the prospect of a rough individual pursuing it at considerable speed, is to tether the pupil with not too much slack on the lead or cord, as it is undesirable for him to be brought to a halt with too hard a jerk. I throw the dummy, giving the command or stop whistle at the very instant that the cord brings him to a halt. I bend over him and surreptitiously remove the slip of the lead from his neck, giving him another 'hup' as I straighten up again. I keep him down a few seconds then send him for the retrieve and repeat the process until he will watch the fall without straining forward. Then I repeat the procedure with him free but at all times position myself strategically in order that I may check any attempt on his part to move unbidden. Position of the dog in relation to the trainer is most important in this exercise. He *must* have his eyes firmly on the trainer when the dummy is thrown.

Variations to give maximum temptation, such as the dummy being thrown from behind him when he is out hunting, can be instituted when basic steadiness has been thoroughly established. There is a subtle difference between the two methods outlined. In the first the pup is stopped from running in. In the second he is shown that he must not run in. I would recommend the latter method to the more inexperienced trainer.

The pup is now quite steady on the thrown dummy, or is he? Set him off hunting if he is a Spaniel and throw the dummy and he will run straight in as though he had never been taught to do otherwise. Why? He has been taught this lesson in a sitting position, concentrating on his trainer. Immediately he is set in motion, his concentration lapses and he has not yet been taught to check his stride when a dummy falls, so this must now be brought about. Again, correct positioning of the trainer is all important. When the pup is well to the left, the dummy should be thrown well to the right, so one has the maximum chance to stop him if he attempts to cut across the front of his handler. Having been well grounded in steadiness in the sedentary position, most pups soon grasp the point that they must be steady to the dummy under all circumstances.

This is a period when the pup can be offered maximum temptation as the variations one can employ are endless. He can be given a long drop, then whistled in and the dummy can be thrown to land a few yards from him as he approaches the trainer at full speed. One can get him hunting really hard in an interesting piece of cover and drop the dummy right in front of his nose until he will drop to a falling dummy without a word from the trainer. He should never be allowed to touch these 'temptation retrieves', but retrieving and marking practice can still be given, throwing the dummy as far as possible into varying cover and making him wait about 20 seconds before sending him, or longer if he has been difficult to steady. If he shows himself to be a naturally poor marker, the waiting period may be substantially decreased but be warned that to send the pup in quickly several times will lead to a breakdown in steadiness, so vigilance must never be relaxed and one must be ready quickly to check the pup when this happens.

13 Introducing the gun

This is a most important and, indeed, crucial period in a gundog's career. I use the term 'period' in place of lesson, as confidence with the gun must be 'built in' rather than taught. In the case of a pup which I have bred myself, I have the advantage of knowing the pup's past history in relation to the gun. I know that since birth, he will have heard gunfire at a distance but will never have had a firearm discharged close to him. In the case of a pup coming in for training from outside, he may never have heard a shot at all, or, as in some cases, he may have had a *12-bore* fired straight over his head 'to see if he is gun-shy'.

It is many years now since I last saw a truly gun-shy dog, as I believe that, like canine hysteria, gun-shyness has practically been eliminated from true working strains of gundogs. The accepted definition of gun-shyness is the condition whereby a dog runs and hides upon hearing a shot. It is thought to be incurable by most trainers but, every now and then, an amateur trainer writes an article in the sporting press, claiming to have cured a pup so afflicted. Whether the pup was actually gun-shy or gun nervous is always debatable and the writer often quite happily discloses information which points to his having probably caused, or at least aggravated, the condition himself. Only recently I read of such an episode. The pup in question was known to be of nervous disposition, yet its first introduction to the gun was to have a .410 fired within 20 yards of it! This is far too close.

By far the most common complication encountered during the period of introduction to the gun is gun nervousness. The pup, on hearing a shot, may flinch, turn his ears back, drop them, tuck his tail down, or run away several yards, glancing over his shoulder but he does not run home or hide right away. On taking him back to his kennel, he may show an unusual eagerness to get there. A pup so affected will usually go out and retrieve a dummy but without his usual dash and enthusiasm. Most cases of gun nervousness are curable but mishandling of this condition can cause it to become permanent. Once a pup shows that he is gun nervous, it is fatal simply to carry on firing shots in his presence in the mistaken belief that he will 'get used to it'. He will not and specific treatment must be given to effect a cure.

A third, and very deceptive complication over the gun, is the matter of the pup who shows no reaction to the first few shots but who, in himself does not care much for a shot. Only an extremely sensitive trainer can spot this condition as, to begin with, the signs are so difficult to detect. He may duck his head slightly when a dummy is thrown, in anticipation of a shot. He may go out to a retrieve with a slight slackening of speed. He may not be quite so persevering in quest of the dummy or he may circle and sidestep when presenting the retrieve. Failure to diagnose this condition at this stage could result in the pup becoming truly gun nervous. I have heard trainers speak of dogs which have 'suddenly become gun nervous after being previously all right'. No such thing. The condition was always there but was not spotted at the crucial and barely perceptible phase. I once asked a friend how a certain Cocker was progressing in training. His answer is worth heeding.

'She's a silly little thing. She isn't gun nervous but fire 20 shots over her in a grouse butt and she would be'.

He is a man of above average ability and perception and meant that a barrage of shots over this bitch from within the confines of a grouse butt would have a cumulative effect as there would be nothing to take her mind off the shots, no bird falling in full view, no retrieve after the shot, nothing to do until the end of the drive.

That plain ungarnished shots fired in succession over a sensitive dog can have a cumulative effect and cause gun nervousness was vividly illustrated when a client, who rather fancies himself as a dog man, brought me three young Labradors to train. I had an exercise pen, bounded on one side by a long brick wall. The dogs were in the pen, prior to being put in their indoor kennels when their owner, standing right by the wall, produced a .25 training pistol and announced that he would 'just see they were alright with a gun'. At the first shot, there was no reaction. At the second, one dog flinched slightly. At each subsequent shot, this dog flinched more visibly until, by the time the magazine was empty, the dog had practically curled into a ball and even the owner noticed something was amiss. The wall had certainly produced a fearful echo. When I started training the dogs, I found there was, indeed, a serious problem with the one which had taken exception to the shots. As the owner had caused this condition by his ignorance and insensitivity, I did not feel disposed to put the matter right, particularly as he was only prepared to leave the dogs with me for three months, so sent the gun nervous dog home. He subsequently went to an amateur trainer of considerable ability who likewise rejected him. The owner eventually took over and after a very long period eventually claimed success. He would proudly exhibit the dog as 'the one Keith Erlandson and H.H. failed to train'.

I will now describe how I introduce the gun, in a manner which I hope will produce no unwelcome reaction but which will enable me to spot the slightest sign of nervousness, should it arise.

I have already described how the echo of a shot can have a disastrous impact on the nervous system of a dog, so I avoid buildings and the steepest of hillsides and choose as level a situation as possible on my mountain pastures. I have no woodland but would advise avoiding a wood, as it will produce an echo.

I sit my pup down and walk a hundred yards away, making certain that the wind is blowing from him to me and never *vice versa*. I fire my blank gun or a .410 and immediately whistle him in to me, having first noted his reaction. He should come bounding up with tail wagging but even if this is the case, I do not imagine that all must be well and fire over his head. I decrease the distance slightly for the next shot and, provided no unfavourable reaction is noticed, I bring him in closer still. Finally, I fire a shot with him seated about 30 yards away and throw a dummy downhill and almost level with him. After a much shorter wait than would be the case in dummy practice I send him for the retrieve. If all seems well, I still do not assume that this phase has been satisfactorily passed but carry on with the same caution for a few days. It is important, I believe, to use the same technique all over again when introducing a large bore shotgun later on in training.

In some cases things do not go so well. The pup may show some fear of the gun or he may even have been made gun nervous before being sent to me. To effect a cure, the basic principle must be the same, whichever method, or combination of them, is used. He must learn to associate a shot with something pleasant, which can be either food or an activity he enjoys, such as chasing game or running in to retrieve. From a trainer's point of view it is better if he can effect a cure with food, as in the case of the latter method, he must create another problem for himself to cure the existing one. In a really bad case, I keep the pupil short of food for a couple of days then enlist the aid of one of my sons, who stands at a distance and fires a shot at a signal from me. As soon as the shot is fired I offer the pupil a piece of tripe which is usually taken. Several more shots are fired and a piece of bait is given after each. The distance at which the shot is fired is decreased each day but the pup is not allowed to see the gun.

A gun nervous pup very quickly comes to associate the actual weapon with a shot, in fact many dogs will show a reaction to the raising of a gun long after they have lost all fear of the report, so it follows that if a pup begins to feel fear at the sight of a gun, the shot will have a worse effect than if it simply hears the sound. When the pup will take food without flinching at a shot fired just over a hedge from him, I will get my assistant to fire a shot and throw a dummy over the hedge from a position about 30 yards in front of me. I send him after a brief wait and build in the idea that a shot also means something which is fun, a retrieve.

I once had a case in which a Labrador had been taken to a covert shoot as a very small puppy and had been terrified out of his wits. To 'cure' him, his owner and a friend fired about 30 beer cans into the air and fired a 12-bore at each. I used my customary tactics but this dog was such an extreme case that he would rather starve than eat after a shot, even though he was a healthy, typically greedy young dog. I changed my tactics and put him in the rabbit-pen which he really enjoyed and when I could see he was mad keen I fired the .410. At the shot he broke off the chase and came in to heel but I managed to get him chasing again. At each shot he abandoned pursuit and came in to me but I noticed he was really finding his rabbits, like a good Spaniel and it was the dog's obvious quality that caused me to persevere. The cure was finally effected simply by walking him at heel with an experienced Labrador whose owner, incidentally, had originally made *him* gun nervous, too, by taking him out on a lead to a shoot at four months old. I threw a dummy, fired a shot and he did not flinch, retrieving the dummy nicely on command, the presence of the older dog seeming to boost his morale.

A word on the dummy launcher may not be out of place whilst on this subject. It is often found that a dog which has become perfectly confident with the gun, will show an unfavourable reaction to the launcher. To understand this, I think we should consider for a moment the working principle of this device. A .22 long rifle blank is exploded within a chamber, the exit from which is blocked by the dummy being fitted over its end. The gases from the cartridge expand to form a terrific compression which launches the dummy. To the dog with its particularly acute hearing, I believe that the sound of this piece of equipment being fired must be heard as a double report, as virtually two explosions take part in one. This may produce the sound of a shot with an echo, or simply be heard by the dog as a double discharge.

My favourite weapon is a simple boxlock 16-bore which I have owned since I was a boy and with which I have trained

22 Field Trial Champions. Every now and then, upon firing the right barrel, it happens that the left will be discharged also, giving me a fearful wallop and causing even the most experienced dog to flinch, which seems to prove that most dogs do not care for a double discharge. I have found that any dog which is sound with an ordinary gun, will, as its experience increases, come to accept the dummy launcher in due course but I do believe that its continued use with a reactive dog in the earlier stages of gun work could well create a problem which might prove difficult to undo, so my advice to anyone who finds their dog does not like the launcher, is to discontinue its use and carry on with an acceptable weapon until the dog is a few months older.

14 Handling the real thing

When training one of my own dogs, the chances are that whilst still a young puppy, he may have shown himself a confident enough retriever of the dummy to have been given a cold bird or rabbit to retrieve occasionally, particularly should he be a Cocker pup, as I find this breed particularly precocious in retrieving.

Should he have come in from a client, the chances are that he will never have handled game, so this is the next step after he has proved his willingness to retrieve the dummy efficiently. A good bird to start with is a dead domestic pigeon. They are far closer feathered than the wild variety, are an easy mouthful for any pup and have a rather rank, bitter scent which can stand a dog in good stead for the future when he is expected to retrieve odd-smelling specimens such as duck, snipe and woodcock. Furthermore, they are relatively easy to obtain at all times of the year. Moorhen, teal and half grown rabbits are all suitable.

I make certain the specimen is quite cold and not badly shot and throw it in full view, as I want the pup to gallop out and grab it before he has chance to use his nose, as he would have to do if it fell in cover. Most pups retrieve their first head of real 'game' without a hitch, never even stopping to decide whether they like the scent of it or not, but sometimes a pup will back away or circle the retrieve if it is a bird, or if a rabbit, lick the ears and tail but refuse to fetch it. In either case, I go in and pick the retrieve up myself and tease the pup with it, shaking it around his muzzle, stroking the top of his head and making encouraging noises. Often he will open his mouth and try to get it round the object. I throw it a very short distance and send him in as soon as it hits the ground. Usually this time he will make some attempt to get it into his mouth, although lack of confidence and experience may cause him to allow the thing to slide out when he is halfway back to me. I continue on these lines until he handles the real thing as well as the dummy.

I do not make more than about four attempts in any one lesson as it most important not to sicken him of the business, should he have any aversion to the real thing. The principle is to build something into his mind and add to it daily until he retrieves confidently. Once he will take the thing into his mouth, he will usually improve with each lesson until perfection is reached. The logical follow-on is to try him with freshly killed game. Having handled cold game, very few pups will refuse the same species when warm, but should this happen, the procedure just described should be followed but success is quickly usually achieved.

After proving he will handle warm game, one or two head may be shot for the pup under controlled conditions. A few pigeon may be shot over him but he must not be allowed to *find* game and have it shot for him as he has not yet been steadied to flush. In the case of a young retriever this is simple. He can be walked at heel round the edge of a covert and a pigeon or two shot for him as they clatter from the outside trees. The object of shooting over him at this stage is to attempt to shoot something for him which may come down as a live bird. I strongly believe that a gundog should retrieve one or two live birds before he is steadied to flush, in order that subsequent steadiness lessons will have their desired effect but will not inhibit the pup to the point of refusing to touch a retrieve with life still in it, as he will already have gained confidence in this sphere before steadiness lessons commence.

15 Steadiness to game

The easiest and, in my opinion, best way to steady a gundog to game, whether he is a Retriever who must be taught to ignore ground game when walking at heel or sitting at a drive and, equally important, when he is well out from his handler searching for shot game, or if he is a Spaniel who must be steady to flushed game under every conceivable circumstance, is by the intelligent use of a rabbit-pen. There is a good deal which can never be taught in a rabbit-pen and can only be instilled by experience in the field but as a means of establishing an essential contact between game and dog, and dog and handler, under controlled conditions, I believe the pen to be unrivalled.

The conventional pen, as possessed by the majority of trainers, is normally a rectangular piece of grassland dotted at intervals with heaps of brushwood for the rabbits to hide in. The basic principle is for the dog to find the rabbits by nose in the piles of cover and remain steady as a rabbit is flushed. He also learns that the rabbit must be pushed out and not caught in the bush and that he must not take the lines of the departed rabbits but break off cleanly and carry on hunting for more body scent. All this, of course, in the case of a Spaniel. A Retriever can be taught steadiness either at heel or while rabbits are driven past him and to pick dummies which fall close to lively rabbits.

My own situation is rather different. My pen is simply a hillside fenced in, about 300 yards long by 40 yards wide. The cover is natural bracken, a few bramble and gorse bushes and an area of rough cocksfoot grass. In the early Spring of the year the bracken is completely flat and the rabbits sit mainly in the old cocksfoot. I have tried piles of brushwood but the rabbits flatly refuse to use them and the answer to this eludes me. During the Summer the bracken becomes far too heavy and I cut paths through it with a scythe, leaving it in square blocks. It is still difficult to work the dogs under these conditions but they really love it and not only learn steadiness but keenness as well. One must normally employ caution and not overdo the rabbit-pen lessons lest the pupils become jaded in appetite, but it is virtually impossible to sicken a keen dog in my pen. A dog running from one stick pile to another, poking rabbits out and watching them run away can become bored with this type of work. In my pen this situation never arises. The dog finds the rabbit and has to push him several yards before he breaks cover, a situation of maximum temptation for the dog and a lesson which is impossible to teach in the stick pile pen. He learns, too, that he must not take the line of a rabbit across open ground or round the pen's perimeter but that it is permissible to line a rabbit until he forces it out of cover. The fact that he may flush a wild pheasant in the pen, or even have one shot for him, all helps to make my pen a highly desirable area.

A few years ago a Spaniel had a most unusual find in my pen. A bird flushed from the bracken, failed to become sufficiently airborne and crashed into the wire. The Spaniel had dropped to flush, so I moved quickly forward and caught the bird. It was a corncrake with one leg completely shorn off below the knee, presumably by a grass cutter but completely healed. It was a lovely looking bird and flew away quite happily on being released. Twelve months later my son Bruce flushed a bird from the top side of the pen and, by his description, it, too, could only have been a landrail.

Dogs which pass through my hands are not always dealt with in the same manner over the question of learning to hunt. If a dog comes in to be trained as a shooting dog, and nothing more, he is never allowed to chase unless he is so lifeless as an individual that I judge the only way to get him moving at all is to let him really find out what rabbits are and have a few good chases. If I train a dog with a view to running it in Trials, I will let it have a period of free hunting and chasing in the pen unless I can see it is one of those rare, brilliant natural hunters who will hunt any piece of ground hard with virtually no stimulation. This is the type of dog which, first and foremost, wants to 'go' and cover the ground. Finding game is an activity this dog must become conversant with later on in his hunting career whereas, with the majority of dogs, the reverse is usually the case; the dog does not 'go' until it has found a fair amount of game, a reason for it displaying enthusiasm, so it follows that it is this type of dog which will benefit most from a period of unrestrained hunting. This type of activity is also beneficial in another and less understood direction. Free hunting allows a pup to 'find its feet'. It becomes accustomed to negotiating varied terrain at top speed, so its balance and movement benefit accordingly. Hunting is surely an example of each case being treated on its merits.

The time has now come when the pup must be steadied. He has either already chased in the pen, so is willing to go out and find something, or failing this he will have exhibited a willingness to move around on gameless ground; one way or the other, I at least know he will leave my feet. The first rabbit he finds or sees he will chase, so I blow the stop whistle directly his movement after the rabbit commences. So soft are a great many modern Spaniels that a very surprising proportion of them stop at the first blast of the whistle, even though they may have previously been allowed a chasing period. In such a case I give the command 'gone away' and work the pup in the opposite direction to the one the rabbit has taken. If the pup persists on the line, I stop him and call him in on the turn/recall whistle.

If he fails to react and still persists on the rabbit line, I stop him again and move in on him. I take him by the throat and pull him towards me, blowing the recall whistle in his ear. This breaks his contact with the rabbit and I send him back into the cover away from the rabbit. In the case of this dog, the lessons continue on these lines until I can stop him on every rabbit he finds and call him off the line with ease. I draw the reader's attention to the fact that the aim is for an intermediate stage in steadiness, so the dog becomes completely stoppable on command but would still chase if left to its own devices. I will explain why in due course.

There is, of course, also a very good chance that the pup will refuse to stop to its first rabbit, in which case I get after him as fast as possible. I can arrange things so he finds his first rabbit at the foot of the slope, so if I fail to stop him he has to run uphill after the rabbit. I can run uphill but I cannot run downhill. The hill slows the pup and with a bit of luck I soon catch him. I take him firmly by the throat and blow the stop whistle in his ear. He must never, at this stage, be punished any more severely than this as a hiding could give him the impression he must not hunt at all whereas a bit of rough handling and the whistle in his ear should illustrate the point that he has disobeyed the whistle. He is made to follow me downhill and is set off hunting again. I should be able to stop him on the next rabbit but failing this I run him down again and give him a hard shaking. Sooner or later, continued catching and shaking will show him that he must stop every time on command. As he has been taught to stop with a minimum of force, his keenness will not be impaired and continued stopping will gradually teach him that he must stop on his own when he finds and flushes a rabbit.

I feel a great sense of achievement when, on a good scenting evening, I have a young Spaniel going at top speed, finally driving an elusive rabbit out of cover, and flinging himself down directly he views the rabbit, without a word from me.

A word of warning over Summer Spaniel training. It might happen that the Spaniel has been steadied in a period of hot weather which, customary to the British climate, might end with a thunderstorm, torrential rain and be followed by a much cooler period. Beware! It will be a very different Spaniel that comes out of the kennel now. Scent will be much better, the air cooler and the dog far keener. Anticipate a breakdown in steadiness as there is a very good chance that this will happen but as he has already been taught to stop to the rabbits, it will not be difficult to come to terms with him again. The important thing is not to be taken unawares and let him get away with it. To obtain the best flush from a dog, a trainer must at all times show the dog that he is vigilant and capable of fairly rapid movement. A dog will respect such a person but will not lose his edge of keenness when working for him. It is not hard to frighten a dog into submission by over zealous punishment but its manner of working will never compare with that of the dog which knows he cannot get away with any misdeeds, yet has no fear of his handler.

The methods outlined are the ones I use to induce steadiness as they best fit my particular temperament and local conditions but I would also like to point out that there are other methods of achieving the same object. To give pups an idea of hunting, some authorities advocate that they should be tethered inside the rabbit-pen and the rabbits hunted past them by experienced dogs. The reasoning behind this practice would appear to be that the pups see the rabbits and become keenly interested but are restrained from chasing, as some people still believe that once a Spaniel is allowed to chase it can never be steadied. I personally do not like the idea of this tethering practice but let me in all fairness hasten to explain that its main advocate has trained at least 20 Field Trial Champions in a long and highly successful career so I do not feel that this method can be altogether dismissed.

I could never advise anyone to hunt a Spaniel on a check-cord, as these snag and tangle but a training cord can be particularly useful in the case of an unusually naughty Spaniel which refuses to be caught after doing wrong. The cord can provide a means of apprehending him. As an alternative to running a Spaniel down when he chases, the pup can be steadied on a short cord. He is simply walked up to a rabbit which the trainer can see and, when the rabbit moves, the trainer jerks the cord and blows the stop whistle. Repetition of this practice can illustrate the point to the pup but the fact remains that, sooner or later, the pup must work free.

The type and behaviour of the rabbits employed in the pen can have a direct bearing on the success or otherwise of steadiness lessons. Tame rabbits in a small pen may be better than nothing but their value is very limited. In a small pen they tend to remain too tame, with the possible exception of the Dutch variety. Pure wild rabbits are good but tend to be uncooperative. Even in a very large pen like my own, they are likely to try to dig out and if they are allowed to dig burrows, spend a good deal of time down them. Wild/tame crosses are ideal. It is essential that a pen rabbit should be fast, both to prevent the dogs from catching it in cover and to provide maximum temptation. These crosses are active and very good at taking care of themselves and are more contented with pen conditions than pure wild stock. An unfortunate limitation of the pure tame rabbits, even when they have become wilder through living in a large pen, is that their scent is substantially different from that of wild rabbits. How can I prove this? Many years ago I had a pen stocked entirely with tame rabbits. One day I shot a wild rabbit and when the dog I was using retrieved it I found it was only slightly grazed and temporarily stunned, so into the pen he went. The following night my old Sausage Dog of the pre-myxomatosis era, burrowed under the wire, hunted him down and killed him. She obviously winded him through the wire and picked him out as legitimate quarry from the tame ones, which never appeared to arouse her interest.

A Retriever which is being trained on conventional lines does not, of course, have to learn to hunt and flush game but he must still be rock steady to fur if he is to become a finished dog. I have had a good number of very kind and easy Retrievers through my hands who, by the time they had been taught complete steadiness to dummies, were so much 'with me' that all I had to do regarding introduction to fur was to walk them at heel round the pen and 'Hup' them when a rabbit appeared in front of us. When I felt that the dog thoroughly understood that rabbits must be ignored, I would throw dummies or dead birds close to squatting rabbits then send the dog to retrieve. Usually he would make a grab for the rabbit if it flushed before he picked his dummy but at a sharp word from me, he would break away from it and pick the dummy. Most Retrievers very quickly grasped this lesson and would soon completely ignore any rabbits either on the way out or coming back with the retrieve.

In the case of a Retriever with whom I do not feel I have such a close rapport, I use a lead and give the dog a jerk if he starts after a rabbit. As a variation, later on in the training of a Retriever, I will place a retrieve at the far end of the pen and direct him to it blind, so he will bump into several rabbits on the way out.

16 **Quartering to a pattern**

The most important function of a trained Spaniel is to find and flush his game within shot of his handler. All authorities agree on this one point and always have done, even in the days when there was a vast divergence of opinion on whether or not his job should end there or if he should retrieve also. Consistently to accomplish this basic piece of work, the Spaniel must have a method of covering the ground which keeps him within shot of the handler and brings him within scenting distance of every piece of cover on his 'beat', or territory the handler wishes him to hunt.

A Spaniel normally flushes his game immediately on contact, so, as he does not normally find his game and hold it on point in the manner of a bird dog, it follows that unless the game is produced within comfortable distance of the handler, it will depart unshot at or, at the worst, cause the handler to take a long distance shot, likely to produce a pricked bird or runner. We are told by some authorities that a Spaniel should never work more than 25 yards from his handler but how many Spaniels consistently cover even this distance when working correctly? A Spaniel going out 25 yards to either side of his handler is covering a beat of 50 yards. Quite a slice of country for a Spaniel.

I think if we look realistically at what actually does happen in practice, either at Spaniel Trials or in the shooting field, it will be found that the majority of Spaniels go out between 10 and 20 yards on either side, depending on the individual dog and the type of terrain being worked. A bird flushed at 25 yards will be 40 yards at least when shot, in other words at extreme killing range and a rabbit flushed at this distance in rushes, heavy grass or bracken, is likely to be quite invisible to the handler.

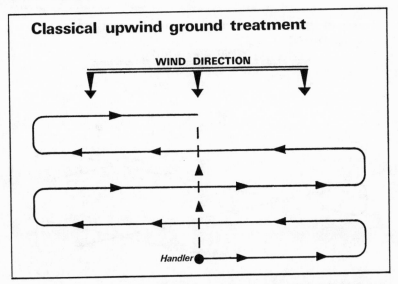

Classical upwind ground treatment

WIND DIRECTION

Handler

Pace is an advantage which is appreciated by all Pointer and Setter people but less often by those who shoot over Spaniels and Retrievers, yet I believe it is essential to top performance in these breeds also. To take the Retriever first. A gun shooting in Norfolk may have his back to a rough 'carr', containing willow herb, brambles, sedge and reeds. The guns are placed in this low spot so pheasants may be well produced from a strip of kale on rising ground in front of the carr. They come over well up and our gun, a typically good Norfolk shot, kills them slightly in front of him or sometimes overhead and the occasional second barrel kill produces a bird which falls a long way back. His birds therefore are likely to all fall behind him in the carr, from 30 to 80 yards out. If he is accompanied by a keen, fast Retriever which will use its speed and drive to really get about the place, his birds will be collected in good time before his host starts shuffling anxiously and looking at his watch, eager to get on the move to the next stand.

A bird dog must have pace or he would never accomplish his task of ranging far and wide over vast expanses of country where the coveys of grouse or quail are thinly distributed. A Spaniel covers his ground, using a similar technique to a bird dog but within the proscribed area already mentioned. To be efficient, he must get on with the job and use his speed to treat his ground.

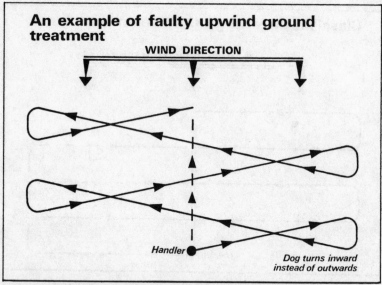

An example of faulty upwind ground treatment

WIND DIRECTION

Handler

Dog turns inward instead of outwards

Some people imagine that fast dogs are 'too fast to shoot over'. Provided a Spaniel does not outrun his nose, pace is an advantage, always provided it is properly channelled. It is absolutely essential for the Spaniel, after he has crossed the front of his handler and reached the extremity of his beat to the flank of the handler, to either turn in on his own or immediately turn to the whistle. The dog's speed is then no handicap as a sharp turn on either side of the handler keeps the dog within bounds. This technique refers to the method necessary to deal with a head-on wind. Side, following and quartering winds require an adjustment in technique and will be dealt with later.

More examples of faulty upwind ground treatment

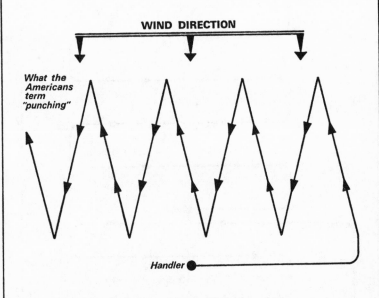

WIND DIRECTION

What the
Americans
term
"punching"

Handler ●

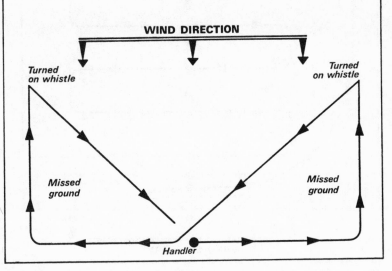

WIND DIRECTION

Turned
on whistle

Turned
on whistle

Missed
ground

Missed
ground

Handler ●

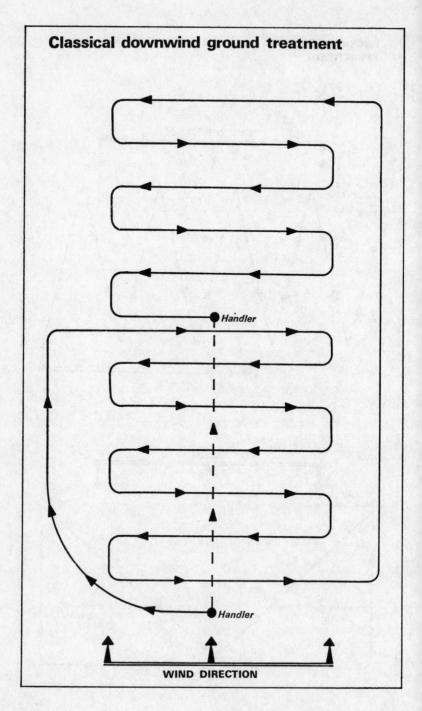

Classical downwind ground treatment

Handler

Handler

WIND DIRECTION

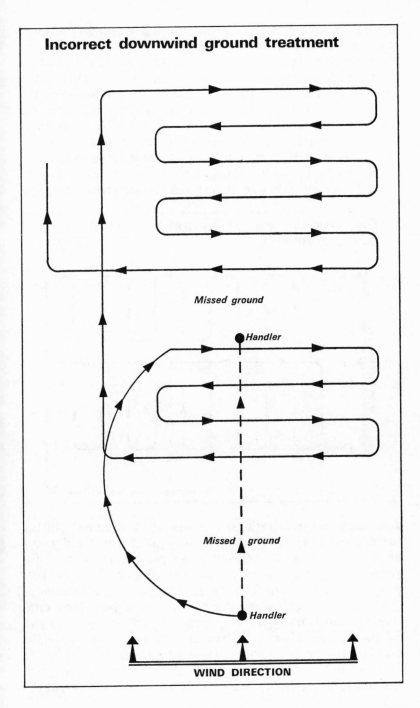

Incorrect downwind ground treatment

Missed ground

Handler

Missed ground

Handler

WIND DIRECTION

There is another advantage in shooting over a fast Spaniel. It will get more game on the move. Not only will it cover more country in a given time than a slower dog, so giving it a chance to encounter more game but it will actually flush more of the game than is present. The Americans have a fetish over the flush of a Spaniel, which is that it must be instantaneous, the reason being that all their Trials are conducted on game farm pheasants, 'planted' at intervals along the Course. Some run in any case and, if heading in a direction the judge feels it will be feasible to follow, the dog is laid on the line and followed, until the bird is produced or lost, the former event giving the

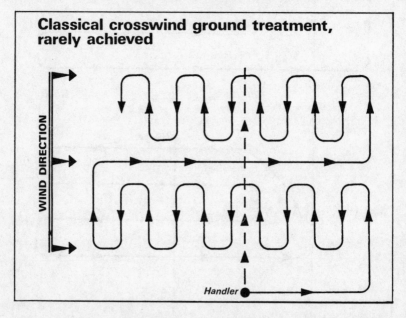

Classical crosswind ground treatment, rarely achieved

WIND DIRECTION

Handler

dog valuable credit ratings, the loss of the 'runner' putting the dog out of the Stake; any birds squatting in their 'nests' must be caught or flushed but *never* pointed, on pain of disqualification. One reason is that the Americans argue that pointing is the prelude to 'blinking' or refusing to acknowledge game, the other is that if a dog hesitates on a game farm bird, the pheasant is likely to creep from its 'nest' and possibly run off the Course, whereas a hard flushing dog would drive the bird into the air, providing a shot and a retrieve.

I have not been brainwashed by the Americans. Our shooting and Trial conditions are entirely different and I resent the

Americans coming over to our Trials and trying to teach us where we are going wrong, as though they invented Spaniels and Trials, which they did not. The British did. I can, however, see the logic in their arguments as they apply to their local conditions and how they can even sometimes apply to ours. If a Spaniel finds a rabbit or bird in this country in a fairly open situation and points it, the game will sit tight until flushed. If, however, the dog should be working in half fallen bracken or similar fairly high cover, holding a population of reared pheasants, it will produce far more birds if it hunts hard and fast than would a slower dog or one with a tendency to point. The

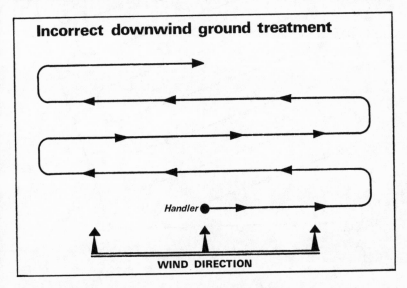

Incorrect downwind ground treatment

Handler

WIND DIRECTION

progress of a slow dog can be noted by the birds, who can run ahead of the dog, but a fast dog will get them up, particularly on a following wind, when the dog goes downwind in front of the handler, cutting the birds off and working them back towards the gun. A similar situation regularly occurs in my rabbit-pen, where the rabbits are dog wise and tend to slip away in front. The inexperienced, or poor quality dogs allow a lot of rabbits to elude them, but take in a really hard going dog and far more rabbits will be seen. They are punched out before they can collect their wits.

I do not like a Spaniel to point as I consider it far more sporting to shoot over a hard flusher. Although rabbits are, happily, coming back, pheasants are still the main quarry of the Spaniel

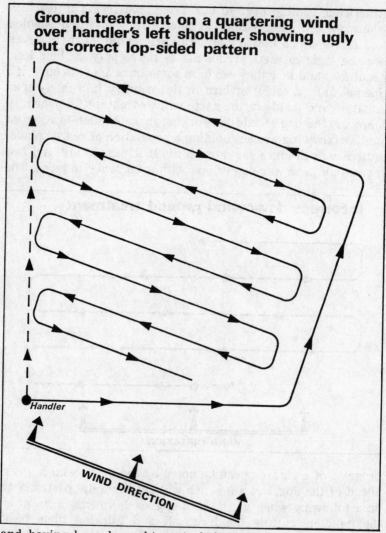

Ground treatment on a quartering wind over handler's left shoulder, showing ugly but correct lop-sided pattern

Handler

WIND DIRECTION

and having been brought up to believe that pheasants should at all times be well presented, I think we require a certain amount of justification to shoot them in the rear. A Spaniel which gives little or no warning of the presence of game before flushing, is to my way of thinking, a more sporting animal to shoot over than one which possesses the 'added refinement' of pointing.

Having decided how a Spaniel should cover the ground to the best advantage of his handler, we must now consider how to bring this about. The rudiments of quartering can be taught in some rabbit-pens, particularly if some thought is given to the distribution of the cover. Stick piles can be placed with geometrical precision so the dog will hunt from one to another so as to describe a quartering pattern. The ideal formation would be to have a succession of rows of stick piles, each one consisting of about five heaps. These should be situated so that the trainer's approach would be straight into the prevailing

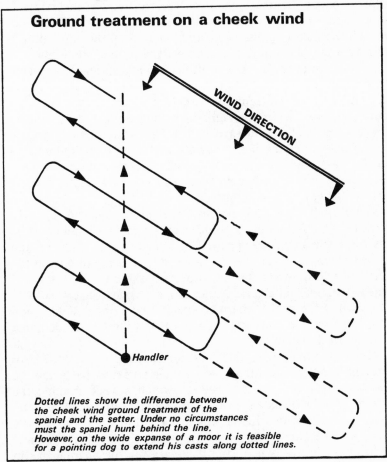

Ground treatment on a cheek wind

WIND DIRECTION

Handler

Dotted lines show the difference between the cheek wind ground treatment of the spaniel and the setter. Under no circumstances must the spaniel hunt behind the line. However, on the wide expanse of a moor it is feasible for a pointing dog to extend his casts along dotted lines.

wind, as a pup's first quartering lessons should always be given with the wind directly in his face. The pup should be cast off in front of his trainer and will automatically make for the nearest clump. After checking this out, he should be directed by a hand signal along the row of piles to right or left. If necessary, the handler should move with the pup and make him hunt each pile, then, when he has checked the bush at the extremity of his beat, he should be given the turn whistle and signalled across to the opposite side of his beat. Most Spaniels react very readily to a hand signal at close quarters, even if they later prove obtuse at taking directions at a distance.

Having hunted out the line of bushes, dog and trainer should take a 'bite' forward and repeat the procedure along the next line of cover. Before long, it will be no longer necessary to move with the pup to make him hunt out each pile. The handler will be able to pursue a straight course up the pen with the pup ranging on either side of him. It is at this stage that the pup is likely to try a few variations of his own and 'go ragged' in his pattern. Instead of moving out to left or right, he might attempt to bore straight forward to the next row. He might hunt one bush to left or right then, instead of carrying on to the extremity, turn forward to the next row, or having gone to the outside of the beat, may attempt to pull out from there to the next row, a practice I describe as 'boring on the turn' and which, under field conditions, causes a triangle of ground and, possibly game, to be missed.

When such a deviation occurs, the Spaniel should be brought back by whistle and made to do it in the correct manner. If he disobeys the turn, he should be stopped, taken hold of and pulled in the direction he was requested to come in on and the turn whistle blown in his ear. Rough handling is best avoided when teaching quartering unless he proves really defiant, although if the same thing happens later on under field conditions, one can be more severe as by that time he will be going with more determination.

My own situation is rather different as in my pen I have natural bracken to contend with. I have a narrow path running the length of the bracken bed up which I walk, making the pup work the block of cover above and then below me and restraining him by whistle should he attempt to bore up the path in front. During the Summer, before the bracken begins to lie over, visibility is poor and it is easy for the Spaniel to slip unnoticed into the next block of cover and beyond. At times, only the movement of the bracken tells me the whereabouts of my dog. In October and November however, my conditions are ideal as the bracken is sufficiently down for me to trace the course of the dog with some accuracy.

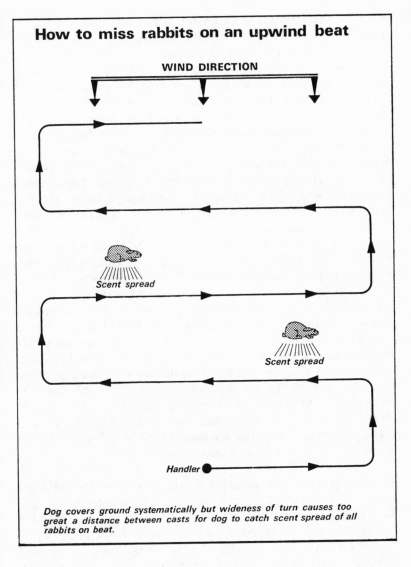

How to miss rabbits on an upwind beat

WIND DIRECTION

Scent spread

Scent spread

Handler

Dog covers ground systematically but wideness of turn causes too great a distance between casts for dog to catch scent spread of all rabbits on beat.

Once a dog has been steadied in the pen and has at least an idea of quartering, continued practice on outside ground should be given. Turnips and sugar-beet can be utilised, working at all times against the drills. Second crop clover and combined stubbles will also serve if you live in an agricultural area. If you live in wilder country–the edge of a grouse moor–rushy fields and areas of white grass are ideal. It is, of course, essential that the areas to be worked should hold at least a sprinkling of game, the idea being that the Spaniel has learned to move and look for game in the pen, so this knowledge must be applied to outside ground and a few finds will soon convince him that the area is well worth hunting. My own logical step from the pen is to hunt the shortest of the mountain bracken on my training ground. This usually contains a few rabbits and hares and I normally choose evening as a time for such ventures. The conditions are cooler, ground game has been on the move so there is no shortage of scent, the pup may have a find or two, or merely get some scent and he almost never views the quarry away, cover being too heavy but he knows there is game afoot, so the idea is projected into his mind that all cover is worth investigation.

When a Spaniel has reached the stage when he will quarter well into the wind, he must be taught to handle every other wind as well, if he is to become a really competent hunter, since it is by no means always possible to work straight into the wind. On a following wind, the pup should be cast out with a hand signal and it will be noted that he will make a semi-circular cast in front of his trainer, further out than he would make if he was cast into the wind. After he has made his circuit and is to one side or the other, the trainer should give him the turn whistle and immediately give him a hand signal to work across his front. On reaching his other extremity, he should be turned in again and cast across. Each time he is turned, he will turn *inwards* towards his handler instead of outwards, as he would on a head wind, so each cast will bring him nearer his handler. The trainer must *stand still* when working his dog on a following wind and remain still until the Spaniel has worked the piece of ground he has taken in right back to his feet, then the trainer must move forward over the ground already made good, casting the pup out again as he moves forward. The pup should take a bigger bite of ground next time and again the handler must remain still until the ground has been worked right back to him.

As the pup's confidence increases he will range further out down the wind and care must be taken not to let his ranging get out of hand. Twenty-five yards downwind is a safe distance; allow him to go further and difficulty may be experienced in inducing him to work the entire piece back to his trainer. He will probably work half the ground back then, with a fair piece

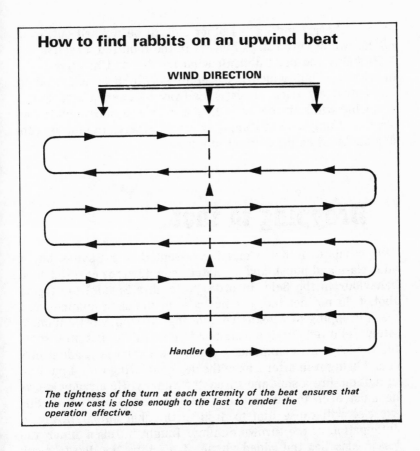

How to find rabbits on an upwind beat

WIND DIRECTION

Handler

The tightness of the turn at each extremity of the beat ensures that the new cast is close enough to the last to render the operation effective.

of ground still uncovered, cast himself forward again quite unbidden. The correct treatment of a downwind beat is impressive to watch and the hallmark of a good hunting Spaniel as it proves he knows how to use the wind.

There is less that a trainer can do to perfect the side wind ground treatment in his dog but if his downwind ground treatment is good, he will obviously possess the ability to work out the side wind technique for himself, which is that he should cast down the wind across his trainer's front, turn and work into the wind corkscrew fashion across the front again. Some Spaniels have a bad habit on a side wind of only working the wind until they come level with the handler, then sinking downwind again for what virtually only amounts to another half cast. The dog must be pulled back sharply by whistle, and the handler must firmly indicate by hand signal that he expects the ground on his other side to be worked out, even taking two or three steps himself in the required direction.

Probably the most difficult wind for dog and handler is the quartering wind, which is easier to work if it is half head on but extremely tricky if it is halfway between a side and a following wind. In this case the dog's pattern must appear lop-sided and ugly and in competition may receive the unjust condemnation of an inexperienced judge.

17 Dropping to shot

This attribute is not completely essential to a Spaniel but it adds class and polish and is another step towards ensured good behaviour in the field. In order to teach a Spaniel to drop to shot, I do not conduct the business in the same manner as I teach dropping to whistle, i.e. blowing the stop whistle immediately followed by the command 'hup'. I do not fire shots followed by this command. I make it a far more gradual process. I bring it in after I have the dog quartering well. I put him in motion, fire a shot and throw the dummy. He already knows he must drop to the fall of a dummy and repetition of this exercise will cause him to drop to the shot automatically in anticipation of the thrown dummy. Taught in this manner, the lesson also has the added virtue of teaching the dog to *mark* to shot. Not every bird shot over a Spaniel is actually flushed by the dog. Snipe, partridges and grouse may get up well ahead of him. A pheasant may be shot to his flank, walked up by the next gun or a Trial official. What an advantage the dog will have if he jerks his head up at the shot and just catches sight of the fall of the bird before it hits the ground, and the dog is able to make a quick marked retrieve of a bird which could otherwise have been a difficult blind.

During the exercises I have just described, the trainer must use the utmost discretion on how often he allows the dog to retrieve the dummy after the shot, as too frequent repetition can cause a dog to become too shot conscious and develop the impression that every shot must automatically signal a retrieve. He must occasionally be called away from his sitting position with the command 'gone away', learned in the rabbit-pen when he was induced to break off departed rabbits. The trainer should move out and pick the dummy himself, then return to the pup and hunt him away from the fall of the dummy. This lesson also proves useful in later field work for teaching a young dog that some birds are missed and must be forgotten, and that others although shot, are not required to be retrieved by him. 'Gone away' is a most essential 'negative' command and in effect tells the dog he must completely forget the last event that happened and accept the next command with a completely open mind, so every time game is missed, this command *must* be given before the order to hunt on, otherwise one may have the situation in which a keen, sharp marking Spaniel, is last seen departing at considerable speed in the wake of a very healthy pheasant, a situation which consistently proved the undoing of one of the greatest potential Trial Spaniels of all time.

18 Handling to direction

Good marking in a Retriever or Spaniel must be encouraged at all times. It saves time and obviously a gundog going out to retrieve in a straight line to his retrieve is far less likely to disturb fresh game than the dog which has to hunt his ground to accomplish the retrieve. It follows that there are many occasions however, both in the shooting and Trial field, when a dog is not in a position to mark or has to deal with a bird on which another dog has failed. To make good the retrieve he must be capable of accepting directions to place him within scenting distance of the bird. Handling has become something of a fetish these past 20 years and more, and some trainers are completely obsessed with this aspect of gundog work, over-handling and overwhistling their unfortunate animals until they lose whatever initiative they may originally have possessed. To a certain extent, although not entirely, working tests are responsible as they specifically encourage this branch of activity. To the devotees of this cult I ascribe the term 'sheep-dog men'.

Nevertheless, no trainer can afford to dismiss this facet of gundog work as in its proper perspective it can prove extremely useful.

I start the pup off by throwing two dummies out into very light cover a few yards apart. He may register the fact immediately that two dummies have been thrown, particularly if he is a Retriever, and retrieve one after the other without hesitation but whatever happens, I introduce a new command. All my dogs are sent for marked retrieves by calling their names *only*, so for this lesson I send him to retrieve by his name followed by 'get back'. If he proves obtuse at going out for the second dummy, I assist him by moving forward with him, repeating the command until he picks the dummy. After giving him a few pairs of dummies, he soon learns to go out to the second one from where I stand and knows that at the command 'get back' he must go out and look for something which he has not seen fall.

The next stage is to introduce the stop whistle. The pup is sent out to hunt, he is stopped by the whistle and the dummy is thrown over his head and beyond him. I raise my hand, move it forward and command him to 'get back'. The object of this lesson is to establish his confidence in the stop whistle, so he will move freely out to the dummy instead of coming into the trainer. When this is established I give him 'going back' retrieves, throwing a dummy a short distance in front of us, walking away a distance and sending him back. Every now and then I will stop him halfway back, then order him to 'get back'. Discretion must now be exercised, or he may anticipate the stop whistle and prove sticky on going back freely, so I let him go back without restraint far more often than I stop him.

The next stage is to give him a retrieve which is completely unsighted, and the procedure I adopt is as follows. I sit him down on familiar ground where these going back lessons have been taking place, cover his eyes and throw the dummy a short way behind him but this time I choose a piece of bare ground. I back away 20 yards, raise my hand, signal and say 'get back'. The chances are he will look a little confused but will usually turn his head to look behind him, spotting the dummy and going back for it. I continue until he will go back freely every time for the visible dummy, then throw the dummy into light cover. His confidence is now developed so he will go back and search for the hidden dummy.

Gradually he comes to understand that if he gets out into the country on the command 'get back' he will find something.

It is terribly important that success is achieved *every* time. If he goes to pieces on a blind and mishandles, he must be taken forward and *made* to find the retrieve, so he realises that his handler knows best and that if he trusts his handler, he will find his retrieve. Most gundogs and, in particular, Spaniels, learn to work to left or right more easily than they learn to get out in a straight line.

I throw a dummy to one side or the other of the seated pupil and give a very clear hand signal towards the retrieve. After repeating a few times I bring in a second dummy. I throw the first one fairly close to him and the second one further out on the opposite side. I signal him to pick the first one, although the second is clearer in his mind as it is the last thrown but as the first is lying fairly close to him, he usually goes for it on being directed but if he attempts to move towards the last dummy, I stop him on the whistle, tell him 'gone away' (I never use 'no' as a command) and repeat my original signal. I now have a dummy still on the ground, so sit the pup a few yards to one side of it and throw my second dummy to the other side of him. This time he may be a little confused as the chances are that he will have forgotten the original dummy which is naturally the one I expect him to get, so I am ready to stop him smartly should he make any attempt to pick the wrong one.

Once the pup is handling confidently on his training ground, he must be tried elsewhere to consolidate what he has learned as it does not follow that because he gets back freely over a certain piece of ground and searches for hidden dummies or birds, he will do the same on any piece of ground. Fresh ground must be utilised and the pup should be sent in as many different directions for retrieves as possible. At this stage, I have nothing against sending a shot in the direction of the hidden dummy. Provided the pup is made to wait an appreciable period before being sent to retrieve, I cannot see that such a practice will encourage him to run in to shot. This is surely a question of management.

⑲ Jumping fences

I live in a country where jumping fences is seldom safe or practical. The standard North Wales stock fence consists of sheep or pig netting surmounted by barbed wire. I will not send a Spaniel over barbed wire under any circumstance, no matter how good a jumper he is and, unless I know he is a very clean and experienced jumper, I have no hesitation in picking up and heaving a 70 lb Labrador over barbed wire. Very few Spaniels jump a high fence clean. The usual technique is to leap for the top strand, hook his front paws over it, hoist his hind feet on to it and leap off from there. If the top strand consists of barbed wire, here lies the danger. The dog can slip and a bad abdominal tear can result or, worse still, a hind leg can become entwined and a muscle or tendon torn resulting in damage which can be permanent.

When I shoot over a dog I want it to find game and put it in the bag when I shoot it. I am not in the least bit interested in seeing it perform circus acts which may put the dog at physical risk. Because I often handle tough, extrovert dogs I think some people automatically assume I am a hard trainer which is pure conjecture as I always train and shoot alone, so nobody really knows how I handle my dogs. What is certain is that I hate to see a dog injured. It is unpleasant for the animal and an injury usually puts a dog out of action for some considerable time.

There are situations in other parts of the country where it is quite safe to expect a dog to jump obstacles, with or without its quarry. Stone walls in a good state of repair are safe enough although a crumbling wall has its dangers, as the dog can dislodge a stone which may catch its hind legs as it lands. Plain rabbit wire fences around Forestry plantations are perfectly safe, even if they are surmounted by plain wire for, in the event of a slip, the dog's leg is most unlikely to become caught up. This can happen in the case of a sheep fence topped by plain wire, as the dog's hind foot can become entwined between the meshes.

We often find at home a long strip of bracken running parallel to a stock fence and which can be a useful place to hunt. It is a very common for my Spaniel to slip under the wire fence and, on being turned back, forget the place it crept under and make a great, foolhardy leap over the top of the fence. Several times a dog has slipped and become hung up on the barbed wire but a prompt dash forward on my part, the dog seized and its weight taken off the hooked up part, has saved it from injury. I can cover five yards ten times quicker than I can cover 50 yards, so had such an accident occurred when a dog was well out on a retrieve, the consequences could have been far more serious.

In my rabbit-pen I have a couple of jumps. They are constructed in the intersecting fence which used to be the boundary fence before I extended the pen. I lowered the wire in two places, stiffening one jump with heavy fencing wire along the top and using larch rails to form the top of the other. The rail jump is quite an awkward one as the take off is on a slope, so I never attempt to teach pups to jump on this one. The other jump is higher up the hill and at one point the take off is fairly level. I get over it myself, pull the wire down a few more inches and induce the dog to follow me over. Pups vary tremendously in their attitude to jumping. Some grasp the idea at once, others take longer and some can be extremely stupid.

Speaking to a client quite recently, he made the criticism that any books on gundog training which he had read, did not tell the reader what to do in the event of an impasse being reached in training over any individual aspect. In the case of the dog which runs up and down the fence and makes no attempt to get over, I call him to me, take him by the scruff and lift him until his fore paws hook over the top. I push my foot into the wire, forming a bulge on his side and squeeze him to me. He dislikes this position and starts to use his hind legs, obtaining a purchase on the wire where my foot has made the bulge. He gives a wriggle of his body and is over. I have shown him the way over and many pups will make the next attempt successfully on their own. Some do not and require more help over the fence before they grasp that they can make it on their own. I familiarise the pup with the command 'get over' during these lessons and give the command just before he follows me over the fence.

The next stage is to induce him to leap the fence from my side. This is usually fairly easily accomplished. I stand close by the fence, tap the top wire and give the command. He is usually keen enough to get over on command as he knows there is more rabbit ground to be investigated on the other side. I progress to making him jump while I am standing further and further from the fence, but bring this in during the course of his hunting lessons. He hunts the bracken patch out my side of the jump, I stop him with the whistle and he comes up to the jump, give him the command, over he goes and carries on hunting. I stop him again, climb the fence myself and set him off afresh. Sometimes I give him a marked dummy retrieve over the fence then, during advanced work, blinds. He soon learns to jump on command, get back and search for the dummy but the natural follow on is most important. He must learn to jump *any* fence on command with his trainer standing well back, not merely the ones on his training ground.

Many young dogs, particularly Spaniels, do not readily convert their knowledge of jumping, learned at home, to getting over obstacles on outside ground. Throw a marked dummy over a rabbit wire or plain topped sheep fence and most will have a go but if one tries to send them over blind, the almost inevitable result will be that the pup runs up to the fence, puts its nose down and runs up and down sniffing. I have never been able to find out what he is looking for. If the fence has cover growing along its bottom he could conceivably be searching for game. If the fence separates two bare, closely grazed pastures, what then? Field mice? Voles? I will never know.

He must be stopped on the whistle, his attention gained and the command repeated. He is still unlikely to jump, unless he is a real 'natural' and loves jumping for its own sake. He may make a half-hearted attempt. Where is the bold, flying leap he has developed on his training ground? More likely he will continue to mouse. One must stop him again, move up to him and tap the fence top to encourage him over, even crossing the fence oneself if he proves stupid. He will eventually cross all fences given encouragement and his confidence will gradually increase with practice.

Supposing during early jumping lessons he has flatly refused to jump at all. Then a special jumping alley should be constructed with the first jump no more than 12 inches high, so he can practically stride across it. The jumps should be progressively higher, a few inches at a time, so the smallest hop is sufficient to get him over the lowest ones and a slight increase in effort will get him over the higher ones. The jumps should be constructed of boards or small mesh wire netting. Rails or pig netting should be avoided in the early stages as he will try to force his head through these materials instead of jumping them.

㉚ Water work

For a shooting dog to become a complete all rounder it is essential that it should be competent in water. There are many aspects of water work. A dog may be required to collect duck from an inland flight pond by daylight, after morning flight, or in the dark after dusk flight. It could be required to make long swims and cross patches of soft mud when working in the coastal regions or estuaries and may have to contend with adverse currents. Inland again, it might on occasions have to cross rivers, either sluggish or swift flowing, for the odd pheasant, flushed from the river bank and falling in or across the river.

Diverse as these activities are, the basic requirement is that the dog should swim. He can be schooled to specific local conditions later. It is a counsel of perfection to suggest that a warm day should always be chosen for a pup's first introduction to water. I certainly agree with this and advocate it myself but a warm day is not always available in the British Summer. If possible, a location should be chosen with a gently shelving, firm margin. A steeply inclined bank or soft mud should be avoided as most pups will be put off by these conditions. I take an experienced water dog with me and the pup. First of all I throw the dummy on land, about a foot from the water and send the pup for it. Next I throw it a few inches into the water so the pup has to wet his feet to collect it but no more. Next I throw it so he has to wade in up to his belly to make the retrieve and the next time far enough out so he has to swim a foot or two.

It is now simply a matter of natural progression to get the pup further and further out until he will eventually cross a river or swim out into a lake the distance of a dummy launcher retrieve, which can be from 40 to 70 yards. However, it is unfortunately not always so easy. Most pups will wet their bellies but some will take a firm stand at this point and refuse to swim. To recover the dummy the older dog must be sent. Theoretically, this should set an example and stimulate the pup into action. I find it seldom does. Most reluctant water dogs say, 'Right, you get it then and I will try to take it from you when you make landfall'.

One method I have used with a reluctant water dog has been to enter the water myself wearing waders and gently towing the dog in after me on a lead. I have carefully towed him out of his depth with my other hand supporting his belly and have shown him that he is capable of swimming a few strokes. Usually he will then swim out a few feet for a dummy. I have taken dogs swimming with me but never with any success. The dog has certainly found itself capable of swimming after me but its dislike of water has remained and it has still refused to swim out for a dummy. I had one exasperating bitch who swam far better than I did. She would reluctantly follow me into the Dee, then would pass me, swimming as smoothly and strongly as an otter, yet I could never induce her to enter water for a retrieve.

I have had some excellent water dogs but I do find that many gundogs seem to be deficient in skill and determination in water work. It is most important that a pup's first retrieve should never be thrown too far into the water. A really bold pup will sometimes fling himself into water because he does not realise what he is doing and when the water closes over his head, may well decide he is not so bold as he formerly imagined. I have made this mistake in the past myself. One case concerned Gwibernant Ganol. She was my own dog so did not receive such consistent or intensive training as my clients' dogs. I had given her a little water work in training, then for months she never saw water. Returning across the moor late one evening we passed a reservoir and I threw a dead pigeon in and sent her. The water was cold and very choppy. She made a great spectacular leap, went right under, surfaced and swam out to the pigeon. For the rest of the season she refused to go in for a thrown bird even though a shot was fired.

Then we had a terrible winter and all the water froze over. One lake some miles away partially thawed out although our own remained frozen. It was essential that she regained her confidence in water as by this time she was destined for American Field Trials where water tests are a feature of virtually every Trial. I managed to kill a bird well out over the

F.T. Ch. Crowhill Spinner demonstrates a perfect delivery and the author a comfortable, one handed, acceptance. Howard Pearson.

A son of F.T. Ch. Crowhill Raffle retrieves a rabbit to Barry Roberts. Howard Pearson.

An Irish Setter, bred in Hungary, retrieving an English partridge on the Frisian island of Texel.

The American system –
a pigeon is 'dizzied'.

– then placed in its
'nest'.

– then flushed for the
gun.

water for her which she retrieved without hesitation. Dogs do know the difference between a thrown bird saluted by gunfire and a *killed* bird. One little monster had this problem exactly in reverse. I could throw a dead duck as far into the river as I wished and fire a live cartridge after it and he would make a magnificent job, but if I shot a duck for him he would swim 10 yards out then turn back, leaving the duck to be retrieved by his older brother, F. T. C. Lancshot Laser, who at that time was my best water dog.

Another canine eccentric was a very large Golden Retriever who was required mainly as a wildfowling dog. He had been performing beautifully, swimming across the Dee for a marked dummy then re-crossing for the other of the pair I had sent across by launcher. One day he had successfully accomplished his mission when we were hailed by a large and formidable lady from the opposite bank who loudly enquired what we were about and informed us that we would disturb the fish. This was debatable. Under some conditions a swimming dog will send fish to the bottom. Under others, a swimming dog will stir up stale fish and cause them to take and I am told that under these conditions some Scottish river keepers will swim their dogs in the salmon pools. Although I had the shooting down to the river I did not argue with the lady, so we climbed into our disreputable Land-Rover and decamped.

From that day on I could never get that Golden Retriever across the river again. With encouragement, I managed to induce him to retrieve from the middle of the river, even in a swift current and consistently at that, but I could never put him on the far bank. He was a morbidly sensitive dog and I am convinced he had a 'screw loose'. I can only assume that he became upset at the lady's tirade and assumed that it was directed at him for his last action, retrieving from the far bank. Subsequently, he made quite a satisfactory dog but his owner confirmed that whereas he was quite good, he was distinctly odd.

I have heard it said that one method which can be employed to persuade a reluctant pup to enter water is to throw pieces of toasted brown bread into the water. I do not like the sound of this at all. Even if it had the desired effect of persuading the pup to go out of his depth, there would be a very good chance that if he attempted to swallow the bread, he could swallow a large mouthful of water as well, some of which would most likely go down his windpipe. That some dogs are aware of this possibility themselves has been illustrated to me in the form of the dog who, for a time, will retrieve from *over* water but lacks the confidence to open its mouth in water to seize a floating bird or dummy, so I would imagine that a throatful of water at a crucial stage could have disastrous effects. In the case of a reluctant pup, a dead bird or rabbit might prove more encouraging than a dummy, but these soon become waterlogged and unattractive, particularly rabbits which, when waterlogged, float just under the surface and are virtually impossible for an inexperienced pup to locate.

A case in point was a working test my wife and I judged. The water test was a tricky one. There were two small rectangular ponds, each about 15 yards wide with a high, narrow bank separating the two ponds. The dogs stood at the side of the first body of water and a deep-frozen mallard was thrown from the bank between the ponds into the second one. My wife stood with the dogs at the starting point. I stood quite a distance away where I could see the retrieve and observe the dogs' approach to the situation when they were over the intersecting bank and completely unsighted from their handlers.

One handler who considers himself something of an authority on working tests, doubtless because of his long association with these events, made a rather sarcastic remark relating to the position I had chosen to place myself in. My reply was to the effect that I would doubtless see many things of both a strange and educational nature from my vantage point, which indeed I did, including the complete nonsense my learned friend's dog made of its retrieve.

Most of the dogs failed this test and, in these cases, the handlers were sent round on to the dividing bank and allowed to throw a stone near the duck to get it picked out of the way. We had only two ducks to play with and after several dogs had made their effort, I noticed one dog nudge the duck with its nose and carry on swimming. The bird was completely waterlogged and riding so low in the water that no dog could wind it, so I had to call a halt to the test and ask for a pigeon (as used in the land tests) to be issued for each subsequent dog.

21 Laying a line

To give a young dog some idea of taking the line of a runner, or a rabbit from where it is flushed to the point where it is killed, or even beyond, should it prove to be only legged, most trainers utilise some form of artificial line, dragging a bird or rabbit along the ground for some distance, in a manner which will prevent the drag becoming contaminated by human foot-scent. Various laborious techniques have been described from laying the line many hours before and allowing one's scent to evaporate, to dragging the retrieve between two people at opposite ends of a long line.

My method is far simpler and, whilst it is easier with the help of an assistant, the system can be operated by a trainer working alone. A long, light cord should be attached to an ordinary hammer. The hammer should be thrown as far as possible, drawing the line in its wake in the manner of a whale harpoon. The retrieve is then attached to the loose end and can either be drawn in by an assistant previously positioned close to the hammer's point of impact or, if the trainer is working alone (as in my case), he can make a swift detour around the line, haul in the retrieve, untie it and make a smart detour back to the starting point, produce his dog and lay it on the line. It is best, after hauling in the retrieve, to put hammer and cord well out of the way as these, of course, carry human scent and one does not really want one' pup to retrieve a hammer in fine style, with yards and yards of cord following after!

For the first few lessons at any rate, it is far better to employ this system when scent is likely to be reasonable, either while the morning dew still clings to the herbage or in the cool of the evening. Once the pup has become competent at taking a line under favourable conditions, it is soon enough to try him when scent is likely to be indifferent. He *must* have his confidence established by success. When working a dog of any age on a line, I never give the command to retrieve or get back once he touches the line but give him the command to hunt. I want him to get his nose down. If he is told to 'get back', he will lift his head and get back, probably cutting the line and missing it altogether.

It is, of course, a different matter if, as a more advanced

lesson, the trainer stands back some distance from the beginning of the artificial drag and directs his dog to the 'fall' as he would under field conditions if faced with an unmarked runner but as soon as the dog hits the right area, it must be given the command to get its head down and hunt.

Since myxomatosis, it is surprising how many Trial handlers on being asked to collect shot ground game, order their dog to 'fetch it' or 'get out'. Often the result is that the dog lifts his head from the seat from which he has pushed the rabbit or hare, makes a bold dash forward and loses the line completely, probably cutting it further on, then working the scent back towards his handler instead of towards the game and making the whole performance look laboured and untidy. The classic way for a Spaniel to deal with a ground game retrieve is to put his nose on the line immediately outside the vacated seat and keep it there until he comes up with the game, following every twist and turn the quarry has made. The reasons are twofold. One is that this is the easiest way to find the game. The other is that when a rabbit or hare is flushed, discounting the very rare occasions when the quarry might be panicked into making a false move and taking off other than on an established run, the animal will stick to its run. Other game does not sit about on rabbit or hare runs. They are used for travel only and have no hiding places, so a dog meticulously following a run will not flush fresh game in the normal course of events. He may pass fresh game tucked within six inches of the run but having his nose right down and full of scent he will not wind it. A dog prancing around with head up would be very likely to get the body scent of this game and flush it, whereas the former dog would leave it undisturbed so it could be worked out and shot after he had completed his retrieve, a weighty consideration should game be thin on the ground.

Experienced Trial judges will give a dog credit for 'taking the line' and mark it down to some extent if it has to collect its rabbit by casting for it on the instructions and signals of its handler although I sincerely hope that few will emulate the Irish judge who had the line bee buzzing so noisily in his bonnet that he penalised a very good Springer for going straight to a hare rolled over in full view of the dog. According to him, the dog should have disregarded the evidence of his eyes, put his nose down and taken the line to the hare. A perfect case of inflexibility making a nonsense of a sound basic principle.

22 Advanced lessons

Towards the end of the training of a Retriever who is to be used on conventional lines, i.e. with more driven game shot over him than anything else, I give a lesson which is also beneficial to a Spaniel which will be used for a certain amount of driven game shooting. I stand at the bottom of a high bank with my dog seated in front of me and an assistant throws dead birds over us at intervals, at which I fire live ammunition. This simulates a high bird drive and the birds fall all round the dog. As each bird hits the ground, I say 'hup' and reload. At the end of the 'drive', I say 'gone away', walk him about 50 yards away then, after an interval of over a minute, I let him collect the birds. Often I have to manage without assistance, so toss a bagful of birds around him myself, firing a shot with each bird. Done quietly and deliberately, this is excellent training for keeping him cool during heavy drives in his future shooting career.

It is a very good idea for anyone who trains gundogs to keep a loft of free flying homing pigeon. They are fairly prolific breeders so one can be shot now and then to provide a natural retrieve for an advanced pupil and a dead bird for use with other pups. Another very useful function of tame pigeon is that a few may be caught at night and placed in a coop. Next day the trainer can put some in a bag and while walking his retriever at heel, can release one at intervals, firing a shot over it and giving the command 'gone away'. These live birds should be interspersed with the occasional dummy or dead bird thrown out which the dog should be allowed to retrieve, so during the course of this lesson the matter is reaffirmed that every bird shot at is not for his specific attention but the occasional retrieve assures him that his handler is not such a rotten shot after all and, on specific command, there are jobs for him to do.

Similarly, they can be tossed over a Spaniel's head when he is hunting but I am not in favour of pigeon being put in cages or under plantpots to simulate a flush. The late John Forbes told me they could be used to good advantage in this manner when training pointing dogs but I do not consider them suitable for Spaniels. A hard flushing Spaniel will charge the cage and become excited by the flapping and fluttering and others dislike flushing pigeon intensely for some reason I cannot explain, unless it is because a pigeon must provide an 'unnatural' flush, for a pigeon never allows itself to be flushed in the natural state. Whatever the reason, I do not think any good ever comes of using caged pigeon. I never use them when schooling a dog for a Game Fair, although I know I will encounter caged pigeon at this event, and as I have won the C.L.A. Game Fair Spaniel Tests twice I cannot believe that my prejudice is too far misplaced.

One rather controversial aspect of advanced training and an exercise well beloved by the working test fraternity is the diversionary retrieve. In a Field Trial, and more especially in a Retriever Trial, more birds than one may be shot at once and a dog may well be asked to pick a bird it has not marked although another has been shot in full view. On a shooting day, a runner may be down and require picking first but be blind to the dog, who has marked a stone dead bird. In this latter instance, if we accept the realities of such a situation, very few shooting men have the inclination or ability to deal with it according to the book, taking the dog off the marked bird and putting it on to the runner but, at any rate, in theory this is what should be done.

There are those who argue that nothing, absolutely nothing, should be done to interfere with a dog's mark and a dog should always be allowed to collect a marked bird first. There are still others who pour scorn on the idea that a dog should even wait for orders when a bird is shot, particularly out wildfowling; yet another man of Field Trial experience can counter with the story of how he dropped a dead duck on the mud and another, a strong swimmer, into an ebb tide and was able to send his dog past the dead bird to collect the live one which would certainly have been lost had the dog wasted time on the dead bird first.

I think we must accept that situations do occur when it is essential to be able to say to a dog in effect, 'No, not that one, the other one over there'. To which the dog replies, 'Which other one?' and the handler answers 'Never you mind, get out over there and you will find out'.

I once trained and handled a Labrador who was particularly good in this situation. He would never persist on the marked retrieve and even if it took him some minutes to collect the blind, when ultimately sent for the marked one, would invariably go to it spot on. Now it follows that any training in this exercise must come as a severe contradiction to a young dog which has been encouraged to mark well, but we must bear in mind that training consists in part of a series of contradictions and we attempt to breed gundogs with temperaments which will stand this type of training. The question arises, however, at which stage of a young dog's career he should be taught diversionary work.

I am certain that to include this in every young dog's initial training would be a mistake as a good many would become confused, to their ultimate detriment. If a puppy is bold, tough and precocious he should then be able to accept this training in his first Summer's work but in the case of a more average specimen, I am sure it would be better if this were deferred until the following Summer, after he had gained confidence in the shooting field the previous Winter.

Earlier directional work will in part have conditioned the dog to accept this training. He has been accustomed to ignore a dummy thrown to one side of him and to collecting a half forgotten one on the other. When commencing diversionary work it is a good idea to use wide angles. The marked dummy should be thrown in an entirely different direction to the one he is expected to collect blind, so there is plenty of time and room to stop him when he makes for the wrong one.

Initially, the blind retrieve should be fairly close at hand and the marked one well out. I give the command 'gone away' and turn my back on it, ordering him to 'get back' towards the blind. It is not unusual for him to get back so far on command, then attempt to veer towards the marked dummy. I stop him on the whistle, command him 'gone away' again and direct him out afresh, moving forward myself if necessary. The main thing is to get the dummy picked, to show him it really is there and that he must get it. At this stage of the proceedings I never allow him to collect the diversionary dummy after picking the blind. This only comes when he has become perfect at ignoring it completely and going out freely to the blind. As lessons progress, the blind can be placed farther and farther away and the marked dummy can be thrown closer in, so whenever he sees a dummy thrown and hears the command 'gone away', he knows perfectly well he must go nowhere near it.

As mentioned earlier, it is most important to study the pupils' attitude to diversionary work and, indeed, blind retrieving altogether. Some dogs, more especially Spaniels and

Cockers in particular, can appear initially stupid over these exercises and the utmost discretion must be exercised to decide whether in such a case, lessons should be discontinued for several weeks or even months or the trainer should continue in the hope that the penny will eventually drop. If the pupil shows signs of sulkiness I think the lessons should stop. He should have game shot over him, some of which he will mark. Regarding retrieves which fall unsighted, the handler has a pair of legs and can walk the dog close to the fall. The dog finds his *raison d'être*, becomes keen and mentally stimulated and reaches a more receptive state of mind for directional work. He finds things to collect which he enjoys handling, so should be more willing to accept the lessons which will help him to find these desirable objects.

A recent case in point applies to a smart little Cocker bitch I recently trained which just would *not* accept directional training; as she was being trained with a view to Trials as well as shooting, it was highly desirable that she should handle reasonably well. I shot a few head of game over her at the end of the season then asked her owner to take her home for the Summer and give her what shooting on rabbits and pigeon he could, as I was quite confident that he would not spoil her. When she came back to me I commenced directional training and she began to see the light but could be deliberately naughty, coming in to me at the command 'get back' instead of getting out and away from me. When it became patently obvious that she was playing me up I would stop her on the way in, move in quickly and slap her face, forcing her out from where I stood. After two or three such episodes she decided to conform and now handles better than most Cockers, a fact which has contributed to her becoming a Field Trial Champion after competing in only four Stakes.

23 Early shooting days

The first few birds which are shot over the young trained dog will make or mar him, according to the amount of commonsense the handler is prepared to apply to the business in hand.

Not every person can train a dog but it should lie within the capabilities of almost every person to take over a well trained young dog and maintain it throughout its working career at a high level of behaviour. This, however, would be Utopia and the sad realities of the matter are that a great many fine young dogs are 'lost' during this crucial transitional period between training and being shot over.

A gundog has certain instincts which must be exploited in order to make him efficient as a gamefinder and the whole process of training consists of channeling these instincts under calm and controlled conditions. When a dog handles his first few head of game there is likely to be a sharp rise in the level of his excitement which may manifest itself in various forms according to his individual temperament. In the case of a Retriever, he finds the handling of shot game far more exciting than working on the dummies and dead birds of his training period. Here is real contact with flesh and blood and there is no human scent on his retrieves to keep the authority of his handler foremost in his mind. He is out on his own. His many generations of working blood now come to the fore and soon he realises that this is his *raison d'être*.

Whereas his retrieving exercises may have been, for him, pleasant interludes in his existence, the retrieving of real game becomes his greatest driving force and unless care is exercised by the handler, he can become so single minded over the collection of game that he may well start to run in and collect it unbidden, or, when accompanying his handler at a driven game shoot, even though he may remain perfectly steady, he may commence to whine. In my opinion, whining suggests a conflict of opinions between dog and master. The handler intends that the dog shall remain seated in front of him until the end of the drive. The dog is not content with the situation and would rather be off after each bird as it is killed. Discipline may remain sufficiently instilled to prevent this from happening but the dog is not happy with the situation and gives vent to his feelings audibly. It is said that whining is, like hard mouth, hereditary. So perhaps it would be safe to assume that the temperament which does not take kindly to being 'held' at a stand is hereditary, yet I am sure that in many cases, whining could be prevented by the handler having a better psychological hold over his charge. This is rather difficult to explain but I believe that if the gun is at all times *conscious* of his dog, even during the heaviest shooting, the dog is far more likely to remain happy, contented and *silent*, secure in the knowledge that after the drive, he will have some work to do.

I believe the finest introduction to shooting a young Retriever can possibly have is for his handler to walk up and shoot a few head of game for him entirely on his own. I do not belong to the school of thought who believe that young dogs should never retrieve pigeon or grouse on account of their loose feathers. Any good young dog should handle these birds with pleasure, although I would not advise giving large numbers of them to a young dog lest the continual shedding of feathers into his mouth should frustrate him and cause him to fumble his retrieves. In any case, after each retrieve, the handler should clear the dog's mouth of feathers, right to the back of his throat. A feather lodged firmly in the bronchial tube or wind-pipe can prove extremely dangerous.

It is excellent post training practice for the dog and gun to walk up the sides of woods and spinneys in late Summer or through parkland containing large trees for the purposes of flushing pigeon. With the trees in full leaf, pigeon will very often sit sufficiently tight for a shot to be taken, particularly the birds of the year. Under these conditions it is usually poss-ible for the dog to mark the fall of every bird. After a success-ful shot, the gun should 'hup' the dog, calmly reload his weapon and make the dog wait at least half a minute before letting him retrieve the bird. Walking up a few ditches and drains in duck country can prove a very beneficial exercise. Here rights and lefts are common, one duck or teal often fall-ing in the water, the second on the far bank. A rapidly climb-ing teal, killed well out into rushes or reeds, the far side of the water, may provide a testing retrieve, particularly as the swim and the negotiation of two banks may cause the nov-ice dog partially to lose his mark on the bird. Here the 'handling' dog comes into his own. Walking up a few grouse is excellent practice for the young Retriever as is walking up October pheasants in turnips (neaps if you live north of the wall) or sugar-beet with a few partridges thrown in if you live in an area where these birds still survive in shootable numbers.

During this kind of foray, ground game may well be shot. A rabbit or hare killed stone dead in cover can be used, but when rolled over in the open, as hares, particularly, often are, it is far better to sit the dog down, walk out and pick the hare by hand. Wounded ground game should always be given another barrel as I would never recommend a wounded hare at this stage; by the end of the season the dog should be sufficiently stabilised mentally to cope with this, surely the most exciting of all retrieves.

However, it is very seldom one really *needs* to send a dog for a hare at all. Hares, unlike birds, do not fall out of the sky into thick cover and can nearly always be picked by hand. If however, the dog will run in Field Trials the situation will be entirely different. It is essential that the dog should have experience of finding, picking and *balancing* shot hares as it is Field Trial procedure to use hares as retrieves. This saves some winged game for one's host and a hare shot up the line from the dog and unsighted, can provide a very testing retrieve, for a stone dead hare often gives off very little wind-borne scent. For ordinary shooting purposes, the retrieving of hares is relatively unimportant.

We now come to the question of how well or otherwise the gun has performed for his dog and I use the words 'for his dog' advisedly as this should be the main object of these early forays—the initiation of his charge into the sphere of shooting proper. If he should have killed the first dozen head or so with scarcely a miss, the dog could well become so retrieving oriented that it may become over-keen and eventually try to run in. After a period when he has shot particularly well over the dog, the gun should vary the proceedings by either deliberately missing some game or by picking a proportion of the game by hand. I believe that few things have a more salutory effect upon an impressionable young dog than killing a bird in full view of him, sitting him down, picking up a bird and walking back to him, making sure he smells the bird before it is put into the bag, thus illustrating fully the point that the gun is just as capable of retrieving a bird as he is and that the whole business of retrieving must be conducted entirely at the handler's discretion.

At some stage in these early shooting expeditions, increasing enthusiasm may get the better of sound training and he may attempt to run in. The gun must continually be prepared for this eventuality and be ready to forestall such an attempt. A young dog running in for the first time does not make the full-blooded, headlong rush of the hardened miscreant we encounter all too often at most shoots, and the time to stop him is not when he has moved ten yards, or ten inches, but as his muscles tauten and his nose moves forward, thereby signalling his intentions.

After *every* shot, hit or miss, the gun should immediately glance at the dog, giving the command 'hup' simultaneously. As already mentioned, the gun must be reloaded and the dog made to wait before retrieving. In the event of a miss, the negative command 'gone away' should be given and the dog walked on. The gun has trained himself to regard his dog at all times, so if and when the dog attempts a break, the handler will be ready. As the dog bunches his muscles to go, the handler must give the command 'hup' quickly and forcefully, catching the dog a sharp slap on the side of the muzzle. If he reacts quickly enough, all should be well; his handler has delivered a shock to him at the psychological moment and he knows he cannot try any tricks and get away with it. If the gun should not possess such lightning fast reflexes, it should still be quite possible to stop the dog by command before he has gone more than a few yards as at this stage he is not, of course, a hardened sinner. The gun should lay down his weapon, seize the dog by the muzzle and the base of an ear and pull him back to the spot he moved from, giving a sharp command 'hup' as he pushes him to his haunches. During situations such as this, I have a great belief in catching hold of the dog's muzzle and holding it shut. A dog's armament is his teeth, of course, and I believe that to render his armament ineffectual places the handler at a great physical and psychological advantage over the dog. Similarly I believe that the rough handling of a dog's ear can be an effective 'natural' punishment. Gundogs seldom fight to kill (with the rare exception of bitches in season) but to establish supremacy. In these cases it is not the throat which is usually the target but the foreleg, lips and ears. It is essential that the handler should be accepted as the dog's superior, the leader of the pack, so to speak. I do not believe in severely thrashing a dog except in the rare case of an old, experienced dog who deliberately steps seriously out of line. In the case of a young, fairly sensitive dog, a painful thrashing, could, I am certain, create such a panic within the dog that it could completely erase the recollection of the original sin and merely leave the dog hurt, bewildered and resentful.

From these few lone forays with a few head of walked up game in the bag, the next logical step would be for the gun to take the dog on several outings with another gun and an experienced, reliable dog. So he is gently introduced to the distraction of other company and will quickly grasp the point that he must occasionally watch another dog retrieve a bird he has seen shot and even see it carried perhaps right under his nose without his interfering with the retrieve.

Prior to covert shooting, the handler may have had the opportunity to flight a few duck over the dog, either on stubble or more likely a flight pond, or decoy some pigeon coming in to laid corn. If so, this will stand him in good stead for covert shooting as the situation is similar, i.e. a long wait with birds shot at intervals and a pick up after shooting has finished.

At his first few covert shoots, a strict procedure should be observed. The dog should be left in the car whilst social pleasantries are exchanged. He should not be let out to run around sniffing at other guns and their dogs but should be confined to the car until the party is ready to move off. He should have a lead placed on him until the gun reaches his stand, then this lead should be removed and the dog seated in front of his master. It is the exact opposite of the all too usual procedure whereby the dogs are immediately turned loose at the meet, allowed to run all over the place on the way to the gunstands and maybe pursue the odd hare that happens to get up, then be firmly anchored before shooting commences.

After a few such outings, the dog should grasp the situation sufficiently to be capable of walking to heel between stands and ignoring other guns and their dogs. When grouse shooting, guns invariably walk in single file up to the butts, usually following a sheep track and an inexperienced dog which becomes separated from his master almost invariably runs forward to the head of the column, searching for his handler, so under these circumstances it is even more desirable that the dog should be kept on a lead until he learns to stick to his handler in company.

The essential difference between driven grouse and covert shooting in relation to the gun's retriever is that it is the former activity which will provide the greatest scope for the dog's talents. Although some keepers burn or cut a wide swathe of heather behind the butts to facilitate the pick up, the chances of birds falling into standing heather or bracken are considerable and a runner falling on burned ground will usually make for the nearest cover so there will usually be plenty of work for the dog after the drive in the vicinity of its own butt. The bird which will defeat a good many retrievers is the one taken well in front which falls within a yard or two of the butt. He will doubtless excel on those birds which fall 30 to 40 yards behind the butt but it is foreign to his nature to work very close in to a butt. In this situation, a Spaniel is usually better than a Retriever.

The occasions when a Retriever is of real value at a covert-side are rather more limited. Many woods are driven across grassland, stubble or ploughland, the majority of the birds falling in the open behind the gun. In situations where the birds will fall into heavy cover, pickers up will usually take care of this stage of the business, so the gun may find himself with several birds down, none of which are of any real value to his dog. Occasionally, at an open gunstand, a runner may be shot which will make for the nearest hedge or ditch, so here we have a situation where a good dog accompanying the gun can prove his worth at the end of the drive.

There is a useful technique which can be employed when shooting driven birds in full view of a young dog, the sensible application of which will 'make' the dog as a no-slip retriever and which, in later days, will allow the gun to concentrate fully on his shooting yet still ensure his dog's good behaviour. The dog should be 'hupped' a few yards in front of the gun, who should keep his eyes in the direction birds are expected to come from. As a bird approaches which the gun decides is his, he should keep his eyes on the bird but as he raises the gun to shoot, he should give a sharp 'hup', even though the dog is seated, to remind it that it is still under surveillance. The shot should be taken and, hit or miss, the handler should glance at the dog as he opens his gun, giving it another 'hup'. This will only take a split second and will not prevent the gun from keeping his eye on the next approaching bird. A little attention as described, on his first few days covert shooting, will provide an adequate answer to those who say a dog will take advantage of a gun absorbed in his shooting. If he is willing to allow it to, it most certainly will if it has a vestige of spirit in it. The remedy is in his own hands.

Some of the wealthier Field Trial competitors shoot in a very big way indeed, sometimes shooting over three or four dogs together and whereas I would not recommend this practice to any but the most experienced, it proves it can be done and anyone should be capable of keeping a trained Retriever up to a good standard of behaviour.

24 Shooting over a young spaniel

There is absolutely nothing which I have written about the young Retriever which cannot be applied to a Spaniel. All the aforementioned practices could not fail to be beneficial when one considers that the Spaniel is, ideally, the all-purpose dog and should be fully capable of being worked as a no-slip retriever as well as doing his specialist job of hunting up and flushing game, retrieving it when shot. In my experience, it is easier to sit a Spaniel down and shoot a dozen birds over it at a drive than it is to keep it within shot, keep it seady to flush and then to the fall, of one head of game hunted up. I do not believe that a bird falling out of the sky is as exciting to a Spaniel as it is to a Retriever. To the latter, retrieving game is the sole object of his existence. The Spaniel's instincts have been deployed over generations of breeding and during his training over a much wider field. For him, the real breath of life is the excitement of the hunt. Hunting, therefore, being his greatest joy, provides his greatest thrill, so to handle a hunting Spaniel successfully calls for a good measure of skill.

If at all possible, I would suggest that the young Spaniel has his first few outings after game with his handler shooting alone or alternatively with a friend deputising as gun. I myself have never enjoyed this luxury and have always shot over my dogs without outside help but that is no reason why such help should not be employed if available. Although the Spaniel will have had some practice by now at working a downwind beat, I would nevertheless suggest that for these first few excursions the dog should be worked into the wind as this technique will give the handler the firmest hold over his charge. The dog should be walked to heel over all non-productive pieces of ground such as bare pasture or short stubble for to allow a dog to ramble about to no purpose on such ground will inevitably lead to a slackness and deterioration in hunting and most dogs will quickly learn to pull towards the nearest cover, which may be well out of gunshot. Far better then to walk the dog to heel until a worthwhile piece of likely game-holding cover is reached.

The dog should be seated in front of the handler and a positive command to hunt given. He should by this time be a proficient hunter, having learned his trade in the rabbit-pen and on game he has hunted up on natural ground, therefore when the first head of game is flushed he should drop to it without any hesitation. As the gun is mounted, the cautionary command 'hup' should be given or a pip on the stop whistle if the handler has a gun shooting for him. In the event of the game being shot, the gun should be reloaded and the dog made to wait about 30 seconds before being sent for the retrieve.

Several factors now intrude, depending on species of game and the nature of the fall. If the game is a rabbit or hare, the Spaniel should be put on the line and encouraged to take it. The chances are that he will have some initial difficulty. At the shot, his head will naturally come up to mark and when sent for the retrieve he will naturally want to bound out with head high, causing him to miss the first yard or two of the line. He should be stopped and made to search for the line with his nose down but, having spent the last six months or so without ever being allowed to take a line, apart from dragged retrieves, the chances of his taking the line right to the retrieve without a check are remote and more than likely he will lift his head from the line and begin to cast. He should be stopped and encouraged to run the line again, the handler moving up the line to assist him if necessary. Most dogs require about six head of ground game shot over them before they learn to drop their noses on the line directly outside the vacated seat and follow every twist and turn of the quarry until the retrieve is reached. This is, of course, a contradiction to which he must adjust. He has continually been pulled off live lines until, theoretically at least, he should completely ignore them but now he is expected to run a line on command after a find and a shot.

A Spaniel ranging out towards a rabbit with its head up on high is highly likely to find and disturb fresh game between the handler and the retrieve. Should this happen in these early days, the game should be allowed to depart unscathed. The Spaniel is, after all, a novice, so the principle of novice Field Trials should be adhered to, namely, that game should not be

Bruce Erlandson with a young son of F.T. Ch. Gwibernant Ashley Robb, of a conformation most favoured by the author, being compact and powerful. Howard Pearson.

Three Springers who made history. L. & R. Hales Smut, his dam, Breckonhill Brando and Brando's daughter, Gwibernant Garreg Wynn, dam of double American National champion Gwibernant Ganol.

A feral reindeer bull near Arvidsjaur, Lappland. An animal virtually unchanged by man.

shot when a dog is searching for a retrieve. The object at this stage should be to encourage single-mindedness of purpose once the dog has been committed to a retrieve, so if fresh game is flushed, the command 'gone away' should be firmly given and the dog cast on again. I believe that at this stage a young dog should be capable of handling a wounded rabbit with little trouble but a wounded hare should always be given another barrel. A Spaniel should be allowed to become familiar with the feel, weight and scent of dead hares before being allowed to tackle a live one.

If a pheasant is flushed and shot, it may fall in an open situation where the dog is able to mark it but, even so, this is no guarantee that the bird will be accurately marked. The dog has no doubt become a competent marker on thrown retrieves and a competent finder of live game but he is not immediately bound to connect the two events. On finding the bird, he will probably glance away and, at the shot, may not manage to relocate the bird before it hits the ground. In this case he will have to be handled to the fall and may not accept direction as well as he did on his training ground. Should the dog go to pieces on the retrieve the handler should move forward and help him to locate the bird as quickly as possible. He must get the bird in his mouth so the connection between the flush and the retrieve becomes implanted in his mind. After a few birds, most dogs quickly grasp the idea of keeping their eye on the bird as it flushes, even turning with the bird should it swing over behind the handler. It is just as desirable that a Spaniel should mark a bird accurately as it is that it should follow the lines of ground game to the retrieve and for precisely the same reasons. It saves time and a Spaniel travelling in a straight line to a mark stands a far smaller chance of flushing fresh game than a dog who has to hunt his way out to the fall area.

Naturally dogs will vary in their ability to grasp the idea of exactly what this business of shooting is all about and when this realisation does come, it will be accompanied by a rise in the level of excitement to which I have already referred. This is the most crucial period of all.

It is important that only a limited amount of game is shot over the dog on these early outings on the real thing. Personally, I never shoot more than two or three head over a young Spaniel at this stage on any one outing but I must admit this practice is governed as much by a limited game supply as it is by my ideas. Nevertheless, I would regard half-a-dozen head as a safe maximum. We are already agreed that shooting over the dog is bound to hot him up, to make him much keener, so the problem the handler now faces is how to cope with this changing animal and prevent him from becoming so hot that he completely takes charge and becomes just another unruly gundog.

As the dog becomes more game conscious, he is likely to 'pull' in his hunting and attempt to cover more ground than is conducive to comfortable shooting. I do not like a Spaniel to produce game at extreme range. The bird is too quickly out of shot and, if shot, is far more likely to be a runner, or at the worst, a pricked bird that carries on beyond the vision of the handler and is therefore virtually unpickable, unless the Spaniel stumbles on it by chance later in the day. It is far better if the game is flushed fairly close to the handler, so he is more in command of the situation and can let the game out to a sensible killing range. A 'pulling' dog, ranging out beyond comfortable distance, may require a great deal of whistle to curb it, at times it may ignore the whistle and attempt to take the lines of moving game which it has, until now, either ignored or broken off immediately on command and a further development can be the inducement to run in when game is shot.

A Spaniel hot on a line may flush a moving bird just inside extreme range. The dog is obviously in motion when the bird is flushed, as opposed to the squatting bird which he pokes out of cover and 'hups' to. The handler must take the bird very quickly before it gets out of range and, if killed, it will obviously fall far closer to the dog than would be the case had the bird been flushed closer in and been killed well out. So we have the combination of a fast moving Spaniel with a hot foot-scent in his nose for several yards, dog and bird both in motion as the Spaniel overtakes it and a close shot bird in front of the dog who is quite a distance from his handler. This, I am told, is the situation which brings about the undoing of many Spaniels in American Field Trials, where, under some circumstances dogs are expected to 'trail' moving birds, so there is little wonder that such a situation is likely to be equally disastrous in our country.

This contingency can be prevented by making sure that the dog at all times hunts well within bounds. The question is how to achieve this object with a rapidly developing dog. It does not matter how hard or fast a Spaniel hunts provided he maintains a correct pattern which keeps him well within gunshot at all times and it is the instant turn, either of his own accord or at the turn whistle of his handler, which keeps him continually flowing in the right direction in relation to the gun. No latitude can be allowed over this most vital aspect of Spaniel work. The first time he disobeys the turn whistle, the stop whistle must be used and the dog dropped. The handler must put his gun down and bear down on the dog with maximum speed. The dog must be roughly seized and pulled in a few yards in the direction he should have turned in and the turn whistle pipped, in his ear. He should be made to sit for at least half a minute to allow the punishment to register, then be cast off again on the opposite side of the handler to the one he has pulled towards. In the rare event of the dog even failing to stop to the whistle and rioting completely, the handler must pursue the dog until he finally runs it down. Even if he fails and the dog has commenced to return of its own volition, the fact that the handler has gone out to meet it to administer correction will have the necessary salutary effect. The dog knows that the handler will not remain rooted to the spot while he trangresses and can expect to be pursued and apprehended should he deviate from his pattern.

On no account should the handler wait for the dog to return and punish him when he does so. This will merely confuse the issue and implant the idea into his mind that he is being punished for returning. A situation then arises whereby the dog riots at every opportunity, finding pleasure in so doing and crawling back to his handler to accept punishment. The dog becomes conditioned to doing as he wishes and regards the ravings of his owner as a natural hazard, as a countryman regards droughts, floods and blizzards.

Assuming that the Spaniel has been kept well within its hunting limits and appears to be going beautifully, the handler must be aware of a possible build up within the dog when it has had a number of retrieves and it may suddenly anticipate the command to fetch and attempt to run in. The dog will seldom make the attempt directly the bird is down. Usually it will wait a few seconds then move. This anticipation of the command is, to my way of thinking, more likely to be a genuine mistake on the part of the dog than a desire to do wrong. The dog has become conditioned to a flush, a shot, a wait, then a retrieve and has forgotten to listen for the command. A great deal can be done to avert such a contingency if the handler trains himself to give the command 'hup' before and after the shot, thus demonstrating his unfailing vigilance to his charge at all times. He must keep his eyes on the dog after the shot, so he can forestall any attempt to move when the dog's muscles tense to go, as previously mentioned. Any attempt to move, however slight, must be dealt with.

The Spaniel, unlike the Retriever at heel, will not be within range of the owner's hand so he will not be in a position to receive a slap. The handler, after stopping the Spaniel, must put his gun down and catch hold of the dog, give him a hard shake and sit him down sharply, then go out and pick the bird by hand. This type of preventive action should preclude any attempt on the part of the dog at a real full blooded run in, right up to the bird but in such an event, more likely to happen in the case of an experienced dog who deliberately takes it into his head to 'have a go', the technique of putting the gun down and getting after the dog as quickly as possible must be adopted. To effect a cure, the handler must never allow the dog to take the bird into his mouth or the advantage will be completely lost.

The dog must never be punished once he gets hold of the bird or he will associate punishment with the act of retrieving and either go off retrieving, circle his handler or bite his birds. The handler in this case must make as much noise as possible when pursuing the dog, so he looks over his shoulder to see what is happening, causing him to slow down sufficiently for the handler to catch him before he gets to the bird. He should be dragged very roughly away from the bird back to the approximate position he set off from and either be shaken hard by the throat, have an ear pulled or be given a hiding with something pliable if he is a really tough character who will not become cowed with such harsh treatment. Soft dogs require softer treatment but if one administers inadequate punishment to a hard dog, he will hold his handler in contempt.

There are times when a dog may defeat the handler over a matter of a run in. It may happen at a Trial, and the handler must accept the situation with a good grace as a dog must never be punished at a Trial or the dog may run in on a piece of difficult terrain where pursuit by the handler could cause the latter a broken leg, or the dog may run in down a very steep slope and no man can match a Spaniel downhill. In any such case, the handler should calmly accept the bird with no show of anger but make sure that he engineers a situation as soon as possible to *make* the dog run in, so the fault may be eradicated.

Once a dog has managed to run in all the way and complete the retrieve, the handler must *never* attempt to merely 'hold' the dog. The problem must be attacked at the root and the dog allowed to commit itself fully, so the full remedy may be applied. This can be accomplished by encouraging the dog to do exactly what one endeavours to prevent it from doing under normal circumstances. One should try to get the dog on to a moving bird, allow him to line it and kill it as close to him as possible. He will almost certainly run in, under conditions when the handler is ready to deal with him.

Another feasible, if unsporting method, which I have had described to me but which I have not used myself, is for the handler to take the dog into a wood at dusk and let him hunt pheasant scent under the trees. When he is really busy, a roosting pheasant should be shot to drop very close to him. Apart from the matter of the ethics involved, I would imagine that few people would wish to disturb a covert at roosting time but I suppose this method could be employed in an outlying spinney.

I once had a 'Cocker afternoon' with some Trial colleagues who, like myself, had some recalcitrant Cockers to sort out and during the course of events I shot a guinea-hen out of a tree almost on top of the heads of two Cockers, both of which promptly ran in, so a situation was created of which we were able to take full advantage.

A Spaniel handler should always bear in mind the prevailing weather conditions and the most likely affect they will have on his dog's performance. It is fairly safe to state that the Springer hates hot weather and is highly unlikely to give a first rate performance under such conditions. In America, Trials are often held in the 70s and 80s, with dogs going flat-out like racehorses. I am told their heat is normally less humid than ours, which apparently assists the dogs and although I have no idea of the average duration of an American Trial run, blank runs of half an hour or more, common enough in our Trials, must surely be unknown in the States as birds are continually 'planted' at intervals ahead of the advancing line.

It is on a hot day in our country that the Cocker scores over the Springer. Why I cannot say but the indisputable fact remains that a good Cocker has far more stamina under hot or humid conditions than his larger counterpart and at the end of a long, hot hunt, a Cocker has usually enough left in him to make a good, clean retrieve whereas a Springer will, more often than not, fumble the retrieve three or four times on the way back. There are, of course, exceptions but I think this can be considered to be basically correct.

On wild, windy days Spaniels are likely to run extremely hot and behave in an unruly fashion. Some say this is because they cannot hear the whistle so well but I do not believe this to be the complete answer as the dog will be found to need more whistle than is normally the case. I believe the wind itself is responsible by having a disturbing psychological affect upon the dog. As often happens after a day of gale-force wind, the following day is often very calm and still and it is my experience that a Spaniel which has behaved in unruly fashion on a windy day, will, if worked the following day when the wind has dropped, behave in exemplary manner, almost as though the wind has purged the Devil from his system.

Neither Springer nor Cocker appears to relish a steady downpour of drenching rain any more than any of us enjoy shooting under such conditions. Game is often absent from its normal habitat. Any game one encounters is wet and reluctant to move, so the chances of the Spaniel catching unshot game are greatly increased.

In my experience, a Spaniel, particularly a Springer, is absolutely at his very best on a day of fairly stiff breeze, carrying a light fine rain, sufficient to keep the Spaniel's coat wet. Under such conditions a fit Spaniel can go for ever. The rain cools him without drenching him to the skin and the dampness appears to keep his breathing apparatus functioning comfortably as he will not 'blow'. Scenting conditions are likely to be at their best and the dog will often catch the windborne scent of a bird many yards away. Scent of shot game carries well too and some very good runners are often collected under these weather conditions.

After a hard frost many Spaniels are willing to hunt keenly but only the most courageous dogs will tackle frozen brambles as there is no 'give' in them, so they become even more punishing. Many dogs will tend to potter somewhat on stale footscent on open pieces of ground and whereas unshot game appears easy enough to find and flush, shot game can often prove extremely difficult to find and runners seldom leave a workable line, so the gun must use his knowledge to estimate the direction the bird is likely to take and work his Spaniel accordingly, hoping to find the bird tucked in somewhere.

Spaniel work can be extremely difficult during and immediately after heavy snowfall. Springers, more than Cockers, enjoy hunting under such conditions but game finding can prove difficult. Many birds, particularly those roosting in conifers, do not come down from their roosts on the first day after a night's heavy snowfall. Those living in hardwood plantations are likely to seek the thickest rhododendrons and some become completely snowed over where they squat and can only be located by a really experienced dog.

I once had an extraordinary experience in a Trial following heavy snow. Game was scarcer than is normally the case on this particular Northamptonshire estate and I had a bitch working in the afternoon who had already had a good run in the morning. She checked at a snow covered clump of rough grass and inch by inch bored her way in. A cock pheasant erupted through a crust of snow and was missed by the right hand gun. 'Oh well, a find, anyway', I thought. Imagine my consternation when the bitch backed out with a dying hen bird in her mouth. I took it from her and quickly felt its ribs and found it be completely undamaged. It was obviously one of those rare specimens which game farmers tell me die of heart failure directly they are handled. This probably accounts for some strong runners which come back stone dead but completely undamaged. Certainly a pellet in a vulnerable area is the cause more often than not, but I am sure that occasional heart failure does occur. Be this as it may, I was 'out' for pegging game. Had it been a normal bird, I could have made the bitch release it with no trouble, so it was sheer bad luck that it 'died on us'.

After the first day of heavy snow, conditions tend to become normal. Pheasants come down out of the firs on to the feed, birds dig themselves out of the snow and tuck themselves into more accessible places and scent is usually very good and runners can be collected.

Under conditions of thawing snow, scent is often excellent

but many dogs are not keen on hunting wet snow, particularly the Cockers. It is generally accepted by experienced people that, all things considered, it takes a pretty good dog to work in snow, movement of game being restricted with a resulting lack of footscent to stimulate the dog. On the other hand, a 'pulling' dog is often rendered more tractable by snowy conditions.

25 Working on runners

One of the most valuable assets in any retrieving gundog is the ability to take the line of a wounded bird or rabbit and make good the retrieve, in fact one of the major arguments for owning a gundog at all is that it puts one in a position to account for wounded game which would otherwise be lost, to die a slow death, to live on permanently crippled or to become food for the local fox population, so, from the points of view of humanity and conservation, a dog which can collect runners is a tremendous asset. I have already described how a Spaniel which works comfortably within shot will assist the gun to kill his birds dead but none of us are infallible and however correctly our dogs work or however well we shoot, a certain proportion of running birds is inevitable. In my own case, I find this works out at roughly 10 per cent, a satisfactorily low proportion due more to the hunting technique of my Spaniels than my marksmanship. Consequently my dogs do not receive a great deal of practice on runners unless I take them picking up but the fewer runners on my own ground that I have to contend with, the better pleased I am. The curse of the high ground in Wales is the sheep fence, with its netting through which a bird can escape and its barbed wire on top to injure a jumping dog.

I have already dealt with how a dog can be practised on lines during training but this can only assist. He must have practice on the real thing to become competent and here chance enters into it a great deal. I am completely opposed to trying deliberately to make runners for a dog as some good shots seem able to do, and I believe one should try to shoot everything dead and rely on those birds which just happen to be runners. Here, the ability to recognise a potential runner in the air is of considerable help. Those of us who are ex-gamekeepers or who have picked up a great deal are at a considerable advantage. One can never be 100 per cent certain whether or not a bird will run but it is possible to be correct more times than not. A bird hit in the middle or tip of the wing usually comes down in unmistakable fashion and obviously very much alive although even these birds are occasionally picked dead where they fall with one pellet in a vital organ. A difficult bird to assess is one which usually comes down feet first with wings outstretched, sometimes falling in a spiral. This bird may remain at the fall and be collected, or it may run, almost invariably getting up and flying off apparently unscathed when the dog finally catches up with it. I suspect these birds to be grazed by one pellet in the head, some more severely than others which would account for them not moving. I believe a good many Trial dogs have been unjustly put out for failing on this type of runner when, in actual fact, the bird has got up again out of sight or even in the open, the judge having failed to appraise the situation accurately.

The most deceptive runner of all is the one which falls apparently stone dead but whose manner of falling is caused by the wing being broken close up by the body; I am confident that this kind of injury is responsible for virtually all those 'dead' birds which disappear. However, they carry a good blood scent and can never become airborne again, as wing-tipped birds can do sometimes. I once stood behind a line of guns on a high shale heap, overlooking a young plantation. A wing-tipped cock landed about a hundred yards behind us in the young trees and I sent my Labrador who hit the fall and took the line for about 30 yards. The bird struggled into the air and just managed to clear a rabbit wire fence about 30 yards ahead. The Labrador stopped at the flush, marked the bird to where it landed in the bed of a small stream and looked up for instructions. I sent him on and he cleared the fence and hit the fall, taking the line downstream, returning several minutes later with the bird. Certainly a most pleasing performance but it proved how severely handicapped a Spaniel, with his much lower eye level, would have been in identical circumstances, particularly if the handler had not been in a position to appraise the situation.

A similar case occurred in my own rabbit-pen. My pen is

divided in two, where an extension joins the original pen. The wire dividing the two sections is lowered in places to form jumps and one day I shot a hen pheasant which fell over the wire into the new pen, obviously only wing-tipped. The dog made a good mark and took a line but, to my annoyance, the bird jumped into the air, took advantage of the fall of the hill-side and glided over the fence. That bird was never seen again.

From the foregoing, it will be seen that not all runners are alike and that they can follow a great diversity of behaviour patterns, so a young dog encountering his first few runners needs a certain amount of luck to bring them to the bag. Ideally, a dog's first runner should fall in full view into a field of damp rushes, should be a hen pheasant, preferably with a pellet in the toe to draw blood, should run into the wind and only move about 30 yards before tucking in. The chances of success under such circumstances would be extremely high and such a successful collection should give a pup confidence to follow birds much further in future. As many runners are likely to be a good deal more difficult, this is where the ele-ment of luck enters the picture, enabling some young dogs to get under way on runners far more readily than others.

Another difficulty a well trained young Spaniel may encoun-ter is a psychological one. He has continually been pulled off live lines and is now expected to follow wounded lines, so small wonder that he may wonder if he is doing the right thing and break off the pursuit. Admittedly he should follow a blood scent but it may be some time before this registers. Not all runners carry a blood scent. In some cases the bird will carry a 'shocked scent' which will occur when a bird is lightly wounded but not bleeding profusely; this is particularly appar-ent when a bird runs over bare ground where there is no cover to collect blood scent from the bird. All the dog has to follow is a footscent but it varies from a normal footscent as the bird exudes a different scent at the impact of the shot. Such a bird is usually only collected by an experienced performer. Some runners are virtually unpickable by any dog. A runner which falls on bare beech leaves with a strong, cold wind blowing leaves no line at all and one can only carry on until the nearest cover is reached in the hope that the bird will have stopped there.

Sugar-beet can pose problems when it comes to finding run-ners as scent usually appears to be very difficult in October (when the majority of Retriever Trials are held) but it can improve later in the season and I have witnessed some very good collections of runners from beet in November and December. Swedes and turnips usually appear to carry better scent at most times than beet but perhaps this is because my experience of this crop has been confined to the northern counties and Scotland, where scent is generally better than the eastern and midland counties.

Theoretically, a Retriever should get the idea of taking a runner sooner than a Spaniel as his attentions have never been diverted from his job of retrieving by having to learn another trade like a Spaniel, therefore he should be more single-minded in his approach to runners; in practice this seldom appears to be the case as the majority of Retrievers appear to have a slower mental development than Spaniels. Cockers often become competent fairly quickly on runners and I believe this to be due to the more independent Cocker temperament. Once away and out of sight I do not believe a Cocker would stop to worry whether he is doing the right thing or not, as might a sensitive young Spaniel or Retriever. They love putting distance between themselves and their handlers so the pursuit of a runner would furnish them with a perfectly legitimate excuse to do just this.

I think the utmost discretion should be used over the numbers of runners a young dog should be allowed to retrieve. Runners are very exciting things to handle and can 'hot up' a pup to an unacceptable degree. Another point concerning Spaniels in general and Cockers in particular is that too many runners, some caught on the move, some pulled out of heavy cover, could cause a dog to become careless over tenderness in handling his birds and produce a case of induced (as opposed to hereditary) hard mouth.

A young dog should never be sent for a runner in an open situation as nothing can be more exciting to him than a long course over a bare field on a bird in full view. Such a performance would defeat its own object as he would use his eyes exclusively and gain no experience at following a line. Even when shooting over a young dog on whose steadiness a careful watch is being kept, he should not be kept waiting more than a few seconds before being sent, provided the bird falls into cover. The dog must be given the maximum opportunity to get to the fall right away, to get away on the line while it is still fresh. Some Retrievers with experience become quite clever at taking a 'cold' line of a bird which may have been down several minutes but the majority of Spaniels need a fairly hot line to enable them successfully to retrieve a runner.

I am fortunate to have in my kennels the best dog on a runner that I have ever handled. His name is F. T. C. Gwibernant Ashley Robb, a son of Hales Smut. As a two-year-old, he never got going on runners at all. His opportunities were limited to one short bird in his first Novice Stake, which he collected and won the Trial, a short grouse he collected in another Trial and two pheasants that he failed on, one shot by me, the other in his first Championship. The following year, when he became a Field Trial champion, he began to show his ability to take a bird a really long distance and at four years of age he became really brilliant.

He demonstrated his ability to take a cold line when I was out on my own mountain late one afternoon. I shot a cock about 40 yards out, seemingly stone dead. I sent a Cocker who never handled too well and it took me some time to get him to the fall. When he arrived at the right area he cast around but produced nothing so I called him in and sent Robb, who had held his mark on the bird. Robb went straight to the fall, in heavy bracken and disappeared. He had been gone some considerable time when I observed him high up on the mountainside to my left but working towards me. This had me puzzled until I saw the cock running downhill across my front within a few yards of me. Upon spotting me, it turned and ran forward towards the original fall. Robb held to the line but crossing my front he spotted me and his head came up, so I gave him a hand signal and he immediately put his nose down again and bored off forward.

Minutes passed, Robb having taken a direction which must have been fouled with his own scent from his previous circuit, then he appeared again on the face of the mountain, working towards me as before. Once more the bird appeared, running strongly through the bracken across my front, this time going down the mountainside below me, Robb on its line like a bloodhound. The bird tucked in and Robb was able to secure it. I had no watch with me but I estimated he was on the line at least a quarter of an hour.

This was undoubtedly the most difficult runner I had ever seen collected, on account of the odd behaviour of the bird. His most spectacular gallery effort occurred a little later in Scotland. During a long and protracted run off, in which hens were not being shot, he was called in no fewer than three times. We were almost out of ground, the bogland cover being finished and giving way to bare, open parkland. He flushed a cock which fell on the far bank of a drain about 45 yards out, sat for a second, head darting wickedly, then set off like a stag. Robb made such a good mark that he nearly had the bird before it got under way but it dodged round a few small gorse bushes lining a bank and Robb went through them, losing the initiative, so he put his nose down and took the line as far as a large tree at the junction of two drains. Here he lost the line and made a huge cast across an open field, failed to pick up any scent so cast himself back to the tree on his own accord, this time going around the far side of the tree and disappearing into a drain. He next appeared, hundreds of yards away, emerging from the drain, crossed some open, slightly rising ground, checked at a very small, isolated gorse bush and pulled the cock out.

The terrain over which he took that bird was completely devoid of cover, in fact a great deal of it was covered in black soil, dredged out of the drains, so there can have been only the faintest footscent to follow, but Robb is one of those determined, arrogant dogs and one could almost sense a personal vendetta between him and that cock.

According to one local authority, never noted for undeserved praise, it was 'the best runner I have ever seen a Spaniel collect'. According to another handler of vast experience, with whom I was actually running off when this incident occurred it was 'the best runner I have ever seen any dog collect in my life and I know my bitch could not have picked it.' Those were the words of a true sportsman.

26 Picking up

Not everyone who loves gundogs and shooting has sufficient access to suitable ground to do as much shooting as he would wish, or to give his dogs as much practical experience as he feels they should have. In fact, I would go so far as to say that I believe more dog handlers find themselves in this situation than in the enviable position of having all the shooting they could desire.

One way around the situation of limited facilities is for the handler to do some picking up on organised shoots. Picking up is not difficult to find as basically there are more vacancies for pickers up throughout the country than there are pickers up available. Picking up, within certain limitations and under certain conditions can provide a gundog with invaluable experience but there are certain snags which may have to be overcome.

On many shoots today, the accent would appear to be on large bags. The main purpose of picking up for a dog handler is to enable him to give experience to his younger dogs on natural game. The main purpose on the part of the shoot in engaging pickers up is to get the absolute maximum number of dead and wounded birds into the bag and here we may have a conflict of interests. Certain aspects of picking up are not good for young dogs and this is particularly likely to be the case on shoots where a large head of game is shot. I have already mentioned that it is inadvisable to shoot too much game over an inexperienced dog on any one occasion, so by the same token it is not a good thing to allow a young dog to retrieve too many birds when picking up, but the picker up has a duty to his host to attempt to recover every bird that falls within the area he is covering. In many cases, though, some of the birds will not be at all beneficial to the young dog's further education.

For a start, there may be far too many birds. This situation can be helped to a certain extent by the handler, who can pick by hand any unwanted dead birds which fall on bare ground. Even so, there may still be so many birds in cover which really need a dog to find them that a young dog working on his own may still have far too many birds to contend with. It does not help if the handler is trying to handle the dog in a specific direction and it finds a bird elsewhere in the process. This proves the handler wrong to the dog, so it is reasonable to assume that a succession of such events could cause the dog to refuse to accept directions in future. Another unhelpful event is the doubtful bird. The handler marks the direction of a wounded bird but cannot quite see it down owing to the nature of the terrain. The bird could be ten yards beyond his field of vision or it could be a 100 or more. It is impossible to handle a dog on to such a bird and the only technique which can be employed is blind hunting. One proceeds in the direction taken by the bird, allowing the dog to hunt where he wishes and hoping for the best. This can be detrimental to his handling and a failure can spoil his confidence, although the handler can assist by surreptitiously dropping a dead bird while the dog is busy, then allowing him to find it, once the handler has decided to abandon the search.

The ideal practice for the picker up is that he should take two dogs with him, an older, experienced dog, ideally a retired Trial dog and the young one to which he wishes to give experience. He can give experience to his young entry on selected birds and he can deal with quantities and doubtful birds with his old dog, who is beyond spoiling, so fulfil his obligations to the shoot.

It should be no problem for a professional trainer, a gamekeeper or an established Field Trial competitor, to take an older dog along to deal with the rougher side of the work but we must consider the one dog owner who has only one young dog, not long out of training, which he hopes to educate on game without spoiling it. I consider that his best solution is to ask the keeper if he can stand back well behind the main body of pickers up, to take the really long pricked birds which travel well beyond the vision of the main pickers up. Here he can serve a dual purpose. He can mark down and collect a few birds which might otherwise be lost and having marked a bird accurately can proceed to within the distance from which he wishes to work his dog, handling him out into the exact area without the hazard of stumbling on to another shot bird. He will certainly encounter live birds from time to time when picking up three or four hundred yards back. If a pricked bird will make for a certain area, it is only logical to assume that unharmed birds will take the same direction. This can be quite a good thing. The dog flushes a live bird when searching for a pricked one, is told 'gone away' and made to carry on with the job, away from all excitement, so learning to accept a fresh bird as a natural occurrence to be ignored. This type of work is absolutely first class for a young Retriever and cannot possibly do a Spaniel any harm either.

Assuming one has the necessary dogs to deal with every contingency which may arise when picking up, the question arises how best one can employ oneself to the maximum advantage. On very highly organised shoots the pickers up may have their positions allocated to them either by the headkeeper or by some other person in charge of the picking up. Often it is left to the discretion of the pickers up where they stand and as the same pickers up operate year after year on some shoots, this system would appear to work well enough.

A picker up should not stand with the guns but at least 50 yards behind, provided this does not interfere with the next drive. At such a distance, he can mark every bird that falls directly behind the gun and the majority of those which plane down and fall further back, these usually being runners. He should observe which of the guns he is covering have their own dogs with them and leave those birds which fall directly behind the stands to them, concentrating on the more difficult birds which fall further back.

The question may well be asked, should the picker up wait until the end of the drive before picking or should he collect the birds as they fall? If he decides to adopt the former practice, he will lose some runners and may find he has not completed his task before he is required at the next stand. If he collects the birds as they fall, he will stand a far better chance of picking his runners but there is the additional hazard that when the young dog is out on a retrieve, a fresh bird may fall practically on top of his head. The individual must decide for himself.

My own practice is to send my young dog for the first bird or two that falls in a useful position, if I am fairly certain they are dead. One can usually get one or two early retrieves before the main flush and reduce the hazard of another bird being shot while the dog is out working. As the drive progresses, I send the old dog for any obvious runners. I do not practise my young dogs on my host's runners. I only send a dog which is reasonably certain to collect and rely on my own shooting activities to produce the occasional runner for my young dogs.

The old dog is often away a considerable time on a runner during a drive, during which time I mark any others that fall and occasionally send the young dog for a bird. I pick the rest of the birds after the end of the drive.

Picking up gives a dog handler considerable experience of shot birds and what they are likely to do, which can prove invaluable when handling at or judging Field Trials. A medium to high bird which lifts perceptibly at the impact of a shot, crumples into a ball, hangs in mid-air for a split second with a puff of feathers at its front end, is one of the very few birds which can be guaranteed dead. The lift proves the impact of the shot has been sufficient to kill it and the puff of feathers at the fore end signifies a hit well forward. Some birds stop dead in the air and crash heavily down but one can often see the eye is open and the head held up out of harm's way. Such a bird usually runs, the wing being broken close to the shoulder.

It is a mistake to assume that a bird which planes with one leg down will stay where he falls. A bird will often go quite a distance on one good leg but not right into the blue. Occasionally a bird will rise almost vertically into the air, then flutter to earth feet first. This is known as a 'false tower' and the bird will often fly again. In the case of a true tower, the bird rises but falls like a stone and is invariably found dead on its back with blood on the beak, the result, I am certain, of a lung injury. I hate to see a bird which gives a wriggle of its tail at the shot. This suggests a hit too far back and such birds will go a very long way and are hard to collect. A bird which carries on after a shot, quite strongly but with a completely silent wing beat, in place of the high drumming note one associates with a healthy pheasant, will usually fall stone dead within 200 yards.

Picking up on a grouse moor differs considerably from the same activity on the low ground and in my opinion can be the most beneficial exercise of all from a young dog's point of view.

Unless a moor is very small, with the drives correspondingly short, the pickers up can usually place themselves three or four hundred yards behind the guns without disturbing the next drive but if in doubt a dog man on a moor should always ask the headkeeper if there is to be a return drive and, if so, just how far back into it he may go. Even if a picker up knows a moor, drives will sometimes be altered, owing to changed wind direction.

Of course, once a return drive has been brought back, the picker up is able to work his dog anywhere he wishes, unless the moor is like one rather odd place in Derbyshire which has only two drives, one over a central line of butts and the other brought back before lunch and the process repeated on the same ground in the afternoon.

Standing well back on a moor, the pickers up may choose their positions according to the geographical features of the particular terrain. There may be a large gully some way behind the butts and in this case the dog men will need to place themselves where they can overlook it as a pricked grouse which makes for such a place will usually turn right or left upon reaching it and follow the contour of the gully so far, or may cross the gully and follow the contour on the far side.

Unless one is in a position to see exactly where a grouse lands in a gully, it can only be a matter of chance if the bird is ever collected. There may be a long expanse of rising ground behind the butts, culminating in a ridge on the skyline which is where, ideally, the pickers up should be. They can then mark anything down in front of them and are also in a position to mark any birds which make it over the ridge. If a wounded bird is seen to disappear over a ridge, it is again a chancy business finding it as there is no possible way of knowing how far it has gone, so it is far better if one can actually command the view on both sides of the ridge. In such a position, however, the picker up must be extremely careful to conceal himself and his dog completely whilst the drive is in progress or the sharp sighted birds will spot him in the background before they reach the line of butts and swing sideways.

The dog handler standing well back on a moor will not be troubled by a confusion or profusion of birds being shot around him so he should not find himself in trouble if he only posesses one young dog. The birds which are killed around the butts can be dealt with by the guns' own dogs or the dogs of the flankers who normally converge on the butts after the drive is over to assist with the pick up. Under these circumstances a few birds may be lost. Wives and girl friends seem to insist on tramping around the butts, trying to hand-pick birds, raising clouds of pollen in the early part of the season when the heather is in bloom and generally ruining the scent. The picker up behind is in a far more fortunate position. Once he has marked a bird he can take his dog to within handling dis-

146

tance and cast it out without any fear of interference. Marking can at times be difficult on a moor as an expanse of heather can look the same everywhere, like the sea. I mark by bits of shadowed heather, caused by irregularities of the ground, pieces of rock, a patch of rushes or bracken or a line between standing and burned heather. When walking towards a long distance bird it is essential to keep the eyes glued on the spot as features can change their appearance as one approaches. The sun may go behind a cloud and so change a shadow pattern.

With the exception of a very hot, still day with masses of pollen about grouse are comparatively easy birds to find. They appear to carry a very strong attractive scent which is often windborne for quite a distance. There usually is a good breeze on a moor and later in the season, scent on a moor is often very good indeed. A running grouse seldom displays the cunning of an old wing-tipped cock pheasant. If he falls on burned ground, he will usually cross it in a straight line and tuck into the nearest standing heather. If he gets on to a sheep path in standing heather he may travel quite a way but is almost guaranteed not to leave it and is usually found tucked in at the side within a foot of the path. A winged grouse that does not run but promptly buries himself in deep heather can be the most difficult grouse of all to find, particularly if someone tramps near to his fall before a dog can approach him but this will hardly be a problem for the picker up well back. He must very carefully watch every pack, covey or single bird, especially the latter, which comes within his field of vision.

Often a covey crosses the guns. Birds may be correctly selected and correctly killed but there is no guarantee that one or two more birds may not have collected a stray pellet at the time and these are the most likely birds to travel a long distance. Some give no indication of having been hit and flight speed is no guide. Perfectly sound grouse appear to be moving quite leisurely, particularly when flying head on into a stiff breeze, so a slow grouse is not necessarily a wounded bird. If a bird is seen to depart from a pack or covey and take an independent line of its own, that is a bird to watch as it is surely hit.

The same invariably applies also to partridges. Watch every bird as it pitches as some can actually be seen to fall over dead when they land; on the other hand, some grouse fly normally, land normally but are still picked up dead on the spot. Obviously anyone would search for a grouse with a leg down but often these will get up and fly again, having no pellet in a vulnerable area.

Spaniels will benefit tremendously from picking a few grouse and a young Retriever can be seen to improve in keenness and efficiency as he pulls off some very worthwhile retrieves on the moor, but the Retriever owner can be in for a big shock and disappointment when he takes his young paragon to the low ground again to work on pheasants and partridges. For a time they can often hardly find their own dinners. As I have mentioned, scent can be very good on a moor in September and early October and a young Retriever can really gallop and use the wind. In early October scent on the low ground is usually atrocious, so it is small wonder that the young Retriever, having been used to a good, windborne scent, takes time to find his nose again. The Spaniel appears to adapt more rapidly, why I just cannot say.

27 Working tests

I am not certain when artificially engineered working tests for Retrievers came into being, whether they commenced some time after the last war finished or whether, in fact, they were held prior to 1939. Certainly, Spaniel tests have only been held for a few years, in fact until the advent of the Country Landowners' Association Game Fair tests, it seemed to be generally accepted that, owing to the nature of a Spaniel's work, convincing tests would be impossible to organise for Spaniels.

At whatever period of time tests emerged, however, I think it would be quite safe to say that working tests have revolutionised dog handling and Field Trials in particular. Whether the revolution has been for good or ill is open to conjecture. The whole question is extremely complex with so many facets that it would require a person of more than ordinary perception to be able to state accurately and categorically whether working tests are a good or a bad institution.

Speaking in favour of them, there can be no question whatsoever that they have stimulated interest in gundog work and training more than any other single factor. For a start, tests have a considerable spectator appeal. They can be held in the close season when there is at least a chance that the weather may be pleasant. Ground is not difficult to come by as the host has no need to sacrifice any of his game for the event. In fact, completely gameless ground is perfectly adequate and it is possible to organise the layout of the course so that spectators have maximum viewing, which is not always possible at Field Trials held on natural game, particularly those Spaniel Trials which are held in heavy woodland cover. Usually held at weekends, they can provide an excuse for a family outing and can be social as well as sporting events.

A working test can be utilised as a stepping stone by the novice trainer between training his dog and using it in the shooting field or ultimately competing in Field Trials. A young dog just out of training can be introduced via the working test to working in the company of other dogs and human beings without the added distraction of natural game and this could hardly be considered anything but beneficial.

Tests allow great scope for the ingenuity of the organisers, as a great many situations may be engineered to simulate various contingencies in the shooting field or Trial. Pigeon may be released from traps to simulate the missed bird which the dog sees, then must ignore and search for a retrieve which it either has the chance to mark or which may be completely blind. A retrieve may be thrown in full view of the dog which the dog must ignore and search for an unmarked retrieve, representing a runner which the dog is required to pick first. A dummy may be fired at when the dog is either on his way out to, or on the way back with a retrieve, which of course he must ignore. A double retrieve may be thrown into water, one of which he is required to collect first as it represents a wounded duck, the other, a dead one. Artificial rabbits or hares may be drawn across the course as an added distraction. Rabbits may be placed in small enclosures to be ignored. Fences can be erected to test jumping powers. To deal with any of these contingencies, a dog must be very well trained, so the handler who aspires to tests will work hard on his dog and his handling ability will improve accordingly.

The public spectacle of tests engenders further competition from many of the spectators, who decide they would like to train and handle in tests themselves. Some will also be keen on shooting but several, including some interested ladies, will not shoot. This will obviously increase the number of owners which means more puppy sales for those who breed and it could lead to an increase of dogs being placed in professional hands for training.

Let us now consider what has actually happened over the years. In Retriever circles, particularly in the south of England, working tests have become so popular that they have become an end in themselves, so much so that some dogs, mediocre by ordinary Trial or shooting standards, have won as many as 30 Open Tests. Some test dogs never work on game and the reliability of their mouths is never proved, even though the organisers use cold pigeon or rabbits as retrieves or even go so far as to kill unwanted homing pigeon and use them while still warm as retrieves. Many hard mouthed dogs will not bite cold game. Others will not hurt a homing pigeon, or anything with a human scent on it but if they had to take a tucked in pheasant out of thick grass or light bracken they would instantly crush it.

There is also the matter of temperament to be considered. Dogs are not complete fools and it is absolutely impossible to stage a test which fools the dog into believing it is really being shot over. A fresh pheasant could be tossed out and a shotted cartridge fired in its wake and the dog would still know the situation was a simulated one. Whether the dog can hear the impact of the shot on the bird, or in the event of a miss, is psychic enough to sense the *intention* to kill I cannot say but the fact remains that a dog knows when it is being shot over and a certain temperament is required to stand the pressures of the shooting field which are absent in the most efficiently organised of tests. A dog could be perfectly stable in a test but completely unreliable as a shooting or Trial dog, so here we have the danger of dogs being bred as test dogs with completely unsuitable temperaments as real gundogs but whose blood could easily infiltrate other members of their breed with disastrous results brought about by injudicious matings.

I understand there has been some campaigning on the part of the Retriever working test fraternity for the granting of the title of Working Test Champion but, thank goodness, the powers that be have denied them the request. It would be so easy, by intention or error, to confuse the title of W.T.C. with F.T.C. in a pedigree which would be dangerously misleading.

Some working test handlers have entered Trials when their dogs have not been sufficiently experienced on game, indeed some dogs have been run in Trials which have never seen a pheasant, taking up nominations which would have been far better filled by genuine gundogs and I am certain that the tremendous pressures on Field Trial nominations which have been present for many years have come about as a direct result of working test dogs being entered in Trials.

When I first came into Trials, working tests for Spaniels were unknown. When the C.L.A. Game Fair came into being, gundog tests were laid on as an added attraction, including tests for Spaniels. This was a good thing. The object was to place gundogs before the public eye as a demonstration rather than a competitive event, although I think the organisers are wise to retain the competitive element as handlers will surely try that bit harder to put up the best possible show. Initially, some test Retrievers did compete at the Game Fair but latterly the organisers have taken pains to ensure that only genuine Field Trial dogs have taken part. In this way tests can do no harm. If only genuine proven dogs take part the argument against test dogs does not apply as the competitors are first and foremost shooting and Field Trial dogs and only do the Game Fair tests as a sideline.

Spaniel tests in their own right have, however, become increasingly popular of late. We had a comfortable situation during my first few years in Spaniel Trials. There were usually enough places for everyone who wished to run, with perhaps two or three reserves in Open Stakes. Now all this has changed and we sometimes have over 40 entries for an available 16 places. The Spaniel working tests have been largely responsible. Some years ago, in the eastern part of the country several interested Spaniel men got together and held tests, gradually entering Trials with varying degrees of success but undoubtedly swelling the Field Trial ranks. These men and women were all amateurs, starting in a very small way, presumably through a genuine interest in and love of Spaniels, but it was found that there was money in trained Spaniels and the situation escalated producing not only a faction of keen Spaniel people but a group of dog hucksters whose original aim of producing a dog capable of winning Trials took second place to their desire to sell one for the best possible price. A similar situation has now arisen in the West Country but as yet the

West Countrymen have not discovered that some Spaniels are capable of swimming the Atlantic. Unfortunately a similar element of rivalry and bitterness has manifested itself in both areas.

Another side effect of the working tests as they become increasingly prevalent, with new clubs being formed, is that out of every group of individual handlers, one or two emerge who are better handlers than their fellows and proceed to win nearly all their local tests and so become the local kingpins. By ordinary shooting or Trial standards, their dogs may be distinctly mediocre but the handler gains a local reputation of being 'a good man with dogs' and the services of his dogs are sought accordingly, likewise his puppies, when in reality his stock may not be particularly good or even sound.

Working tests are here to stay for good or ill and whether some of us like it or not but when we consider the possible benefits and argue the case for them accordingly, we must bear in mind one hard indisputable fact—we are unlikely ever to see better dogs and handlers in the future than those of the past. When we consider dogs like Spy O'Vara and Silverstar of Chrishall and men like Joe Greatorex, John Forbes and John Kent, we must remind ourselves that they did not need breaking in gently to Trials via the working test with its lack of shooting pressures to make things easier for them. They graduated via the shooting field and made good; on the other side of the coin we must recognise that whilst some good handlers made their initial debut in working tests, the test has never produced one truly great handler of the calibre of the three I have mentioned.

28 Field trials

I do not pretend to possess an extensive knowledge of the early history of Field Trials and as there is such a dearth of reliable literature on the subject of Trials at any period of time, my information is rather sketchy.

I believe that the first Trials ever held were for pointing dogs and were quite simply conceived. One estate owner in

Scotland informed his neighbour that his own dogs were better than the neighbour's. The latter gentleman disagreed, so they arranged to run their dogs together in competition with an uninvolved party, a local headkeeper, as judge. I have no information on the outcome but this event saw the inauguration of Field Trials and I believe that by 1860, Pointer and Setter Trials were firmly established. The Retrievers took the field later in the century but the Spaniels did not make their debut until after the turn of the century. The reason why Spaniels were last into the competitive field was because for an appreciable period, no two sportsmen could apparently agree on what was the correct function of these ancient dogs.

We have conclusive evidence that in the 10th century, the progenitors of the Cocker and the Welsh Springer were flushing game for the hawks and falcons of the Welsh king, Hywel the Good, and it is also thought that they were employed during this period and later, in flushing game which was then taken in strategically placed nets. The woodcock, owing to its flight and habits, lends itself to being captured in a net placed across a ride or glade and I believe the Cocker Spaniel's name is derived from this early use of the Spaniel and not because the Cocker was developed mainly for woodcock shooting.

It would appear, then, that from the earliest times, the function of a Spaniel was that of a gamefinder and flusher, pure and simple, so any ideas that a Spaniel should retrieve would be regarded as a distinct departure from established tradition by the purists, or even downright heresy. Nevertheless, the revolutionaries persisted with their idea of the retrieving Spaniel and, by about 1905, the first Spaniel Trials were held.

What began as a simple competition was recognised by those far-sighted enough to be an institution which could improve the standard of working gundogs. As Trial dogs were expected to display a high standard of behaviour and polish in addition to natural gamefinding ability, the aim became to produce an animal which was highly tractable and trainable without inhibiting the drive and natural ability of the dog. I believe that over the years Trials have succeeded in their object. Admittedly, some who participate in them have long forgotten the original aim of Trials, tending to regard them as an end in themselves or a means towards increasing the value of a particular animal or its progeny. Yet, for all the kennel blindness, fanaticism, bad sportsmanship and commercialism which is inevitably sometimes encountered, as Trial people simply represent a cross section of the human race, there has always been present over the years, a hard core of dedicated, knowledgeable and realistic sportsmen more likely to regard their swans as geese and able to recognise the strength and virtues of their opponents as well as their weaknesses. These are the people who have made Trials and consistently produced a nucleus of top quality dogs, whose excellence has always been available through their stud services and puppies to the man who shoots and aspires to own the best possible animals to assist him in his shooting.

Trials can never be perfect and obviously never have been and possibly some of the criticisms levelled by those who do not compete in them may be justified but the point must be taken that nobody has come up with a better idea to maintain, let alone improve, the standards of our present day gundogs.

There are two commodities essential to the production of a kennel of Field Trial dogs–knowledge and money. Of these, knowledge is by far the most important as it is possible for a knowledgeable person with restricted finances to produce several good dogs but the project is rendered far easier should financial matters be of secondary consideration. There is then no compulsion to sell one's best dogs. Whole litters can be reared and run on until training age and the entire litter discarded should they not come up to expectations. There is no temptation to breed from a sub-standard bitch in the hope of recouping some of one's expenses.

The period between the wars saw the heyday of the private Field Trial kennel whose object was to produce better and better dogs and which did not have to concern itself with the production of dogs for sale. Names like Banchory, Adderley, Bryngarw, Rivington, Blair, Ware, Avondale, Beechgrove and, most famous of all, O'Vara, became household words. This was the autocratic period in the history of Field Trials when wealthy owners employing private trainers vied with each other. If a certain dog belonging to a gamekeeper was fancied by a kennel owner it was bought and no such thing as the owner refusing to sell was tolerated. There were ways and means of persuading a working man to comply. A gamekeeper running his dog was frowned upon and I am told by some who competed during this period that a Second was the maximum award a gamekeeper could ever hope to win. However, despite certain practices which would be considered outdated and un-democratic by today's standards, these were the formative years of Field Trials and the large private kennels were stabil-ising forces. These last 20 years we have reaped the benefit of their efforts.

Today the situation is the complete reverse of the one obtaining 50 years ago. There are perhaps five or six privately maintained Retriever kennels in the country where a trainer is retained but there is not one such kennel of Spaniels left and it is correct to say that there is not one real strain of Spaniels left. There are, of course, a good many 'lines' of Spaniels, in fact I have had a line of Springers for about 20 years but I do not feel that I can claim to own a strain.

Trials have now become more democratic, with competitors of more modest means entering the ranks and several private kennels in existence at the beginning of the war were never revived at the cessation of hostilities. Professional trainers would occasionally win a major event with their own dogs and more gamekeepers now entered into competition. George Curle won the first post-war Springer Championship with F.T.C. Breckonhill Bee. John Kent won the Cocker Champion-ship in 1950 with F.T.C. Newton of Chrishall. Joe Scott won the event in 1952 with F.T.C. Shawfield Glenfire. In 1957 Jack Windle triumphed at the Cocker Championship held at Grimsthorpe with F.T.C. Jordieland Bunty but it was the season of 1973–74 which saw the ultimate triumph of the professional owner/handler when Frank Clitheroe won the Retriever Championship with Hedenham Park Holcot Fay, Peter Stewart won the Springer event with F.T.C. Crowhill Raffle and Speckle completed the hat trick by winning the Cocker Championship for me. The wheel has turned full circle.

During the golden age of Trials judging was almost exclus-ively in the hands of the wealthy amateurs, just as it is in America even to this day but in this country the post-war years saw the emergence of the professional judge, in the shape of men like Bill Brunt and Andrew Wylie.

At the present day, professionals are most eagerly sought after as judges, indeed a good many amateur handlers state with no hesitation that they would far sooner run under profes-sional handlers than other amateurs. We have some very good amateur judges but there are many others who fall down in their ability to appraise a situation quickly and accurately. I feel confidence in a judge who, the moment a bird staggers at the impact of a shot, says 'That's a runner–get after it'. So many amateurs seem to think all the runners are dead birds and all the dead ones are runners!

It is completely illogical and exceedingly naive to pre-suppose that all judges are the sons of Heaven and therefore incapable of any dishonesty. Judges simply represent a cross section of human nature with all its peculiarities and frailties and the wonder is that they turn out as honest as they usually do! No potential newcomer to Trials should ever allow himself to be dissuaded from entering competition because he feels he will not stand a chance with the judges. If he is unlucky enough to receive less than his dues on one occasion, provided his dog is a good one, the law of averages will put the matter right and if all goes well with his dog in its next Trial, it will most likely win something.

Handlers have occasionally turned to me in frustration when their dog has put up a winning performance and only been awarded a Certificate of Merit, or been put out of the Stake for an imagined misdemeanour and said, 'What do you have to do to win?' My answer is invariably the same. 'Keep on running, and next time you will run a worse Trial than you have run today but you will win'.

Only last season a friend ran a Spaniel in Scotland which was head and shoulders above anything else there, the only bitch of comparable quality having failed on a most awkward short distance retrieve. He was put out for missing a rabbit which flushed on its own before the dog had a chance to even get within scenting distance on the right side of the wind. Normally a man of most equable temperament, on this occa-sion he practically exploded. I delivered my homily and at the next Trial his dog became a Field Trial Champion. His next Trial was the Championship which he won most convincingly, thanks partly to the commonsense of one of the judges. In a very 'gamey' patch in brambles, a bird got up on its own to one side of and slightly behind the handler. My friend mentioned this point to the judge after the event who replied:

'I gave him full credit for it. You were working a following wind and your dog had done the right thing in swinging out in front to work the cover back to you. Birds were creeping about everywhere and this one came back to you from your dog'.

This was a piece of Spaniel judging at its best but many judges would have put him out for missing game.

We have always had lady owners of Field Trial dogs but to what extent they actually handled their own dogs prior to 1939 I cannot be certain. Certainly Miss J. Wykeham-Musgrave handled her famous 'Poddle' Cockers in the 1930's and possibly before and I believe Mrs. Quentin Dick, later known as Lorna, Countess Howe, handled her 'Banchory' Labradors herself. The post-war years however, witnessed a tremendous influx of lady handlers into Trials, particularly in Retriever events and some extremely competent female handlers emerged. In 1952, Jean Train won the Retriever Championship, followed in 1954 by June Atkinson. Later, I believe Mrs. A. Radcliffe placed Second in this event with one of her Yellow Labradors. Sometime in the 1960s Lady Joan Hill-Wood won the Championship (not for the first time by any means). Of more recent years, Mrs. Gabrielle Benson, one of the most consistently winning handlers of all time, won the Championship with a very young dog, Holdgate Willie. Shortly after the war, a veteran handler Mrs. A. Wormald, made up her yellow dog, Dual Champion Knaith Banjo. Countless other lady handlers have done extremely well in Retriever events but for quite a time Spaniel Trials were male dominated. Then the female element began to infiltrate the ranks and some proved extremely competent. Some lady handlers are completely realistic in their assessment of their animals and will come out of the line telling you what an idiot their dog made of itself but there is a female element (as of course a male element) which is completely unrealistic and totally kennel blind. Their temperaments appear to be completely wrong to cope with the vagaries of fortune encountered in Trials. They complain that they can hardly ever obtain a nomination in Trials. Yet Mr. X has been able to run his nasty little dog in several Trials. I later have the opportunity to observe Mr. X's nasty little bitch and personally rate it as very nice. Some come to a professional trainer practically in tears over some problem created by their own incompetence and beg his assistance. Being gentlemen, these professional trainers give them all possible assistance and the woman achieves some success, then before we know where we are she is putting us all to rights and letting us know exactly how Trials should be conducted. Instant experts however, are by no means confined to the female sex.

157

29 **Retriever trials**

Of all the gundog breeds run in Field Trials the Retrievers are, without doubt, numerically the strongest, with Labradors leading the field, Goldens following up and just a few Flatcoats being run.

As my first gundog was a Golden, I do not find the temptation to refer to Retrievers as 'Labradors' as many people do, simply because we see more Labradors about than other Retrievers.

Very occasionally, Retriever Trials are held in August on grouse and very enjoyable these grouse Trials can be. There have been Trials held in September on partridges but owing to the decline of the wild partridge in many parts of the country, these September Trials can be rather hazardous undertakings as the game supply may prove inadequate and the judges may not be able to bring the Trial to a successful conclusion. October and November, therefore, are the most important months in the Retriever calendar and the Championship is normally held during the first week in December.

Retriever Trials probably attract more criticism from the ordinary shooting man than any other form of Trialling and when one considers the manner in which many Retriever Trials are conducted, such criticism is at least understandable even though it may often be unjustified. A great deal of money is spent annually on pheasant production and on all efficient shoots the emphasis is on presenting the birds as well as possible to the guns and this does not entail shooting them from the rear, yet the majority of Retriever Trials are held on walked-up birds in roots. If the purpose of a Trial is to find the best shooting dog on the day, it may seem a little illogical to some that the dogs should be tested on a form of shooting in which the average shooting retriever owner does not normally indulge. It is also argued with some truth that Trial Retrievers seldom have any cover tougher than sugar-beet and stubble to contend with, the inference being that the courage of the competing dogs is not tested and that if Retrievers are bred to work solely in this type of country, they will inevitably become soft as a breed. Again, the logic in this argument is immediately apparent.

I particularly enjoy the story about a very famous Labrador

stud dog who was running in a Trial held in the eastern counties. It was said that there was one bramble bush, a few square yards in area, in a hundred square miles and one pheasant made it his business to fall dead in this thicket. The dog made a brilliant mark, covering the open ground at tremendous speed, took a huge leap right into the middle of the bush and an even mightier leap out again, minus the bird. As his handler put his lead on he philosophically remarked: 'Ah well, he never did care for brambles much, I'll take him home now.'

The average shooting man is unlikely to walk up game with a Retriever at heel except on very odd occasions but he is likely to shoot a good deal of driven game over the dog. At some stands his birds will fall on to stubble, grass or plough and the pertinent question may well be, does he require a dog at all? Pricked birds and runners should have been dealt with by the pickers up behind but his dog will come into its own when he stands with his back to another covert or other rough place. The gun will now need his dog to get out and work brambles and rhododendrons, most of the time unsighted from his master. Fancy precision handling will be of little help. To be effective, his dog will need to go in the direction indicated and work the ground on its own initiative, just as it would if its master has several duck down in a thick reed bed. It is argued that walking up in roots, with the accent on marking and hand-ability will hardly test a Retriever in the type of work I have just described.

Some Retriever Trials are held on ground where all the game is driven but these are in the minority. On other grounds, particularly in Scotland, the Trial may be a mixture of walking up and driving. A bog or moss might be walked up, then a field of roots, then a fir covert driven out over the roots, the birds falling in the cover, and so on. In my own opinion, this is Retriever Trialling at its best.

There are two systems of Retriever judging, the three judge and the four. Under the former system, the three judges work independently, each having a dog and handler on either side of him. The judge has two guns shooting for him, situated on either side of his two dogs. During the first round, dogs are normally tried only on game shot by their 'own' guns, although if a bird falls close to his dogs, a wise judge will offer the bird to a co-judge and, if not required, have it picked by hand. The first retrieve shot by his guns is given to his right hand dog, the lower number. If the dog picks it, the next retrieve is given to the left hand dog. Assuming that two retrieves are being given to each dog, the next retrieve shot will be given to the first dog who will have then completed his round and be taken up. The left hand dog will now be moved to the right of the judge and a fresh dog will take its place on the left of the judge, being the higher number. The next bird shot will then be given to the right hand dog to conclude his round. If a dog has not had a retrieve and his opposite number fails, he will be tried on the retrieve, so his first retrieve is actually a second attempt. The next bird shot will be automatically his, for if it should be given to the opposite dog and the dog fails, this would mean that the other dog would have to take two consecutive second attempts, which is considered unfair.

If both dogs with any one judge should fail on a bird, the judge may offer the retrieve to another judge who may use it at his discretion and if the next two dogs should do no better, a fifth and even a sixth dog may be tried. During the course of events the judges will evaluate the performance of the competing dogs. When walking up, particularly in roots, good marking should receive full credit. It enables a dog to get out and back with the game quickly and a dog going out in a straight line is far less likely to become involved with live game than one which has to hunt for the bird. Good marking can, however, be something of a two edged sword. To an inexperienced judge, a good marker can appear to do his work too easily. He cannot visualise the complicated situation which could arise had the dog failed to mark and started flushing live birds. Of the good marker he might say, 'He had two easy birds and nothing difficult to do', yet another dog which has failed to mark and got into a bit of trouble with live game but been put on the right lines again by a clever handler, will probably be rated higher in his book as he 'was good under temptation and handled very well'.

Another situation which crops up occasionally with a normally brilliant marker is when the dog, on odd occasion, mismarks. The dog, thinking it knows best, can be very difficult to re-direct, although normally a good handling dog on completely blind retrieves. One top class Labrador man has told me that it is better to have a dog which walks tight in to the handler and does not mark but which can be quickly and accurately handled on to the bird. Some good intelligent

*The late Lady Auckland's championship winning Pointer F.T. Ch.
Swift of Cromlix with Mr Angus McLaughlin.*

Mr John Nash's Pointer F.T. Ch. Moanruad Don.

markers tend to develop the habit of walking in a position in relation to the handler which will put them in the best position to mark but this may not coincide with the judge's ideas of what constitutes walking correctly to heel. The best position for the dog to walk in to enable him to command the maximum field of vision is with his tail to his handler's knee but such a dog would run a grave risk of being put out for bad heel keeping.

Each dog, whether it has failed or not must be given a chance under another judge in the second round, provided it has not committed any of the eliminating crimes, which are: Failing to walk to heel, running in, damaging game, whining or giving tongue, chasing, hunting out of control or failing to enter water on command. During the second round, in Open Stakes, the judges can vary proceedings by exchanging birds, giving the dogs some tricky retrieves up and down the line. It is normally harder to handle a dog down the line at an angle than it is to get him out straight in front or directly behind the line. Birds frequently break back when walking up in roots and are killed behind the line. In this situation, the wise handler quickly turns round so his dog turns with him, the better to mark the bird if it is shot. On a bird behind the line, the dog will have fouled ground to contend with and under these circumstances a runner can be particularly tricky.

Throughout the proceedings, the judges keep a wary eye on the steadiness of the dogs under them. It is generally accepted that if a dog attempts to run in but stops instantly on command it will be put out of an Open Stake but not out of a non-winner Stake. Each bird is handled by the judge who will pass it to his next judge if he believes the bird has suffered damage from the jaws of the dog. Some judges are absolute fanatics over the question of hard mouth and never take into consideration any outside factors which may have been responsible for the damage to the bird such as a close shot, a heavy fall or striking a stone wall, a tree or an upright stub.

After each dog has been under a second judge and in some Trials under a third and been allowed another two or three chances of retrieves, depending on the game supply, all three judges compare notes and have a discussion on the individual performances. In Retriever Trials, assessments by individual judges vary tremendously and it is sometimes possible for a dog to make a mistake which would automatically eliminate a

Spaniel, yet still receive a place, if not a win. It is not unknown for a Retriever to fail on a bird and have its eye wiped but later recover its lost ground by a brilliant piece of work. This never happens in a Spaniel Trial. The retrieving aspect of a Spaniel's work is regarded as of far less importance than its hunting, yet if a Spaniel fails on a retrieve, many handlers will withdraw the dog, secure in the knowledge that they can win nothing and some judges will, quite incorrectly as it happens, put a dog out of the Stake for a failure and deny it a second run.

Most Retriever judges are rather lenient over the time factor when a dog is out on a retrieve and seldom is a dog seriously down graded for taking a long time to collect a bird, provided he finally picks it. I once earned some adverse comment when judging a Retriever event. A dog had made a bad mistake on a straightforward bird in roots and was not doing itself a great deal of good in my book, when an obvious runner was shot. Again the dog made a very poor effort and did not settle to the job at all; when it became perfectly obvious that the dog stood no chance of picking the bird, I called it up, in accordance with Kennel Club rules and tried a second dog which took a short line and quickly found the bird. Apparently I was castigated behind my back for not giving the first dog longer on the bird. Being an experienced handler myself, I was able to see in a very short space of time that the dog was having an 'off' day and was just not 'with it'.

Some judges will call a dog in after it has been down on a bird for several minutes but if the dog finds the bird on the way in, will credit it with the retrieve, yet other judges will still count such a performance as a failure as, according to their edicts, the dog's time was up directly they instructed the handler to call it in. Personally I think the latter procedure makes sense.

Occasionally, a bad scenting day is experienced and not one runner is collected in the entire Stake. This is usually due to extreme lack of moisture in the ground during a dry spell in October, or conditions of hard frost later in the season. It will sometimes happen under such circumstances that Retriever judges will completely ignore failures on runners and judge the dogs on the work they do on dead game. I can see the logic of a dog winning a Stake after failing first dog on a runner under terrible scenting conditions, yet fail on such a runner in a Spaniel Trial, and you will usually be out of the Stake without even a certificate.

After the three judges have finally sorted out the failures, the eye-wipes and the other positive work, they will normally find they have some 'A' dogs in their top flight and two or three 'B' dogs, which at that moment are not standing to win much more than Certificates of Merit, but which they keep in reserve in case any of their 'A' dogs come unstuck during the run off.

When lining up for the run off, judges tend to place themselves closer together in the centre of the line, so all three are in an equal position to witness each individual piece of work. Again, the competing dogs are placed in the line with the lowest number on the right and the highest on the left and whereas it appears to be the basic procedure to send the dog with the lowest number for the first retrieve and work up to the highest number as the game is shot, judges are under no obligation to conduct the run off in this manner and can send any dog in any order, to collect game shot by any gun, in any part of the field. It is during the course of the run off that some of the best and most interesting work of the Trial may be seen. With the dogs being situated near the centre of the line, birds may be shot by the more distant guns which provide longer and often more testing retrieves than those shot directly over the dogs during the body of the Stake. Owing to congestion of handlers, judges and dogs towards the centre of the line, it is often impossible for even a good marking dog to mark because his vision is obscured. Here the good handling dog comes into his own and some long blind retrieves may be pulled off. However, interesting and spectacular as such work may be, would it be of any practical value in the ordinary shooting field? Occasionally it happens that a 'B' dog is brought into the run off and by a lucky combination of circumstances plus good work on its part, builds itself up, defeating the 'A' dogs and winning the Stake.

There is also the four judge system of judging in Retriever Field Trials and opinions are somewhat divided as to which is the better method. It can certainly be claimed that the four judge system saves time and game as should a dog put up an inadequate performance without committing an eliminating fault, under the first pair of judges, it can be discarded forthwith as the Kennel Club rule has been fulfilled,

163

namely, that each dog must be seen by at least two judges.

One of the most potent arguments put forward in favour of this system is the one which claims it is the best possible system under which novice judges can be initiated as it is, of course, possible to team up an experienced judge and a novice together, in order that the latter may benefit from the wisdom and experience of the former. This is an irrefutable argument but could it not mean that under a double set of such circumstances in any one Trial, the net result could be that the Trial would be judged under a two judge system? Even should all four judges be more or less equally experienced people, it is felt by some that of each pair of judges, one is bound to be the more dominant, so the system is still virtually a two judge one. Despite the arguments for and against, the four judge system is definitely here to stay and seems to be the one favoured in all the major events, such as the Kennel Club Open Stake, the International Gundog League Open Stake and the Retriever Championship. Certainly this system should help to eliminate human error, as should one judge happen to miss a point of some importance the other should spot it.

Regarding Field Trial dogs in general, the words 'pace and style' continually keep cropping up. Certainly, without pace a bird dog would be of little use as he just would not cover sufficient territory in a given time and even though it is conceded that an English Setter is faster than an English Pointer, the latter can really cover the ground with his peculiar, distinctive canter. Style, for those who can appreciate it, is an added refinement as it continually draws the eye and stimulates interest, giving the gun something to follow when game is scarce.

So it is with the Retriever. Most of his time is spent walking at heel or sitting at a drive but a fast, stylish dog is far more pleasurable to work with, although what a Retriever does, rather than the way he does it, will be taken more into account when he is running in Trials. It is possible for a moderately paced and not very stylish Retriever to win Trials, whereas his counterpart in Spaniel Trials would not rise above a Reserve or Certificate of Merit. So much can be done to educate and experience a Retriever. He can be forged into an efficient and polished performer even though, in himself, he might be quite a moderate dog. As one lady of my acquaintance, remarking on the supposed decline of the Field Trial Labrador, remarked:

'Labradors these past few years have had rather too many good trainers'. The inference was that too many mediocre dogs had come to the top by good training and had accordingly been used at stud, passing on rather limited qualities in several cases.

I am not heavily involved with Labradors myself. I do not breed them or run them in Trials nowadays and only train those which are required as shooting dogs. Basically, those which come to me are well away from the mainstream of Field Trial breeding, so I do not feel qualified to comment on the present day quality of the breed and I do not pay too much attention to hearsay evidence but, according to some informed associates, all is not well with the breed either from the angle of the hip and eye trouble currently affecting many specimens of the breed, or from the alleged decline in working ability.

In spite of any alleged trouble the breed may be in, and hereditary physical defects extend to Golden Retrievers too, one cannot deny the current popularity of Retriever Trials and organising societies are consistently receiving three and four times the number of applications which they are able to accommodate.

30 Spaniel trials

In my earlier days as a gundog trainer, I found myself faced with the choice of trying to run Retrievers and Spaniels simultaneously, to the possible detriment of both, or concentrating entirely on one breed. I ultimately decided on the latter course for a variety of reasons. The main one was that I had to decide with which breed I really preferred to work and, without any hesitation, I chose the Spaniel. Geographical location certainly entered into my choice. Wales is Spaniel country, with its preponderance of rough cover and relative game scarcity, except on the large reared bird shoots. Here it is possible to shoot over a Spaniel and give him sufficient education to take him to the top in Trials, but to build up a Retriever to top Trial standard in Wales is a good deal more difficult. There is plenty of picking up to be had locally, both on the grouse moors and at the many shoots, so a Retriever need never go short of game but, as I have already mentioned, the majority of Retriever Trials are held walking up in roots.

In Wales we do not have many roots and virtually no sugar-beet. We do have rape but the only walking up is practised by those very few Retriever enthusiasts who are fortunate enough to have shoots of their own and are able to have a couple of hundred or so pheasants shot over their dogs in the rape fields in addition to extensive picking up at stands. Experience in roots is so essential to a Trial Retriever as its performance and technique in roots differs from other conditions, particularly when being directed on blind retrieves. It must learn to go out in an almost straight line, either across the root drills, unwind, downwind or crosswind, or down the drills, stopping on command and casting right or left across the drills, with head held at the correct height to wind its game. But most important of all it must stop instantly to the whistle at all times and for some reason there is a tendency for a Retriever to come 'off the whistle' in roots, far more so than in any other type of country. This is why practice in roots is so important as the handler can get after the dog in a rootfield if it disregards the whistle and persuade it that the whistle is there to be obeyed, even in a crackling sea of beet tops.

Not having access to extensive rootfields put me at a disadvantage in Retriever Trials and I believe in running to win. The element of chance is ever present in Trials without increasing the odds against success through running a dog which is not quite proficient in a department. With the Spaniel, this problem was not of the same magnitude. Some Spaniel Trials are held in roots but the majority are not, so one is able to be selective over where one runs. I can always find one or two turnip fields where I can at least teach a Spaniel to hunt in roots, even though he may be extremely lucky ever to find a bird in them as, for some reason, pheasants are hardly ever found in the rootfields on my small hill shoot, any more than the grouse ever come on to the stubbles from the adjacent moor. I find this rather odd, as on almost identical terrain in Scotland, I could guarantee that pheasants would be found in the roots and grouse would certainly use the stubbles and rough fields. Nevertheless, I manage.

I shoot quite a few pheasants in the dingles and on the steep mountainsides. The occasional woodcock makes a mistake, and I shoot a few hares, sufficient to familiarise my young dogs with the weight and scent of these creatures. I do not find it easy to give experience to a young Spaniel, but with a lot of hard work and the right type of animal to suit my local conditions, it can be done.

I have run in a great many Spaniel Trials over the past two decades, so can claim to be conversant with this branch of sport to a greater extent than with any other competitive activity.

Whatever the critics may have to say about Retriever Trials and how far divorced they are from ordinary Retriever work, it can be claimed that Spaniel Trials follow more closely the procedure employed in rough shooting over Spaniels.

Two judges are employed, sometimes with the addition of a referee, who is expected to be seen and not heard until his opinion is asked. In this eventuality he has the casting vote in a case when the two judges find themselves at variance over any matter.

I have found that in Scotland and Ulster a referee is always present. In England and Wales this is not always the case, though why this should be so I have no idea.

The right hand judge takes the lower number and sticks to the odd numbers until he has seen all the odd numbered dogs. The left hand judge does likewise with the even numbers. Two guns normally work with both judges, one on either side of handler, dog and judge. The dogs are cast off and the line moves forward. Theoretically the dog should cover all the ground between the two guns but this procedure is subject to variations depending on terrain. In very open country guns sometimes tend to straggle, particularly those unused to shooting over Spaniels, so a Spaniel would have to range like a Pointer to make all ground good. On other terrain, the guns may be bunched together, so a Spaniel covering a normal beat may extend beyond his two guns. It is up to the wise judge to employ a certain flexibility in his judgment and take into account all such prevailing factors.

In open country such as rushes, heather, roots or rough grass the handler should pursue a straight course between the guns and the dog should do the work; this applies also in woodland where the bracken and brambles lie in a fairly even carpet about 18 inches high. In broken country, where the dog is often unsighted from the handler, both handler and judge should move with the dog between the guns to keep it in view. Hunting clumps of gorse, rhododendrons and large high bramble bushes calls for an entirely different hunting technique to that employed when quartering more even ground. In bush country, it is permissible for the handler to assist his dog to 'do its ground', moving from bush to bush and trying all likely game holding places. This is, after all, what a handler would do if he was shooting over his own dog yet some judges will penalise an experienced handler who tries his best to produce game in such a manner.

When a dog finds game it should flush it without any attempt at catching it and either sit or stand immediately the game is moved. It certainly looks better if the dog drops automatically to flush but some perfectly good and reliable dogs, by nature, stand. Sitting is completely foreign to their nature. Some handlers automatically blow the stop whistle when game flushes, simply as a reflex action from training days. This should not be penalised unless the judge can see for himself that the dog would have moved after the game had the whistle not been blown. A good judge who has handled many dogs himself can 'read' the intentions of a dog and judge it partially by its attitude and approach to the business in hand.

Game occasionally does not flush freely for a variety of reasons. A pheasant may push itself headfirst into a clump of bracken or brambles from which there is no exit. A rabbit may wedge itself between the exposed roots of a rhododendron or, being hard pressed by a Spaniel inside a gorse bush, may make a false turn and come up against a solid wall of prickles. Both birds and rabbits are reluctant to move when soaked with rain and rabbits are apt to behave rather stupidly when they have been 'stunk out' of their burrows. Hand-reared pheasants are apt to behave at times in a manner which is not conducive to good Spaniel work. Some stroll ahead of the line, avoiding clumps of thick cover and causing the competing dogs to attempt to hunt the lines instead of quartering the ground and hunting out the cover. On the other hand, some may tuck in tightly and refuse to move, allowing themselves to be caught.

In this country, the deliberate catching of unshot game constitutes an eliminating offence. This is reasonable enough. A Spaniel's main function is to get the game on the move, thus providing a shot. If the game is caught, it cannot be shot and Spaniels can become extremely clever poachers unless firmly checked, so the anti-pegging rule is a valid one but must be interpreted intelligently in order that Spaniel Trials should make sense. It must be borne in mind that such Trials often take place under circumstances far removed from the usual conditions under which rough shooting over Spaniels is conducted.

The main purpose of the Spaniel is to hunt up game where it is relatively thin on the ground and where the birds are either wild or are reared birds which have left the main coverts and taken up residence on outlying ground, where they quickly become as wild and cunning as true wild birds. One does not normally take a Spaniel into a covert full of reared birds, as one naturally keeps the main coverts for a different sport. Yet these are the conditions under which a Spaniel must often work at Trials. There are some excellent grounds, notably in Scotland and Ulster, where it is possible to run an entire Trial in natural rough shooting country. A hare, a rabbit and a pheasant come to hand, then a grouse and sometimes a snipe. This pattern is repeated during the course of the Trial. There are no large flushes of birds and game is seldom caught under these conditions. Names like Glenwherry, Clandeboye, Abington, Corsewall and Crathes immediately spring to mind. In other parts of the country large natural tracts of Spaniel ground are absent and generous hosts often place their coverts at the disposal of Spaniel Societies, where the population of reared pheasants can cause the type of hazard I have mentioned.

If a Spaniel strikes hard and viciously at game and can be seen to make a determined attempt to get the bird or rabbit into its mouth, this is not to be tolerated. If the game is brought to hand the dog must be discarded. If it can be made to release the game, it must still be downgraded. If, on the other hand, a dog enters a thick piece of cover and can be seen rummaging for a few seconds at a particular spot, then backs out with game in its mouth, it can be assumed that the dog has attempted to push the game out but it has refused to move. If the dog releases the game on command and it is able to fly or run without impediment, the dog should not be penalised. If the dog refuses to release the game on command, the judge should carefully examine it for possible injury by dog or shot. If it is injured by the former, the dog should be put out of the Stake and the judge does not need to go into the academics of whether the game was shot or unshot. If the game is sound the judge must look for shot damage. In the case of a bird, the judge should look inside the beak for blood from a lung or breathing tube. He should examine the legs and feet and open both wings. If one wing or tail feather is broken by shot, giving a splintered effect with the white core visible, the bird should be assumed to be shot and the dog must be excused. If the dog brings in a rabbit or hare, ears and toes should be examined for shot. The entire skin should be examined with fingertips for pellets embedded under the skin. If no shot can be detected, the palm of the hand should be rubbed hard over the fur and examined for blood. In the case of a hare, injury should be fairly easy to detect as these animals bleed more freely from small shot punctures than do rabbits. It should be the object of the judge to try to prove the dog innocent and not continually to be looking for an excuse to eliminate dogs. This is negative judging and should be vigorously discouraged by organising societies who should be extremely careful not to invite those judges whose object appears to be to eliminate as many dogs as possible.

The Spaniel should at all times keep up a brisk movement between the guns. A really fast dog is always desirable provided the rest of its work is sound, but it is most essential that speed should be coupled with game-finding ability. A fast dog is pleasing to watch and exciting to handle but drive is more important than pure speed and a dog moving at a steady canter which really tears the cover apart is far more desirable than a real racer which flashes about and skirts the rough cover. It has been said that a fast dog nearly always has a good nose and is fast because it can trust its nose but I cannot entirely agree with this. This is a generalisation and generalisations can be dangerously inaccurate when applied to any living creature. I find that noses vary in effectiveness from one individual to another, irrespective of the pace of the dogs concerned and, in any case, a worthwhile animal will regulate its pace in accordance with prevailing scenting conditions.

If a Spaniel covers its ground at a steady trot it is said to be 'just not going' or 'pottering' and should not be tolerated. It is also undesirable that a Spaniel should periodically stop and sniff a specific piece of cover at great length. This is timewasting and accomplishes nothing and often signifies that the dog is mouse hunting. Another annoying animal is the persistent false pointer. I have never been troubled with one myself but I have observed this trait in some Spaniels when judging or competing. As I shoot in country where game is fairly thin on the ground, I expect a Spaniel to produce something when it indicates game. If a dog were to false point then quickly make several finds, the false point might be hardly noticeable but if a false point is made at the end of a long hunt and no game is forthcoming, this is likely to have a demoralising effect upon the gun, who could be excused if he missed the next chance.

A Spaniel's basic function is to locate and flush game for the gun to shoot, so if it passes game and fails to acknowledge it, the dog may be justifiably accused of failing in its duty; it is small wonder that according to Field Trial rules, the passing of game is a major fault. I believe that passing game is regarded more seriously nowadays than was the case in the pre-myxo era. A dog would probably have several finds in one run, so the passing of one rabbit might not be regarded too seriously by some judges. H. Carlton in his classic *Spaniels, their breaking for sport and Field Trials* states quite plainly that he would sooner have a Spaniel that went with style and dash and just occasionally missed the odd thing, than work with one which went about its work in a slow and uninteresting manner and never missed a thing. Carlton contended that the good going dog would ultimately find more game as its pace would allow it to cover more terrain in a given time. It is not hard to see the logic in his argument.

Sometimes when game is missed, there may be extenuating circumstances. A dog may find a rabbit which is missed by the gun. The handler gives the command 'gone away' and hunts the dog away from the line. After breaking off the rabbit, the dog may take a second or two before it settles down to hunt again and a rabbit sitting close to the original one may easily be missed. Similarly the dog might make a retrieve and, as it comes in with the game, the handler might unconsciously take a step or two forward to meet the dog, so if he is ordered to hunt the dog on, could miss a small piece of ground which might just hold a bird or rabbit.

One of the hardest pieces of ground for a Spaniel to find game on, particularly rabbits and hares, is an area of sparse white grass or short stubble. Apart from the fact that game scent appears to be very localised on bare ground, as opposed to thicker cover, many dogs appear to experience difficulty in holding themselves in sufficiently to take a small enough bite of the ground, even when working into the wind, to bring themselves within scenting distance of every tuft and tussock. If the dog makes anything bigger than the tightest turn at the extremity of its beat, its next cast will automatically be further reaching than it should be, leaving too great a gap between casts for its hunting to be completely effective.

Under these conditions, it is comparatively simple for a judge to prove beyond doubt when a dog has missed game. He can see exactly where the dog has been in relation to any game that may get up and, in the case of ground game, the vacated 'seat' is there to show exactly where the game has flushed from. When a judge discredits a Spaniel for missing game, he should immediately draw the handler's attention to the situation on the spot. Too many judges keep completely silent about any such event until after the Trial. The handler may imagine he has had two first class runs and when he receives nothing at the end of the day feel justifiably puzzled and disappointed. If he asks the judges where he went wrong and one replies: 'Well you had an A plus run under me but my co-judge says you passed a rabbit under him', he might well feel that he should have been told at the time, rather than be allowed to continue thinking he had done really well.

Where the cover has folded over to form a canopy, as happens with bracken, or in the area of brambles, assessments over passed game can be extremely difficult. Game, and pheasants in particular, can creep all over the place under these conditions, so a bird getting up some distance behind a dog need not necessarily have been missed. A dog under these conditions should always be given the benefit of the doubt, yet many judges will penalise a dog if a bird gets up anywhere behind the line at all.

When game is found, it is desirable that the dog should drop on its own and the handler remain silent, although a pip on the stop whistle should not be penalised provided the judge can see for himself that the whistle is merely used as a reminder and not to restrain a potentially unsteady dog. When ordered to retrieve he should operate exactly as though he were out shooting with his handler, taking the line of ground game, or accurately marking the fall of birds. One essential difference between a bird shot by his handler and some birds shot by guns at a Trial, is that the position of a Trial gun in relation to the flight of the bird frequently causes the fall of the bird to be considerably longer than would be the case if his handler was shooting and birds may often fall at unfamiliar angles, so he must take these varying situations in his stride. Occasionally a bird may be shot by an outside gun which has actually flushed on its own well off his beat and which he has probably been unable to mark. Under these circumstances, the judge must be sure to give the Spaniel what constitutes a logical retrieve. A Spaniel should be assessed mainly as a hunter and gamefinder and his retrieving should merely complement his ground work, so it should never be the object of the judge to try to prove how good the dog is on blind retrieves. The dog should be taken to within reasonable distance of the bird before being cast out but 'reasonable distance' can vary according to circumstances.

If there is a good deal of thickish, potentially game holding cover between the dog and its retrieve, which a Spaniel would normally want to hunt and where the disposition of the cover might make it extremely difficult for the dog to see the handler and vice versa, I would say 30 yards would be far enough to send the dog. Where visibility is better, such as in rushes or roots, a dog should be capable of getting out 40 yards, and on bare ground, with no cover to 'pull' the dog, such as pasture or Winter wheat fields, I would expect a Spaniel to get out 60 or 70 yards if the situation arose.

In discussing the subject of Trials, I make no distinctions between Springer and Cocker Stakes, except for the proviso that when judging the latter breed, a person should take into account the lower eye level of the Cocker when assessing marking and handling ability. All other things being equal, a Cocker should be capable of doing a real Spaniel's job and, despite the fun I poke at the breed, I have respect for their ability. They particularly commend themselves to me because they make me laugh. We Scandinavians are a sombre people and in bygone ages required large quantities of Danegeld, ale and plunder to make us merry, so a dog that amuses me has an added attraction.

If a Spaniel fails on a retrieve, its bracemate should be tried and, if successful, should receive a little extra credit, so that if its hunting in the final analysis was rated equal to that of another good hunting dog, the eye-wipe to its credit should tip the balance in its favour; such an event should never, never advance an indifferent hunter in the estimation of the judges. It is not customary to try a third dog on a retrieve should the first brace fail. The judges should then make a search for the bird themselves and, if unsuccessful, should ask an official picker up to look for the bird when the line has moved on. If the bird is picked up dead or tucked in close to the fall area, both dogs must be eliminated. If the bird is never found, the first dog must suffer some penalty but nothing should be held against the second dog. If the bird appears to have run and the first dog makes a determined effort on the line but reappears without the bird and the second dog is unsuccessful, the first dog tried should receive a certain amount of credit for the attempt and not be automatically eliminated. Its overall performance should be assessed and, whereas I would go so far as to say it should not win, with a first dog failure against it, I agree with official policy which states that such a dog could still win a place.

I once saw a Spaniel win a major event after failing first dog on a runner in the run off though this animal never got as far as the fall, so the academics of whether or not it took a good line never arose. This event left a nasty taste in many mouths.

In the event of two dogs failing on a legged rabbit, I think the judges should adopt a slightly different attitude and allow the first dog to continue without prejudice as legged rabbits very frequently manage to get down holes, provided of course that the first dog has been seen to take a good line out of sight. When a really strong runner comes down and is seen to take off into the distance, it is very seldom that a second dog ever collects such a bird. The delay caused by the attempt of the first dog plus the disturbance of the scent usually results in an unworkable line for the next dog to try on.

I have collected runners second dog down by pushing my dog out in the supposed direction of the bird and have occasionally been lucky enough to have my dog wind the runner where it has tucked into a piece of cover. Only once has my dog taken a cold line on a runner right into the distance and returned triumphant. This was during the course of the 1973–74 Cocker Championship. I was running a very young Field Trial Champion, Diasan Meg who, despite having won four Open Stakes that season, was still, by my book, relatively inexperienced. She had never collected a runner and only one legged rabbit, so when I was asked to try for a runner second dog, I rated our chances of collection as nil. Meg hit the fall, put her nose down and disappeared up the wood at speed and was gone quite some time, then our host called 'She's got it' and back she came with a very lively hen. Such is the unpredictability of the Cocker.

Occasionally when a dog is out on a retrieve, another bird flushes. In Open Stakes it is generally accepted that game should be shot under these circumstances but I think it is a pity that any gun should shoot a bird directly over a dog out on a retrieve as I feel this jeopardises a dog's chances to an unreasonable degree. This has happened to me on several occasions and, more often than not, I have survived but I still do not think the practice should receive encouragement.

It is accepted custom not to shoot at all when a dog is on a retrieve in a Novice Stake but occasionally guns forget, or plead that nobody has informed them that the event is a Novice Stake. Whatever happens, the position is a delicate one as one must bear in mind that guns are normally the guests of the host. I have seen a handler openly abuse a gun during a Championship and get away with it and I know of a case where a handler made a silent protest to a gun and was banned from the particular club's Trials for three years.

When both judges have seen every dog in the Stake, with the exception of those which have been guilty of eliminating faults under their first judge, notes are compared and usually the first question asked is 'Which is your best dog?' If both judges come up with the same answer the matter is easy. They have found the overall winner without further trial. More often than not, what is the best dog under one judge, may be the second or third best under the other so the situation often arises that two dogs are under consideration for first prize, each being the best dog under one judge and rated 'Clean' under the other. The judges may well also have a pair of dogs of lesser quality, each judge rating one higher than the other, so in such a hypothetical case the judges are left with two pairs of top dogs which they must separate. Opinions are divided on how the run off should be conducted. My own view is that provided the supply of game has been sufficiently adequate during the body of the Stake to test all four dogs in steadiness and retrieving, no game should be shot in the run off as this can cloud the issue. It is easy enough to shoot something at this stage for the best hunting dog in the Stake which neither he, nor any other dog could collect, so we could easily find the best dog in the Stake is shot out of the Trial and the also-rans are not subjected to the same hazard.

When a Stake is reduced to four top dogs I believe it is unwise, unfair and positively dangerous to shoot over these dogs. One may be ultimately faced with the choice of bringing potential Certificate of Merit dogs into the awards or withholding some prizes altogether, neither course being fully acceptable.

In a Stake of very high standard, the judges may have six or eight really outstanding dogs to separate, all standing more or less equal. In such a case, I think shooting is not merely desirable but essential and I believe the run off should be regarded more as a third run. If a good dog fails or puts up a poor performance on a retrieve, he can be down-graded and an equally good dog can take his place but in the final stages of such a run off I still believe a halt should be called to shooting and the four top dogs remaining be separated on hunting ability.

There are several points to look for when two dogs are hunting close together. One dog may have a smooth, natural pattern while its bracemate may require a good deal more assistance by whistle and signal to make its ground good. Both dogs may hit a hareline and one will, with a minimal amount of persuasion, carry on quartering across the line whilst the other pulls ahead. One dog may thrash every bit of cover in its path, the other, running jealous, may extend its beat and skirt the cover which the other dog is penetrating. Under these circumstances the latter dog may often score a find ahead of the other but should not receive undue credit for so doing. A dog should work tidily at all times and a find at the extremity of its beat is not what is wanted. Then there is sheer pace and style. A dog that has a fast, even sweep, coupled with a beautiful tail and body movement, should, all other things being equal, always take precedence over a more moderately paced, plainer actioned dog. When out shooting on fairly barren ground, it is the fast, eager, stylish dog which inspires the gun to keep on going and remain alert for the chance which may next present itself. Perhaps one must be a purist to appreciate true Spaniel style, in which case I believe it is the purist who receives the maximum enjoyment from shooting over his Spaniel.

*Mr John T. Pirie Jnr. of Illinois, U.S.A. with his double National
Championship winner (1964 and 1965) Gwibernant Ganol.*

The late Mr Frank Thomas's championship winner, F.T. Ch. Mark-down Muffin. More handsome than any show springer and a pillar of his breed.

F.T. Ch. Dinas Dewi Sele. Winner of 10 trials.

The author with F.T. Ch. Gwibernant Abereithy Skip.

31 Good mouths and bad

It is generally accepted that a retrieving gundog should possess a tender mouth, in order that the game it retrieves will be delivered intact. There are degrees of damage which shot game can suffer. Some dogs deliberately mangle their game, breaking the bones and digging deep into the flesh, rendering the bird virtually unusable. Some dogs give a bird a sharp nip across the ribs, leaving it fit to eat but impairing the hanging and keeping qualities as the bird will commence to putrefy at the site of the bruising caused by the dog's jaws. Some birds suffer skin damage in the course of being extracted from heavy cover and others similarly affected are strong runners trying hard to evade capture.

I find it interesting to consider how we are able to breed an animal which has a mouthful of sharp teeth, primarily designed for killing, to retrieve tenderly at all. I believe this ability, which every carnivore, large or small must possess, stems from their faculty for carrying their own young without damage, either when danger threatens, or as a matter of convenience when moving from a fouled earth to a clean one. This ability to carry a creature smaller than itself is inherent in the make up of every dog, gundog or otherwise, and I believe that over the decades, we have exploited this instinct and encouraged it by selective breeding, so we now have our main gundog breeds possessing good mouths with the exception of a few individuals who are either confirmed biters or, more commonly, bite the occasional retrieve. It seems to be accepted without question by all gundog authorities that hard mouth, or occasional hard mouth, is hereditary and my own experience bears this out. This is where Field Trials have done a tremendous service. As hard mouth is not tolerated in Trials, it has encouraged all but a lunatic fringe of competitors to discard any animal showing an unreliable mouth during training or early shooting days; many such animals, quite properly, have thus never been entered in competition. It must be admitted that several dogs have run in Trials which have been in the habit of damaging the odd bird. Some have done well, even becoming Field Trial Champions but inevitably they have been put out for mouth sooner or later, some several times. The word gets around and informed breeders leave such dogs severely alone. A dog may only be guilty of nipping the ribs of a bird but if it is bred from, particularly if it is mated to a bitch with the same fault, there is a very good chance that the next generation will be even worse and become manglers.

There are some people who are not as careful over the question of mouth as they might be. Some take the defeatist attitude that 'they all do it sometimes' and will breed from an animal whose mouth is less than perfect. They leave a trail over the years of dogs discarded for mouth from time to time and so pay the penalty for their lack of foresight. My own attitude is that if a dog deliberately bites one head of game before it is six years of age it should never be bred from. There are, happily, several other like-minded people in the country who follow an identical policy and they are the people who can quite truthfully tell you that their fourth season dog has never bitten a bird in its life.

It is most important, however, for both handlers with dogs in preparation for Trials and judges in Trials, to be able to differentiate between deliberate and incidental damage. In my book, a hard mouthed dog is one which comes up to a dead bird or rabbit on a grass-field, a stubble or a rootfield and gives it a deliberate bite, or which, if it has a runner to contend with, kills it stone dead. Game does, however, very frequently fall into heavy cover from which it can only be extracted with the greatest difficulty and a bird may often be very badly torn during the process of extraction by a soft mouthed dog. Skin damage should be ignored and a lively runner in the open is also capable of tearing itself against the dog's teeth. Occasionally a strong runner will be pulled out of heavy brambles and one side of the ribs will sometimes be pushed in but the indentation will have no sharp edges and the bird will be alive: A sharp bite across the ribs kills a bird outright but a gradual push in does not. The important thing is the *intent* of the dog towards the bird.

The danger of having ancestors with dubious (or really bad) mouths in the pedigree of a gundog is that the trouble keeps on cropping up and when this does happen it is far more likely to occur in an animal of exceptional promise than a mediocre specimen; it appears that fire and drive are highly likely to be coupled with hard mouth when this is present in the background. Unfortunately, the trouble is likely to remain dormant until the dog is well advanced and has had a lot of time and possibly game wasted on it. Without any doubt, hard mouth is the worst fault of all as, even when it is improved through selective breeding, it still lurks in the background.

There is no permanent cure for hard mouth, despite what any bright young men may claim. It is said that top American Spaniel trainers can 'control' hard mouth most of the time, by means of which I have no knowledge and I know an Irish trainer who claims he can cure it for one day, long enough for a show dog to gain its Field Trial qualifying certificate and so become a full bench champion, but the fact remains that even if it could be cured, the fundamental cause would still be present, to the future detriment of the breed.

32 Gundogs abroad

British gundogs have been exported in the past to many parts of the world, mainly because of the high reputation they enjoy as competent workers and also on account of this country's strict quarantine regulations, which means that a country which is free from rabies can safely allow a British bred dog in without imposing a period of quarantine. In many countries rabies is endemic but at least they can be sure they are not bringing in a fresh source of infection when they allow a British dog to enter.

Many years ago, considerable numbers of English Pointers and Setters went to the U.S.A. and a number of Irish Setters too. The result is that the Americans have bred some very fine bird dogs from British stock and, numerically, bird dogs are stronger in the U.S.A. than any other gundogs. They are used mainly on quail but some are used on pheasants too and most bird dogs used by shooting men will also retrieve. Bird dogs also have a very strong Field Trial following and the Pointer and Setter Championship is indeed a mammoth event. The dogs run so hard and wide that judges, handlers and gallery follow on horseback. Deer are assessed as a natural hazard and provided a dog does not give tongue while in pursuit of deer and is back within a certain time limit, he is not penalised for taking off after deer. The competing dogs in the National Championship have to run three hour heats and the entire Trial takes about three weeks to run. It is almost invariably won by an English Pointer but history was made four years ago when the event was won by a 56 pound English Setter.

The Labrador, too, has made its mark in America, mostly from imported stock. They do not have driven game shooting except where some wealthy individual decides to model a shooting preserve on British lines, so the Labrador is used mainly as a duck shooter's dog.

Trials for Retrievers are very artificial compared to ours, with the accent being on very long water retrieves; in fact from what I can gather, American Retriever Trials resemble very elaborate working tests with live boxed up game being shot instead of dummies thrown. Some British Labradors have gone out and done well in American Trials but they must be retrained for local conditions and I believe the majority of Trial winners are American bred and trained.

The Springer Spaniel has a certain following in the States, more as a Trial dog than as a rough shooter's dog and although there are more Field Trial Spaniels in America than there are in this country, the breed is numerically weak compared to the vast numbers of bird dogs in the U.S.A. Nevertheless, there are close links between the Spaniel fraternity in America and Spaniel people over here and we are better informed in this country on what is going on in the American Spaniel world than we are in their other gundog spheres. This is mainly because so many British imports have done exceptionally well in American Trials, particularly in their National Championship, winning this event a total of 14 times out of the 26 years it has been held. The most notable winning run is held by the late Bill Sheldon whose two exports, Micklewood Scud and Ludlovian Bruce won the event four consecutive years between them, from 1953–56. My own Gwibernant Ganol is the only imported female to win the National two years in succession, 1964–65.

American Trials differ from ours both in the way they are conducted and in what is required of the dogs. For a start, to ensure an even supply of game, pheasants are placed or 'planted' at regular intervals ahead of the dogs. As the success of the Trial is not dependent upon wild game, the most convenient cover can be utilised. Flat, open fields are generally used and cover can vary from rice stubble to tall grass. Dogs are normally worked into the wind and occasionally on a side wind but, as far as I am aware, they do not use downwind beats. The beats are marked out by stakes driven into the ground and whereas American Spaniels are expected to range considerably wider than would be expected in Britain, they must not cross the stake line on pain of disqualification unless ordered by the judge to 'Take a runner'. A runner, as we understand it, is termed a cripple and to the Americans a runner is a planted bird which has left its 'nest' and taken to its heels. At the start of a run, the judge will instruct the handler to 'Take runners going straight up the course' or alternatively to 'Take all runners'. In the latter case, the dog is of course allowed over the stake line. The handler, judge and one gun follow the Spaniel while the rest of the line remains stationary.

Field Trial rules state that a Spaniel must not cause his handler to run after him as this would show the dog to be hard to control but I understand some American handlers can walk awfully fast after a lining Spaniel. In Britain, under similar circumstances, a dog would be expected to quarter over the line, still searching for squatting game and the running bird may only be flushed by chance if the dog should come up with it, or it may be flushed by a subsequent dog but in America the 'Taking of a runner' is a serious commitment and, once committed, a dog must ultimately produce the bird or be disqualified. The dog must stick to the line and when getting towards extreme range, must stop to the whistle to allow the human participants to catch up. For the handler to be capable of stopping a dog with a noseful of bird is regarded as the hallmark of good training by American standards, whereas we tend to take this for granted in this country.

If the 'runner' enters a briar patch, the dog is expected to enter and either flush or catch the bird. These are the only circumstances under which American Spaniels are expected to face briars. Birds cannot be planted in thick briars. They would just push further in and refuse to flush, as they would in bracken, so the cover Spaniels are regularly worked in over here is avoided in America as being impracticable. The successful following, flushing and ultimately retrieving of a runner is regarded as a top performance in America, provided it was preceded by a good fast hunt until the bird was first indicated.

In American Trials, the accent is on speed and keenness and more whistle is tolerated than is the case in Britain. If a dog turns instantly to the handler's whistle at the extremity of its beat every time this extremity is reached, this is satisfactory, but in this country we would downgrade the dog for 'pulling' as we expect a dog to make a good number of turns entirely on his own. The Americans deliberately train for speed. They train in open cover with no tangled masses of cover to impede the dog and as it becomes conditioned to working a wide course, this factor in itself increases the speed of the dog as it gives it room to build its speed up.

Planted game encourages a Spaniel to work with its head up and a high headed Spaniel can run far harder than one with its nose down. Also, during training and conditioning for Trials, dogs are given short, sharp runs, with quick finds and retrieves of planted birds, then are put back into the kennel before they begin to slow down. Repeated throughout a Spaniel's career, this maintains his speed into late middle age, whereas the equivalent dog in this country will have had too many hard shooting days behind it to be still racing about like a two-year-old.

Following in importance after fast, wide ground coverage, are hard flushing and accurate marking. A soft flush or a flashpoint is an eliminating fault and a missmark a serious fault.

Regarding the flush, American Spaniels must go in hard and flush instantly or catch the bird; in fact the dogs are conditioned to catch and a flush is simply the result of a bird being too quick for the dog. Study any action photograph of an American Spaniel going in to flush and you will see its mouth open like a crocodile. The Americans flatly refuse to believe that a British Spaniel is ever capable of driving in hard and striking game a hard blow with its nose without having any designs on the bird. I think they sometimes forget that Spaniel work evolved in Britain and that they are still comparative newcomers to the sport.

During a Trial, only pheasants are shot. Quail and rabbits are ignored, likewise any pheasant which is not flushed by the dog. A 'wild flush' ahead of the dog will be taken if the gun is sure the dog is working on the bird but the essential consideration is that the dog must have every chance to mark the bird. When the bird is shot, the judge does not make the dog wait long before allowing it to retrieve. Providing he can see it has honoured the fall, he sends it, in order not to break its mark. Small wonder, however, when dogs are conditioned to go in to retrieve quickly after a shot that the incidence of dogs anticipating the command and running in is higher than in this country. Having a dog which will take hand signals well is no great asset in America. If a dog fails on a retrieve, its bracemate is not sent to look for the bird and blind retrieves are not shot for the dogs. In the event of a missmark, about two signals to correct the dog are the allowable maximum. Dogs must mark accurately.

Although no penalty is attached to catching game, if a dog should catch every bird on its course it will not receive an award. Having no mark and retrieve, it will be dropped for lack of opportunity, as happens when a dog has a blank run, as if it does not indicate any 'runners' it will be assumed that it has passed game, a heinous crime in America as it is over here. It is customary for the guns to let the birds well out before shooting them and as most Trials are held in open country, the problems of snap shooting among trees seldom arise. Heavier cartridges and loads than used in Britain are normally employed and I believe it is for this reason that the attitude to hard mouth is more lenient than in this country as a fairly high proportion of birds are damaged by shot.

At one period, it was quite usual for a Spaniel which had done very well in this country and probably gained its title, to go to America and after working for a time on planted game and having its pattern widened, begin to win consistently but in recent years the pattern appears to have changed. Some very mediocre, or even downright poor Spaniels, by our standards, have been exported to America and have done very well.

Some breeders have concentrated entirely on a type of Spaniel with American Trials only in mind and have produced a light leggy animal, not particularly good in punishing covert or otherwise adapted to a working life under our conditions. Fortunately, however, the tendency to export our best Spaniels seems to have been averted. More owners seem to be taking a pride in their dogs for their own sakes rather than because they represent several hundred dollars and I have heard of examples of substantial American offers being refused for British Spaniels.

There was a time when Cockers featured as American Trial dogs and some well known owners, including the late Dean Bedford and the late Clark Gable participated, but Trials for

Cockers faded out in the States some years ago. A few Americans still shoot over Cockers; in fact I sent a Field Trial Champion bitch, Monnow Mayfly to Texas a couple of years ago. I recommended her as she worked particularly well in hot weather and it has been confirmed that neither heat nor sandburrs trouble her. I do not know what a sandburr looks like but am led to believe it is something nasty which dogs dislike. Apparently she has done sterling work on mourning doves, working as a no slip retriever and retrieving from high grass under indifferent scenting conditions.

Springers have been popular in Canada for some years now, both as shooting and Trial dogs and several British dogs have been imported. In Canadian Trials, both wild and planted pheasants are employed but I understand dogs are not penalised for pointing. A Canadian Spaniel can also become a Field Trial Champion on a points basis, which certainly finds the consistent dogs but I would imagine not necessarily the brilliant dogs.

British gundogs, particularly Spaniels, find their way to several other parts of the world. The Belgians buy quite a few Retrievers and France imports a number of Spaniels. I have exported a Spaniel to Korea, where they apparently enjoy excellent pheasant and duck shooting and I have sent four to Malaya to work on driven and hunted up pheasants and green pigeon, said to be the most difficult and sporting bird in the whole world to shoot. One was unfortunately fatally bitten by a cobra, which rivals the incident in Canada in which a Scottish Spaniel was eaten by a wolf.

A Welsh Labrador is performing good work in Jugoslavia as a servant of the State, after a local shooting man spent a shooting holiday behind the Iron Curtain, pronouncing the shooting fantastic but the local gundogs deplorable, so made a present of the dog to the State for a specific gamekeeper to handle. Marshal Tito himself purchased a brace of English Setters when on an official visit to this country many years ago.

Holland has purchased Labradors and Golden Retrievers and a few Spaniels are beginning to find their way to the Low Countries and by all accounts should never be short of work as Holland is rich in assorted game. Partridges are scarce but pheasants, wildfowl and snipe are in abundance.

Creation of new polder does not assist snipe and wildfowl, as several extra thousands of acres of their habitat are lost for all time, but such an operation is beneficial to the pheasant. After draining, the polder is planted with reeds which stand for five years to consolidate the ground. Pheasants use these vast reed beds and breed unhindered during this period of consolidation. It is impossible to shoot pheasants in a huge sea of reeds so the birds remain unmolested. When the polder is broken up into farms the reed pheasants gradually adjust to a new habitat of farm crops and drain banks and live an identical life to the pheasants of the north Lincolnshire coastal farms.

33 Breeding: theory

Any form of activity involving the production of either livestock or plant life is heavily dependent upon policies of selective breeding in order that the quality of this product should be at least maintained or, if possible, improved. I possess a copy of Hagedoorn's *Animal Breeding* but this work is far too scientific for my unscientific mind and in any case deals with the production of food animals, whereas the working gundog breeder must breed for something which is totally unique in animal breeding. Armchair gundog breeders frequently quote something to me which they call Mendel's Law. I do not know what it is and my attitude to it is somewhat akin to Rudyard Kipling's caveman, 'Who couldn't read and couldn't write and didn't want to and lived cavily in a cave'.

From the foregoing, it will become abundantly clear that I know nothing at all about breeding but, if past records are anything to go by, I occasionally finish up by breeding better stock than some of the experts. Being rather dim, breeding-wise, I have to rely on my knowledge of a dog's parents, grandparents and more distant forebears and rely heavily upon the excellence of the individual. I have come to various conclusions through trial and error, as to which dogs can be line bred to and which are likely to produce faults if this practice is adhered to.

One thing I have learned is that, whereas one should adopt a firm policy over breeding, one must never be dogmatic, as the rules of gundog breeding can never be hard and fast. When breeding farm livestock, the object is to produce an animal which grows rapidly and has a high conversion ratio of food consumed to flesh produced, or produces the highest possible milk or butterfat yield. The requisite qualities in the gundog are that he should have a sound constitution and an active body and, apart from a keenness and aptitude for work, he must have an even, trainable temperament, the equivalent of which is not sought in any other animal, with the possible exception of some horses which are schooled for highly specialised equestrian events. It is so much more simple to breed solely for pure physical characteristics. To combine mental and physical excellence is much harder. In the opinion of one armchair breeder of my acquaintance, it is perfectly in order to breed from two mediocre, or even poor specimens, provided both go back to a common ancestor of great quality. In some cases, this policy may work but I would never dare risk it myself and would feel far happier if both parents were of proven excellence, both going back to a great ancestor, preferably not too far back. An exception to this procedure might occur in the case of the mediocre daughters of a really brilliant bitch. Within the confines of my own experience a truly great bitch, as opposed to a very good bitch, seldom produces pups as good as herself, or even nearly as good but provided her daughters are sound, with no real faults, mated to top class sires these daughters often prove to be excellent breeders. Although I have had considerable success with the progeny of the daughters of my best ever Springer bitch, who never bred a top class pup herself, I much prefer the idea that a brood bitch should, ideally, be the favourite shooting bitch of the owner, as advocated by William Arkwright in 1914.

It is recognised by all livestock breeders that the soundness of the female line is of paramount importance, but I have found among gundog circles, several people who are so fanatical over the theory of female superiority that they would have us believe that the sire is of little importance and that a first class bitch will consistently produce good pups by any reasonably good dog. I find this reasoning somewhat hard to follow, as surely anyone in possession of a top class bitch would seek the best possible sire for it. Some people attempt to assess the relative importance of sire and dam by percentages. Some say the bitch is 75 per cent of the mating. Others say it is fifty/fifty and this is the most prevalent American idea on the subject; strangest of all is the theory which ascribes 51 per cent to the bitch and 49 to the dog.

With the exception of some persons of proven knowledge who, having committed themselves to a certain unqualified statement, will not deviate from this statement even though they are aware that in the light of alternative evidence, it should be qualified, I regard people who attach percentages to the importance in the mating of dog or bitch, as normally lacking in knowledge. There are too many facets of gundog breeding for one neatly to categorise the procedure into hard and fast rules. My experience strongly suggests that in one mating the bitch proves the dominant partner. Mated to a different dog, the pups may take far more after the sire.

Then again, we have the case of the dominant sire who appears able to stamp his own qualities on the majority of the pups he sires, no matter to what bitch he is mated to. In fact, I know of one particular sire who was so strong that he has even sired some first class progeny from downright poor bitches. There is also the strange phenomenon of the repeat mating. In some cases, a proven mating can be repeated several times with equal success yet in other cases a repeat of a successful mating is a failure, the pups very often being physically smaller than the last litter besides proving deficient in quality when training is commenced.

There are theories relating to the ages of the parents. I do know for a fact that young or middle aged ewes produce better lambs than aged animals but am told that old dairy cows can produce first class calves but that the same does not appear to apply to the beef breeds (nobody seems to have come up with any theory on dual purpose breeds, like the Lincoln Red or the Friesian). Some say an old dog and bitch will not produce good pups and that a famous old stud dog should only be mated to young bitches and that an old brood bitch requires a young dog.

I know a case of a ten-year-old Championship winner who was mated to an eight-year-old bitch and two Championship winners were produced by this mating. In my establishment, this theory is never tested. I breed from my bitches when they are young, usually in their second heat and keep them hard at it until they are seven years old then never breed from them again. By this time they owe me nothing whereas I owe them much and I would never exploit them into old age. This is a private policy based on appreciation rather than sentiment.

My opinion is that however good are the bitch and her forebears, the dog is most important and I have strong views on the qualities he should possess. When breeding high performance animals, which would include Trial dogs, racehorses and fighting bulls, man must endeavour to breed an animal above the norm for his particular purpose. Nature, unaided, has a strong and inevitable tendency to revert to the norm. Consider the case of wild pheasants, isolated from any rearing programme. The cocks revert to a set type, with colours less gaudy and iridescent than reared birds but with distinctive mauve wing coverts and the inevitable ring round every neck.

For a start, a gundog sire should look masculine. I dislike light, whippety, bitchy headed dogs. They may often be excellent working dogs in their own right with qualities of speed, stamina and gamefinding ability but I like to see a good heavy skull and strong bone in a stud dog. The qualities most easily lost in gundogs are drive and style so, to maintain these attributes, I believe the breeder should seek them in the sire. The dog must be a first class gamefinder with a well proven mouth. Speed, drive and a beautiful tail action are of little use unless the front end of the dog is of comparable efficiency. Provided a dog is not downright pig-headed or dishonest in a tempting situation, I do not mind if he is a little headstrong. It takes a certain amount of experience to differentiate between a hard dog and a hot dog but there is all the difference in the world. A hard dog will ask for punishment repeatedly and when he receives it will still commit the original sin when he can. The hot dog may boil over once in a while, take his punishment and behave impeccably for several weeks. He is hot enough to make a mistake but sensible enough to acknowledge it when it is pointed out to him.

This brings us to the essential point of the purpose of Trials in relation to the shooting man. A certain amount of hypocrisy exists in some quarters regarding the supposed requirements of that ambiguous creature 'The average shooting man'. There are some who are incapable of producing top Trial dogs and spend a good deal of time decrying those who do, on the grounds that the top Trial dog is far too difficult to handle for the 'average shooting man' and claim to be doing the shooting man a service by producing their own mediocre animals especially for his use. I am the first to admit that handling the really top specimens in the shooting or Trial field is a job for the specialist and most shooting men might find such an animal too much for them. It must, however, be borne in mind that comparatively few of these top specimens are produced and these, if in the right hands, become the top Trial dogs and the stallions of the breed. What is not always appreciated is that hot sires and dams only produce a limited proportion of progeny as hot as themselves and for the rest, there is an excellent chance that they will inherit the working qualities of their parents but will be easier specimens to handle.

If one continually breeds from generations of soft dogs, very soon they will become too soft to be effective to the shooting man, so infusions of good hot blood must be employed in order that the shooting man's Spaniel can still get through its bushes. Ideally, I suppose the shooting man's Spaniel should have terrific drive in cover, the stamina to hunt all day and do a duck flight in the evening but require no handling at all. A rather unrealistic order, so it is only logical to presuppose that a compromise must be reached. If the shooting man requires nose and drive, he must be prepared to do a little to keep it within reasonable bounds. If he only shoots in turnip and rush fields, possibly a very soft Spaniel with no ambition ever to move more than ten yards from its handler's feet would suffice. The advocates of the super easy Spaniel invariably appear to assume that no shooting man could possibly handle any other type. We have been brought up on a diet of soft-boiled Spaniels, largely because some authorities can only handle this type. It does not appear to have occurred to them that some shooting men, with a little gundog education, could become good handlers, capable of keeping on terms with a spirited dog. An American writer and ex-Trial competitor, Charles Goodhall, takes a rather different view to some in this country and is a firm advocate of the fast, hard-going Spaniel for the shooting man and endeavours to help his readers to keep on terms with such an animal, explaining how much more rewarding it is when properly handled than a potterer. Some shooting men are such poor handlers that no amount of education could ever improve them and in their hands even a soft Spaniel would develop such a head of steam through contact with game that it would become more of a menace on the shoot than an asset. As hard as we may try to suit the individual with a suitable dog, the final remedy is in his own hands.

What must be remembered is that no Trial handler enjoys

handling a really difficult dog and although a pig-headed animal might fluke one or two wins, or even the Championship, as once happened, to win consistently under a wide cross-section of judges, a gundog must have a basically kindly nature, however hard he goes. Those who continually strive to bring such animals to the fore deserve full credit rather than the condemnation of those who can themselves make no contribution to the improvement of the breeds.

34 Breeding: practice

Bitches normally come into season twice a year but some only reach this condition once a year, others every nine or ten months. Some come into season every six months whether they have been bred from or not, others after rearing a litter, come in season six months after the birth of the pups, or eight months after the last heat.

Bitches also vary in age when they experience their first heat. I once had a terrier which had its first heat at five and a half months and then again I had a famous Springer bitch who came in season for the first time at 18 months, thereafter coming on regularly at six monthly intervals. I find that the majority of bitches have their first heat between eight and ten months and it has become established practice in most parts of the world to breed from a bitch no earlier than her second heat. Twice I have had bitches come into season for the first time at 12 months and have bred good litters from them but, in spite of intensive care and a really good diet, both bitches lost condition after the weaning of the pups, so it appears the theory of not breeding until the second heat is more than an old coon hunter's tale.

There are usually several days in a bitch's heat during which she can conceive, varying from the seventh to the 21st day but again bitches vary enormously. Some bitches have been accidentally mated within about a couple of days of coming into season and others are still not safe from conception after a month, but 10 to 14 days sees the majority of bitches just about right for the dog. The bitch herself is the best guide. With my own, I try her with a dog (any dog) until the day when she stands, then I give her a couple of days for good measure and have her mated. I seem to have very few bitches who fail to 'hold'.

The condition of the bitch, or any other animal for that matter, is important and a bitch is far more likely to conceive if she is not over fat. My bitches are always lean and hard when mated and the fact that I only breed from reasonably young animals probably accounts for my high ratio of conceptions. About three weeks after mating, an experienced **hand** can usually tell whether or not the mating has been successful, particularly in the case of a bitch which has been bred from before. Low down in the abdomen can be felt, between finger and thumb, one or two small spherical swellings. A maiden bitch is often so hard muscled around the abdominal region that nothing can at first be detected and some dogs tense their muscles when turned over on their backs in any events but gentle massage of the abdomen usually causes them to relax.

The bitch should have her diet increased at about this period, two feeds a day being given instead of one, with calcium and vitamin supplements. The pups are normally born 63 days after mating but if the bitch becomes really huge and heavy, pups may be born up to a week early with no adverse effects. It is always a good idea to use an infra-red lamp when pups are expected as it helps to dry them out quickly and prevents chilling after birth, I also believe it alleviates shock in the bitch. I give the bitch plenty of newspaper in her box two or three days before the pups are due. She amuses herself by tearing it up to make a nest and it is absorbent and easily disposed of after the event.

A bitch will usually show signs of impending parturition by panting, turning round in the box, scratching the box floor and whining occasionally. The bitch's temperature drops when the birth is imminent, something which few persons outside the veterinary profession seem to know. The bitch looks hot, with her panting and general restlessness but her temperature will be about 98°F instead of the usual 101½°F. After the temperature drop has been noted, the bitch should commence whelping within 12 hours. If nothing is forthcoming, the vet should be summoned immediately. As a primary remedy, he will inject pituitrin and wait 20 minutes. If the pituitrin does not cause the bitch to whelp a pup, she must have the pups removed by surgery. This is a simple operation *if performed in time* and the bitch has not been allowed to weaken herself by excessive straining. The incision should be made high up on the bitch's flank, well out of the way of the feeding paps and, if correctly placed, there will be no drag on the sutures when the pups feed.

In the case of a maiden bitch, a psychological complication can arise. As the bitch has been under anaesthetic when the pups were removed, the natural process of the pup arriving, the umbilical cord being cut by the bitch and then being thoroughly cleaned by her, does not occur. Coupled with the effects of the ether plus post-operative shock, some bitches just do not know what the pups are and are terrified of them. The owner must be prepared to spend up to several hours stroking and soothing the bitch, holding a pup close to her ,and letting it suck from her. I believe that once a certain amount of colostrum is drawn from the bitch by the pups, with the assistance of the owner as described, this triggers off a natural process and her maternal instincts begin to function.

Assuming however that there are no such unpleasant complications, the bitch will normally attend to everything herself without the need for assistance and, providing the pups appear to be arriving at fairly regular intervals, she is best left alone to get on with it with a minimum of interference.

After the bitch has finished whelping there remains one vital job which can be done by an experienced owner himself but over which professional assistance should be sought if the owner doubts his own capabilities. This is to check the bitch for a retained pup, a most dangerous condition which spells certain death for the bitch if it goes undetected. After appearing to whelp normally, some bitches retain one or more pups which they are unable to get rid of unaided. If no assistance is given, the pup quickly putrefies, gangrene sets in and the bitch dies. I give my bitches a through examination after whelping appears to be over, feeling up under the ribs, where these retained pups usually appear to be. If nothing can be detected and the uterus, being empty, has started to contract, the organ can be detected like a piece of spongey rope in the centre of the abdomen and must not be mistaken for a pup, as the latter would be much harder to the touch. If at all in doubt, get help.

As someone who formerly reared pups on three or four wet mixed feeds daily, as we did our pheasants on the open rearing fields, the idea of hopper feeding when it was first advocated, filled me with horror. Pups would gorge themselves and become pot-bellied for life! Of course I was completely wrong and there are now several excellent proprietary feeds on the market which rear excellent pups when fed dry from a hopper and I am now completely converted to hopper feeding with the addition of some fine pieces of bullock's tripe later on.

35 The wildfowler's dog

By definition, wildfowling is the pursuit of duck, geese and waders along the coasts and estuaries, as opposed to shooting duck on inland ponds or geese on their feeding grounds, so obviously water is the main element the wildfowler's dog will have to contend with. He will at times be subjected to several immersions, often under vile weather conditions. He may have to negotiate steep-sided gutters and at times seek his quarry in dense reed beds, completely unsighted from his handler. He may have to pursue a wounded duck far out to sea on an ebb tide and must have the strength to fight his way back against the current.

Gales and vile weather are helpful to the wildfowler as these conditions help to bring his quarry down to a reasonable height and render the fowl less wary. Under these conditions even stone dead birds may be carried a great distance beyond the gun and winged birds plane down a quarter of a mile away. So, coupled with a love of water, it is most essential that the wildfowler's dog should possess marking ability second to none.

Any old, keen Retriever whose manners render it unfit for use at the covert will have a certain amount of usefulness on the foreshore but such an animal can never become a wildfowler's paragon. As with all forms of shooting, manners and controllability will pay dividends under some circumstances. I have earlier mentioned the controversy which was raging in the sporting press over wildfowling dogs when I first began to sit up and take notice. Peter Moxon stated that a fowler's dog should run in directly a bird began to fall but should not career round at every shot. Dugald MacIntyre said that a fowling dog should be just as steady as any formal retriever, pointing out that the command to 'go fetch' only requires a split second to give.

Quite recently, I have used an experienced Spaniel for picking up at big pheasant shoots in exactly the same way that MacIntyre advocated for the wildfowling dog. He would remain perfectly steady to anything that fell but marking every bird, then when an obvious runner began to fall, I would send him in at once, sometimes several times in one drive. In this way he collected the maximum number of runners but his steadiness never suffered as he was thoroughly conditioned to await the command to fetch. So it is when wildfowling. If dead birds fall on to land or into still water, the dog can be held so there is no risk of turning birds away which are heading straight for the gun but when a bird begins to fall which obviously should be collected right away, the dog can be sent by an instant command.

There is the question of the ideal breed for the wildfowler's use. Some Spaniels are undoubtedly used for coastal wildfowling with success, usually large, powerful specimens but I believe any Spaniel, however courageous, is at a disadvantage when faced with this work, when compared to a Retriever. Not only is the Retriever a larger, stronger dog, with a much longer history as a water dog (remember, the Spaniel was originally essentially a land animal) but he can better stand the continual immersion in ice cold water and subsequent shivering waits, than can the Spaniel. Colour needs a certain amount of consideration too and a deep fox red can be considered ideal as it blends with the marsh turf and other cover, whereas pied or cream coloured dogs stick out like beacons and must be carefully concealed, even a black dog is conspicuous to duck at night.

36 Hill country training problems and advantages

At the beginning of this book, I mentioned how I first became interested in gundogs when living in large agricultural areas which held a good game and rabbit population and, in fact, started my career as a professional trainer in Lincolnshire.

Then, it was no problem to find a few birds or rabbits to 'get a Spaniel going' and even in the close season one could always shoot a couple of pigeon or a hare for a Retriever. Local farmers, too, seemed glad enough to share their shooting, a situation which a good colleague of mine informs me obtains in North East Yorkshire, where he trains under identical circumstances to those I experienced in South Lincolnshire.

After I moved to North Wales, I found I had some very rapid adjusting to do if I was to continue to train gundogs successfully. Game was altogether much scarcer, a pigeon would be shot now and then and hares were always at a premium. A Spaniel had to be built up on far fewer finds than was formerly the case and the rabbit-pen became three times as important. Even ordinary hand training posed problems. Most of my work is done on steep hillsides, through absence of level ground and this can cause difficulties over dummy work. Hillsides can cause strange air currents and often a young dog will be in a position relative to a dummy where it should be able to wind it but is unable to owing to a quirk of the wind. The contours of a hillside also make it far more difficult for a dog to get out and use its ground than is the case on the flat. Our mountain climate is severe and the rabbit-pen becomes an inhospitable place during the winter and even more so in the early Spring when food and cover is scarce. I appear to have built my pen on a hillside which is a natural run for stoats and suffer frequent invasions and subsequent loss from these little beasts.

I love to see buzzards floating over the valley but they can hardly be termed benevolent birds when the first young rabbits of the year are born in the pen. The main disadvantage of my hill ground is the shortage of cover and lack of scent on the windswept acres during early Spring. The bracken dies away to nothing and becomes useless as cover and the gorse becomes hard, dry and uninviting. How I long for some fields of nice damp rushes! I have conditioned myself to accept the fact that at this time of the year I must forget about the hunting side of a Spaniel's work, concentrating solely on obedience and dummy work and await the coming of the new bracken as eagerly as my pagan ancestors awaited the lengthening days which followed their Festival of Light in late December.

With the coming of the bracken, the place is reborn. The ground will then hold scent again and the lush green growth gives the young Spaniels something to tear into. One wild rabbit in a bed of short mountain bracken will really set a dog alight and by July I begin to feel my advantages over my lowland colleagues. July is usually a bad month for dog training in England. The weather is normally hot and humid or wet and humid and there is little cover to hunt a Spaniel in as the hedgerows are choked with nettles, the bracken in the coverts is six feet high and there are fields of standing corn everywhere. Here, our altitude keeps us relatively cool and although parts of the mountainside are unworkable owing to four-foot bracken, there are patches of short bracken where it is possible to keep a Spaniel in view and find a rabbit or hare.

One difficulty I find is that, owing to the closeness of the country, it is hard to get a dog out on a really long blind retrieve as he is all too soon lost to view. I can usually find a situation open enough to get a Spaniel out as far as I need to, but there is not sufficient room to get a Retriever out 150 yards; as I do not train Field Trial Retrievers, this is not too great a disadvantage.

37 Conclusion

I have tried to show, throughout this book, how I have achieved more than average success in the sphere of gundogs and Field Trials with the minimum of outside assistance. I have never attended a training class, although I do not decry them and mention the fact merely to point out that results can be obtained by a keen man who is willing to work out for himself the inevitable problems he encounters. I have trained myself to shoot over a hard going Spaniel, so my concentration on the dog does not lapse when I mount my gun and fully reverts to the dog when the shot has been taken. I have done a lot of picking up but, during one period, I did no picking up for five years. This was to prove to myself, should nobody else find it of interest, that I could consistently maintain a team of Field Trial Spaniels, with new dogs coming on each year, by shooting every head of game over them myself in preparation for Trials. There is so much nonsensical propaganda spread by the uninitiated in some cases and those who should know better in others, that successful Trial dogs are poles apart from the ordinary work-a-day shooting dog and that Trial handlers deliberately produce an animal which can only win Trials and is no good on an ordinary shoot. How pleased I was when the Editor of a sporting journal said recently that, yes, there is a difference between an ordinary shooting dog and a Trial dog when both were out shooting. The Trial dog is a great deal better.

A Trial dog is a shooting dog which is simply behaving as a shooting dog *ought* to behave. The sad thing is that so many shooting men seem content to settle for so much less. Some are incapable of handling any dog, having a blind spot just as I have a mathematical blind spot but others cannot be bothered to handle their dogs properly and would rather stroll off to look for a bird when their particular dog has been trained to get out, obey signals and find it for them.

Another disadvantage of a Trial dog is that for the duration of his run he is under a spotlight and is likely to be assessed by the uninitiated solely on what happens during that run. It is the judge's task to assess the run, purely to reach a decision on the day but a reporter who does not know his job can paint a completely false picture by dwelling on the mistakes made by individual dogs during their runs, being unable to assess quality in spite of possible wrongdoing. There is all the difference in the world between a Stake consisting of poor dogs and one consisting largely of good dogs, a proportion of whom slip up during the course of events. I get an entirely different impression of American Field Trial reporting in the U.S.A., it is frank, analytical and down-to-earth. The reporters dwell more on the excellence of the dogs than their shortcomings and often have kind things to say for quality dogs which go wrong in the Trial.

I believe it is a great mistake to overestimate the intelligence of a dog and credit it with a reasoning power actually beyond the capabilities of its brain. The handler must be in charge at all times and there is a great deal of commonsense in the remark which was once made: 'Make up your mind what you don't want your dog to do and see he doesn't do it'.

I abhor the dog which cannot get on with his job for staring at his handler, but a dog should ask a question once in a while. If he crosses the front of his handler, quartering in the right direction and glances up as he passes, I give him a signal with my hand to confirm that he is doing the right thing. Actually he knows he is but this small signal keeps us in contact.

If a handler takes on a dog which he has had trained or purchased, he should make sure he learns the correct commands and stick rigidly to them. It is all right for a professional who takes over a trained dog from another professional to run in Trials for a client, to change the commands and whistles to his own but he will know what he is doing and will first ensure that the dog has really accepted him, then will make the change gradually but the ordinary owner/shooting man should stick to the original commands. These commands should always be very clearly given and never in profusion, but one at a time. If a dog has been stopped to the whistle, he should always be given a few seconds to collect his wits before being given the next command.

Then there is the vexed question of punishment. It seems that only a few people are capable of giving a dog the correct amount of punishment. On the one hand we have several shooting men who never get out after a dog and punish him when he really needs it; on the other hand we have some Field Trial handlers who are far too brutal and will thrash a dog really hard with a stick or chain when bare hands, properly applied, would be more than adequate. Female handlers can sometimes be harder on their dogs than their male counterparts, particularly if they should have a male audience.

This book has required a great deal of effort to write and has taken nearly a year, as it has been done in my spare time. During its production I have carried on with my normal business, training several shooting dogs, breeding five litters of pups, making four new Field Trial Champions and winning another Cocker Championship. I will not end with the pious hope that if this book will promote the better understanding between only one gundog and its owner, my task will not have been in vain. I want this book, now and in years to come, to help hundreds of handlers to get the best out of their dogs. My happiest times are when I go out alone with two Spaniels, one at heel and one hunting, to shoot a bird or two—then I can wish Field Trials and their human element a thousand miles away.

I have had the best from my dogs and there can be little out of the ordinary about me.

Go thou and do likewise.

38 **Some great dogs**

GOLDEN RETRIEVERS

F.T.C. Treunair Cala. Cala was a great character with the most marvellous temperament–and temperament with me is of prime importance in a potential gundog–a spot-on marker and I would be justified in saying that his nose was second to none. It never failed to astonish and delight me and certainly won him the Championship where, under appalling scenting conditions, he was the only dog who never had a failure. He used his head too and slowed down a little to cope with the very bad conditions.

He was so much at one with me that he needed the minimum of handling and seemed to possess that uncanny instinct as to where game lay, which I think is the hallmark of 'a good one'. He had tremendous determination and always persevered. He never came back and said 'I can't find it'. He would go on and on, hunting out his ground until I felt compelled to call him up. He was very keen but calm and reliable, facing any cover and performing consistently well on land and in water, either shooting or Trialling.

He was the first dog I had ever trained out of the first litter I had bred. He was Third in our first Trial and he was never out of the awards that 1950 season (he was born December 1948), finishing with a win in the United Gundog Breeders Association Non Winner Stake. In 1951 he received two Awards of Honour and a certificate in the Open Stakes I entered and in 1952 become a Field Trial Champion in five days. I decided not to run him again until the Championship which he then won, thereby winning three consecutive Stakes. The Championship judges in their report said 'That he must be the most delightful dog to shoot over' which of course he was and I retired him from Trials. He was a natural pointer as a young dog and he would point a wounded bird before going in to retrieve and I used him as a Spaniel. He was most useful walking up grouse as he would come up to a covey and remain pointing until told to move in and flush.

My father (Sir Landale Train) bought his dam for ten pounds when she was three years old, her only claim to fame being that she went back to F.T.C. John of Auchencheyne on her dam's side. His sire, Treunair Ciabhach was of our own (at that time my father's) home bred line of really good shooting dogs. His grandfather, Treunair Darach being our first of the line and he was bred by Joan Gill out of Speedwell Dulcet by Weyland Viking. Cala lived to over 15 years of age and remained very active right up to the end.

Cala's grandson F.T.C. Treunair Texa whose dam was by Cala out of Cala's litter sister was my next notable dog but he was never as consistent a performer as Cala although he won three Open Stakes. I really consider the bitch I have now as the best I have had since Cala. She is just three years old, a daughter of Texa out of Stubblesdown Della. She has much the same temperament, persistence and nose. Her name is Treunair Strathcarron Crion. She has had no outstanding wins but in her two seasons Trialling, has never been out of the awards. Last year (1972) her first in Open Stakes, she was second, third and Certificate of Merit in the only three Stakes she ran in, all open and variety Stakes.

Jean Lumsden, *Little Millbrook, Nutley, Sussex.*

F.T.C. Mazurka of Wynford. F.T.C. Mazurka of Wynford won the Retriever Championship in 1954 at two and a half years old and was second in the 1955 Championship, the only two three-day Championships held. He won the Rank/Routledge Trophy (for the highest overall performance) in 1957, the first Golden to win this award. His mother, Musicmaker of Yeo was my first Golden and every one of my Field Trial Champions have been direct descendants of his, or very closely related.

As to my next best Golden, that is a very difficult question. F.T.C. Holway Bonny was uncanny, she was so clever. She won seven Open Stakes, including the International Gundog League, before she died at five years old. She was by Haulstone Bobby, out of Melodymaker, litter sister to Mazurka.

F.T.C. Holway Gaiety has won the Rank/Routledge Cup two successive years, 1970 and 1971 and is a brilliant bitch, with the most wonderful nose and absolutely fearless in the thickest of cover but also super to handle. She is out of F.T.C. Holway Flush who is one of Mazurka's last offspring. Gay is five years old now (1973) and has won eight Trials.

June Atkinson, *Holway, Cattistock, Dorchester.*

FLAT-COATED RETRIEVERS

CH. Claverdon Jorrocks of Lilling. This dog came as close to becoming a dual Champion as it was possible to without actually accomplishing this feat. As his title implies, he was of course a Champion on the bench and also won one Open Stake. He also won at least one second in Open Stakes, so only just fell short by one place of the necessary requirements.

I saw Jorrocks win the Retriever Game Fair Tests in 1961 on the Earl of Bradford's estate at Weston-Under-Lizard. This was a most exacting test with clouds of homing pigeon released as a distraction and he made a very convincing win.

F.T.C. Hartshorn Sorrel. This bitch from Northern Ireland is the only Field Trial Champion I have ever seen of this breed. I saw her run in the Retriever Championship which was held at Cromlix some years ago and I remember her specifically on a bird which was never picked. A doubtful bird from a drive was thought to be down somewhere on a large open pasture and she was asked to try for it. She gave one of the best displays of precision handling that I have ever seen and could be placed absolutely anywhere at tremendous distances. Coupled with beautiful style she was the most spectacular bitch to watch.

ENGLISH SPRINGER SPANIELS

I have seen more Springers in action than any other breed. There are great dogs of the past whose names have become household words among Spaniel people and who have contributed much towards the make-up of our present day Springers and indeed the great Springers I am about to describe. There are names like F.T.Cs. Daud, Spy O'Vara, Sarkie O'Vara, Breckonhill Bee and Rivington Glensaugh Glean but one cannot live too far back in the past, so I will only mention in detail their descendants of whom I have personal knowledge.

Conygree Simon. Simon was by Slam O'Vara, a dog whose eyesight and chances in the field were ruined by an attack of hardpad, out of a very small lively bitch called Conygree Minnie. Simon was never handled to full advantage and only won a Novice Stake and placed second in one Open.

Nevertheless, I can state without fear of contradiction that more Field Trial Champions have issued from his line than from any other in the history of the breed. He was not a large dog but was lean and spare and perfectly balanced. He had the most terrific drive and spectacular style and possessed the undoubted ability to pass on his qualities. He was a perfect example of all that was best from the great O'Vara line of which he was a perfect example. Events have also proved that he can be heavily line bred to without producing undesirable qualities which has actually been proved through his son, Hales Smut. Line breed to Smut and, of course, one line breeds to Simon.

Hales Smut. If old Simon laid the foundations, it was his son, Smut who really put the plan into operation. Discussing Smut with an admirer of his, I stated that Smut is as good as he is because his breeder is thick! Had I been an expert geneticist, I would have found a sire for Smut's dam by charts, graphs or perhaps even the stars and the chances of this sire being Simon would have been remote. I simply mated the easiest and most honest bitch in the country to the most stylish and fiery sire, bearing in mind that between them they went back three times to F.T.C. Sarkie O'Vara, a particularly sound dog in his own right. Perhaps another factor to be considered when assessing the excellence of Smut as a stud force is that he came from a strong litter and was not just a flash in a panful of mediocre brothers.

Among his brothers were Gwibernant Cadwaladr, not as clever as Smut but a terrific hunter and sire of F.T.C. Willie Snaffles. There was F.T.C. Jontis Gwibernant Gynan, a very level-headed Irish dog who won about six Open Stakes. There was Gwibernant Garnedd, a dog who never ran in Trials and who never had a decent bitch to him but as a worker was quite up to Smut in quality.

Smut suffered the same handicap as old Simon in the field as he was never really handled to full advantage. He was just too high powered for anyone's first Trial dog and I doubt if any novice Trial handler could have coped with him. He had a lightning fast reaction, which, as it was not quite channelled, got him into trouble on several occasions. Having built up such a head of steam, there were occasions when he gave tongue and this fault lost the Championship for him and caused many fingers to be pointed at him. Happily, this trait has hardly ever manifested itself in his progeny and a great deal can be done to prevent the fault arising through sensible training, really screwing the dog well down in obedience at the outset and later firmly building complete steadiness into the dog.

Although Smut never won a Trial, he did a great deal for Spaniel Trials by bringing a new breath of life into them. He delighted spectators and judges alike by his spectacular, flamboyant hunting and his brilliant marking and retrieving. The speculation was always 'What will he do next?', which gave the proceedings a rare air of expectancy. He might get a brilliant runner, he might execute a spectacular run in but whatever Smut did, there was nothing cheap or nasty about it. He did it with class.

Smut has sired 13 English Field Trial Champions, an all-time record and a number of his progeny have won their titles in America but I have never bothered to record these as the requirements are, as I have already explained, so different from ours in America that I believe true Spaniel quality can only be assessed by what a dog does in our bramble patches and gorse clumps. American triumphs should only be assessed as a bonus, not as an end in themselves.

F.T.C. Pinehawk Sark. Sark can be truthfully described as the 'First spectacular Spaniel after myxomatosis'.

I first saw him in January 1957 when his handler ran him in an Open Stake at the age of nine months and I was immediately taken by the brilliance of his expression and his erect, mobile ear carriage. Ears can be as expressive in a Spaniel as eyes and tails. His handler assured us that Sark would be a good one and, as it turned out, this was no idle boast.

He matured over the summer and came out like a tiger the following October. He did not win his first Trial but looked extremely dangerous and soon won a couple of Stakes, to gain his title. He was also placed second against Labradors, working as a no slip Retriever in a utility trial. Sark was a very fast dog with real drive in cover and a brilliant gamefinder, marker and retriever. When marking a bird he had a speciality entirely of his own. When the bird was shot he would mark it in a glance, then rivet his gaze upon his handler. If the majority of Spaniels adopted this habit, it would mean missmarks a-plenty but Sark had an uncanny knack of going to the bird spot on.

After a few Trials, Sark's reputation spread far and wide, so small wonder that a knowledgeable veteran handler from the North Country wanted a good look at him. Sark proceeded to thrash an area of dead bracken in his customary manner and after a while my colleague remarked: 'Yon dog's just galloping' Sark evidently heard him, stopped and poked a rabbit out. It is interesting to note that he was put down to a Certificate of Merit at this particular Trial because one judge during summing up announced to his colleague, 'I could not shoot over that dog'. Yet in a long and successful career at stud, Sark sired very many Spaniels which made kind, excellent shooting dogs which bears out my theory of the desirability of using fiery sires for the good of the breed.

Sark sired four British Field Trial Champions including the tiny but spectacular Jonkit Jandy and the sweet, ever reliable Criffel Melody. Only one of these four had the speed and drive of Sark, a truly fantastic dog who must remain nameless. One of his daughters, out of F.T.C. Wivenwood Fofo was a real handful but mated to Hales Smut, produced litter after litter of quality progeny, many of whom have had outstanding success in America, in fact some of Sark's direct progeny have achieved consistent results in the U.S.A. Sark was by International F.T.C. Ludlovian Socks out of a Garwgarreg bitch and had a beautiful hunting brother, F.T.C. Pinehawk Spur, whilst another brother, Garwgarreg Socks, held the Welsh Marches against the English, another example of a strong litter.

F.T.C. Markdown Muffin. Once upon a time there was an evil little Springer called Ludlovian Diana. A brilliant hunter but a real monkey, it was decided to use the late Colin Thomson's F.T.C. Rivington Glensaugh Glean on her to cool things down a little. Glean, though brilliant and spectacular was also kind and easy, so the logic in the choice was fairly obvious.

The mating was a success. It produced one Championship winner for me, Micklewood Slip, who still retained much of the devilry of her dam, a big promising dog and some very useful also-rans. The dog's name was Markdown Muffin, a big short coupled, hairy dog with a beautiful head and expression–a real old fashioned 'China dog' Spaniel.

Muffin's rise to fame was not so rapid or spectacular as Slip's but it was more consistent. Hampered by ill-health during his first season, Muffin began to win in his second season and impressed me with his wonderful gun sense when cover was sufficiently heavy to prevent his marking. He had an effortless way with brambles, seeming to float through them without fuss, as opposed to the crash of Hales Smut. He was a deadly game-finder, who frequently pointed his game, a spot-on marker and could get out and handle well. He was rather unlucky not to win the Championship at the end of his second season. However, we came back with a vengeance in his third season, winning the Championship convincingly at Blenheim against a good quality field.

Muffin has sired nine British Field Trial Champions and at least two of his sons have won the Championship. His progeny have not done so well in America as some have showed a tendency to point—sudden death to a Spaniel's chances in the States and an additional factor is that Muffin's progeny tend to be methodical hunters rather than racehorses and are marginally slower than some. As a beneficiary of the breed in this country he has few peers.

F.T.C. Dinas Dewi Sele. Bold, tough, challenging, hard going yet amiable, completely honest and quite indomitable, this was without doubt the best Springer I have ever handled, although others have run her close. She was a big bitch with an even, flowing pattern, completely at home on any terrain, hitting gorse and brambles like a tank, yet holding herself in with no effort in light rushes. She did not believe in 'off' days. When cast off to hunt she hunted without question for the sheer love of moving, never questioning whether the game supply was plentiful, sparse or non-existent. I did a good deal of shooting over her and had some wonderful outings on very varied terrain. With Sele out in front, it was possible to concentrate on the shooting without paying her the slightest attention when game was flushed, so honest was she, combining superb drive with the most perfect temperament.

She won nine Open Stakes and several seconds, seldom placing lower, although occasionally winning nothing.

She never bred a pup as good as herself but some of her daughters, mated to the sons of Conygree Simon, produced top quality stock and subsequent generations still show some of her qualities. In fact I ran a most spectacular descendant of hers whom I described as 'the best bitch I have seen since Sele'. She became a Field Trial Champion quite easily but for all her quality, was not Sele. When Sele was made, somebody dropped the mould.

F.T.C. Denhead Walnut. Many years ago, a keeper to one of the hereditary Clan Chiefs in the north of Scotland came out to a Novice Stake with a couple of large show Springers. So superbly trained were these animals that I ventured the remark that should this keeper ever get hold of a decently bred animal, some of us had better look out.

The keeper came out eventually with a son of Muffin and what a pair of characters they turned out to be. The dog's name was Denhead Walnut and he was a thickset, powerful animal with tremendous drive and game-finding ability but little style and a high tail action. He won four Open Stakes but in every instance he won them on two superb gamefinding runs and was never brought into a run off when it was his day for winning. His owner would candidly remark that he would always lose a run off when down against a more stylish dog and I recall an amusing episode when I was down against Walnut with Micklewood Story during the closing stages of a run off. Straight in front of us we had a wonderful piece of Spaniel ground, open bracken interspersed with whin bushes, with an area of solid whins to our left. Story was a lovely mover, really eye catching in the open, so I headed straight down the middle of the course, Story quartering the bracken with drive and style, splitting the whin bushes as we encountered them. Walnut and his handler began to edge to the left and out of the corner of my eye I could see Walnut being pushed into heavy whins, which he tackled with enthusiasm.

When the Trial was over, the verdict having been given in Story's favour, I tackled my colleague over his deviating from the course in front of us to seek heavy country on the left, pointing out how I was attempting to display my dog, whereas he was trying his best to hide his!

For all his lack of style, Walnut sired some good stylish progeny including one bitch who, for a period, was rated 'The best bitch in the country', but more of her anon.

F.T.C. Saighton's Stinger. Stinger was never quite my type of dog but in attempting to describe the Spaniel scene, I feel it is my duty to present the picture as fairly and accurately as possible and feel I would be guilty of the sin of omission were I to leave Stinger out of this section simply on account of a personal, purist view. Stinger has written his own vivid page in the history of the English Springer Spaniel and, this being the case, must receive recognition.

Singer was a large, leggy, bounding, precocious type of puppy and won his first Open Stake at the age of about 16 months, maybe less. He gained his title under me at the Spaniel Club's Trials and won the Trial most convincingly. He won a third Stake that same season and the following year won the only Open Stake in which he competed, then won the Championship at Thoresby Park, among the mature oak trees of the original Sherwood Forest. Stinger never ran in another Open Stake in Great Britain. By virtue of his winning the Championship, he was automatically qualified to run in the following Championship, held at Clandeboye in Northern Ireland. He came close to winning this event for the second year but a running cock pheasant on frosty ground, shot during the run off, caused his downfall; he was lucky enough to receive third place.

Stinger was a dog of undoubted ability and really could put his shot game into the bag but extraordinary good fortune attended him in the five Stakes he won. Every retrieve he had to deal with was first found by him, then shot in front of him. He never had a second dog bird or a blind retrieve shot away from his beat to contend with. Had things been otherwise, it would probably not have made the slightest difference to his final placements but I mention it in passing as being quite extraordinary that he only had his 'own' game to deal with. He was a most amenable and level headed dog under pressure of game and would completely ignore fresh game flushed when searching for a retrieve.

In addition to his Trial successes, he won the Game Fair one year and also the Irish Game Fair, doing some fine work across the Liffey, I was reliably informed.

Stinger did not appear ever to be placed at public stud and it seemed that few Trial people used him, but he sired F.T.C. Harwes Silas, a most consistent Trial winner and former Game Fair winner and Silas's daughter, Harwes Silver, in her turn won the Spaniel Championship at Thoresby Park in January 1973.

Stinger went to the States for a period to compete in Trials, collecting only one fourth place but managed to complete all series in the American National Championship before returning home. It may be that his 'English' method of hunting let him down against the wide sweeping American dogs. As a sire of American Trial dogs, Stinger has a reputation second to none and for a period his progeny completely dominated the Trial scene in the U.S.A. His son, Saighton's Sizzler, winning the National in 1970 and 1971, under the veteran handler Clifford Wallace.

F.T.C. Shineradee. This dog was born in Shropshire, sired by Scamp O'Vara out of Ninadee and had a most successful career, winning six Open Stakes. He was a really good stamp of Spaniel with great all round quality and real determination. He was particularly good on blind retrieves, in fact his handler swore he was capable of winning the Retriever Championship.

He went to America when over four years of age, quite an age in fact for a Spaniel to adapt itself to new methods and his rise to fame on that continent was hardly meteoric. He contracted heart worm in America and this condition hindered his career until successfully treated. However, he finally won his title and was placed second in the American National in 1963.

F.T.C. Drumbro Daisy. When I was about to cross the Dee, to the side where I have now lived for the past eight years, a mighty giantess arose in Morayshire. Hardly a giantess in stature but a giantess in quality and achievements. Her name was Daisy and she was sired by the redoubtable Denhead Walnut, out of Reece of Elan. I had seen her as a young puppy in her owner's kennel when visiting the North and had been immediately struck by her unusual style, a most peculiar body wriggle combined with a lively tail action.

I beat her into second place in her first Novice Stake with a rather nice Smut bitch called Lady of Ardoon and in her first season, Daisy did not do a great deal, in fact she did not become really impressive until her third season, then she began to carry all before her. With experience, she developed great drive but was kindly to handle, with marvellous game sense and when Daisy was put down on a runner, the bird was as good as in the bag. She was placed second in the Championship in January 1970. She won the Game Fair in 1969 and I felt I had achieved something when I beat her in this event in 1970, with F.T.C. Lancshot Laser, as we had come to regard her as virtually unbeatable.

I am particularly grateful to Daisy for producing Auchtertyre Donna for me, who, although she never became a Field Trial Champion, was one of the most consistent bitches ever to run in Trials and the perfect epitome of that favourite shooting bitch from which Arkwright suggests we should breed.

F.T.C. Coppicewood Carla. I know very little about this bitch except for what I could see of her myself. I first saw her on Shadwell Heath where I was impressed with her wide, full pattern and a style so brilliant that it compensated for her rather dark, drab appearance. I thought she ran a good Trial but, as she was unknown, it appeared that the judges did not recognise the obvious quality in her. The following year she won an Open Stake, shortly followed by winning the Championship at Cromlix in January 1971. This was a most convincing win. All too often we have seen the Championship winner run a clean, simple Trial which any good Novice could have equalled, whilst better dogs encounter complications but, in this case, we were all convinced that the Championship was won by a quality bitch.

F.T.C. Bricksclose Scilla. Some years ago, a beautiful black and white Smut bitch came into my hands for further training and Trials. Scilla was just my type. Fast, stylish, happy and intelligent with just sufficient devilry in her to make her an adequate challenge. She was a fine bitch to shoot over, although lacking the drive, in really sharp low brambles, of Willie Snaffles and Sele.

I ran her in 18 Trials during her first season, winning 16 awards, most of them places. She ran a superb Championship at Clandeboye as a puppy, finally being thrown out of gear by a gun who, through lack of attention, failed to shoot a bird for her which she found during a crucial period of the run off but won a Diploma nevertheless.

Her owner took her over at the end of that season and for two years Scilla did nothing, but in her fourth season, bitch and handler seemed to find each other and a brilliant career ensued, Scilla winning six Open Stakes and a third in a Championship. Like Drumbro Daisy, whom she preceded, she gained the title for a time of 'The best bitch in the country'. True to the pattern of several brilliant bitches, Scilla has never produced a pup as good as herself, although she has been mated to several notable sires, but a grandson did win the 1973 American National.

F.T.C. Crowhill Raffle. Farsightedness is an essential quality in the breeder of top class livestock, plus the ability to recognise the mating that has gone wrong and the ruthlessness to act accordingly.

The breeder of top class Ayrshires, upon observing a field of sub-standard heifers, does not breed from them on the strength of their illustrious pedigrees. They become beef.

Of like mind is a friend who at one time was a moor keeper in Yorkshire and is now a very successful gundog trainer. I used to spend some time with him when he lived on his West Riding moor, picking up a few grouse and shooting some rabbits and dogging about in general. Several years ago he asked me to find him a decently bred Springer pup, so I approached a breeder who had three bitches for sale, by a son of F.T.C. Willy of Barnacre out of a daughter of F.T.C. Pinehawk Sark. The wily breeder wanted to show the pups to me round and about his premises, where the hedges were riddled with rabbit runs, a fact I knew these eight-month-old pups would be perfectly aware of, so I requested that the pups should be loaded into his car and taken to 'the sand hole', a dry sandy area with a few Scots Pines and a bit of heather.

We tried the pups individually and one would not hunt at all, appearing nervous and inhibited. Another made some sort of attempt to hunt but the third got down to it quite well and had a natural quartering pattern, so this was obviously the one which went to Yorkshire. She made a good working bitch. Fast, wide and a deadly rabbit finder, a lovely retriever with a good mouth.

At this time Micklewood Story was a young Novice Stake winner in my kennels but he was much admired by my friend for his wide, graceful hunting method, his great speed and superb style, so requested a service for his bitch, Flirt. Story never made a top class sire but in this case the mating was a success, even though it did not produce another Story. The question eventually arose as to which sire should be used on the best of the bitch pups but there was little doubt in my friend's mind. He had always been a great admirer of Hales Smut, whom he considered a godsend, bringing a much needed *joie de vivre* into the Spaniel scene at a period when things were beginning to look rather tame. Discussing the amount of good Smut had done, he remarked: 'But we will lose it if we are not careful', so with no hesitation whatsoever he mated the bitch, Tart, back to her own grandsire, Smut. This line bred mating certainly worked as far as appearances went and a dog pup was retained which was a complete replica of Smut in conformation apart from a darker body coloration. Very soon, the Smut drive and style manifested itself but his owner never attends many Trials so the dog, Raffle, was seldom seen. However, he won his first Novice Stake and at three years of age won an Open, and was placed second in the Championship at Blenheim in 1972, by virtue of this qualification. The following year I only saw Raffle run one Trial, when dog and master parted company in the run off, then at five years of age, he won his essential second Stake. He ran a superb Trial at Elkstone in January 1974 and was subjected in both runs to heavy pressure of game, which he withstood in a manner that the detractors of the Smut line would have us believe would be impossible. He defeated the best and joined that small but exclusive number of Championship winners who can claim to be truly great dogs.

In a most lucid and analytical article, 'The Wonderful Family of Conygree Simon', an American friend, Paul Diegel, of Oregon, states that nearly every great dog leaves behind him one son who has the ability to pass on the excellent qualities of the line and poses the question at the end of his article 'Will it be that a son of Smut will carry on where he left off?'

So far no such son has proved itself. Story was virtually a failure. My son's Smut dog, Gwibernant Gi Bach, sired one Field Trial Champion before he died, aged four. Jonkit Joel went to America early in his career and F.T.C. Gwibernant Ashley Robb who is in my charge has sired some good ones but appears to be terribly dependent on the bitch he is mated to, so I would not term him pre-potent.

Spaniel people are only just beginning to sit up and take notice of Raffle, so could it be that we have found a successor to Smut?

GREAT BIRD DOGS

F.T.C. Blackfield Gem. I saw Gem run during one of my infrequent appearances at Pointer and Setter Trials in 1965. She was far faster than the other Pointers present, who worked at a steady canter. Gem really galloped, with a flashing style and a tail action which would have rivalled any Spaniel's.

She won four Open Stakes and the Championship in August 1968. As far as I can make out, she won nine firsts at Championship shows and a Reserve Challenge Certificate at eleven and a half years of age, although I must confess, I am not certain what a Challenge Certificate is!

The Moanruad Bird Dogs. It is very difficult to go back memory lane over 25 years and say who was the greatest and who were the ordinary dogs among the many which have passed through one's hands. One is always conscious of the fact that many dogs were sold or died before they reached their full potential, but when all is said and done I think the pride of place must go to the Irish Setter Int. F.T.C. New Square Red Lassie, as 'being the noblest Roman of them all'. She was a smallish bitch, very good-looking by working setter standards; she had a super nose, always carried a high head and had great intensity on point at a time when this trait was not predominant among Irish Setters. She was one of the few dogs in my experience who could go fast or slow, wide or narrow as the occasion demanded. She came from a very good line being by that very pre-potent sire and milestone of the breed The Blacksmith, and her dam Rena of Burtown, Field Trial Champion herself, was by the great International Champion Garry of Burtown. She only bred twice as she died at the early age of six years, but she left Moanruad Ambassador who become a Dual Champion Irish Setter in Canada, one of the greatest stud forces that there has been there, both in field and bench. At home she gave us Moanruad Admiral, Field Trial Champion himself and a very pre-potent and successful sire. Also Moanruad Sheila, an Open Stake Winner who herself founded a very good family of Irish Setters in the hands of the Rev. A. S. O'Connor of Dungannon whose prefix was Maytown. It is almost impossible to get a working or Field Trial Irish Setter in practically any country of the world which does not place directly to New Square Red Lassie.

In second place without a doubt must come the Pointer Field Trial Champion Moanruad Don. A dog bred from Swedish and Italian stock he was a big black and white who seemed to have the ability completely to demoralise any opponent against whom he was drawn. He outpaced them and cut them off from any ground likely to hold birds and they were reduced to the fact that they were only anxious to back. He was a very precise dog about birds and I and many others will recall that on one occasion he indicated, without moving his feet, two widely separated coveys of grouse on the Dublin Mountains. He always carried a high head, pointed with great style and intensity and was a good roder and always delivered his birds in the shortest possible time. He was not widely used at stud because many owners felt that he was almost too much dog, and they were afraid that the next step would be untrainable. This did not come about in fact. They tend to average out, and among his better gets in this country were Queen of Moanruad–a Pointer which became a Champion in both Ireland, France, Belgium and Italy. Also Mallow Road who became a Field Trial Champion of Ireland and was herself a successful dam. His brother Moanruad Dandy though not a trial dog himself, was used at stud in the absence of Don who was exported as a three-year-old. Moanruad Dandy was also a very successful sire and seemed to convey many of the traits of his more illustrious brother to his progeny.

In third place I would put the Irish Setter International Field Trial Champion Una Moanruad. She was a real Irish Setter in every way, in both looks and in temperament. She had great style in her gallop and on game, very high head and very good nose. She was very wilful and, if anything, lacked the ice cool brain of her great grandam. She was exported to Switzerland where she became a Champion and founded many good lines. Before she left for Switzerland she left one pup Moanruad Lone Survivor who himself was a very pre-potent stud and sire of the very important brood bitch Moanruad Leaf.

Next in line one must place the Irish Setter, International Field Trial Champion, Patricia of Killone. Patricia had much of the old red and white Irish Setter blood and had the race-horse Hyperion's colours in a white face, white socks and a white tipped tail. She lacked the blinding speed of some of the others but she was very precise around game, always gave the appearance as if she were on her job and looking for birds, and handled them as a true Irish Setter or great one would.

Closely following Patricia would be her brother, the all red Moanruad Dan. Dan was a very good dog, very consistent and equally good sire. He was exported to America at an early age where he became a top class grouse dog which at that time was and still is, a very scarce commodity in America. The ruffed grouse is not like the grouse in the heather but keeps to the woods, and is very touchy and consequently requires a dog that will stand back well with a very discerning nose and handling perfectly. His owner, Mr. McCluskey, who has a great experience of grouse dogs always claims that he was the best grouse dog in his 50 years of grouse shooting.

I would place next International Field Trial Champion Bena of Maytown, by Ballymac Eagle ex Sheila of Moanruad, a smallish bitch with great pace, drive and nose. A wonderful backer and her ground treatment was of mathematical precision. She could take game a long way off and had a great competitive spirit, so much so that we always felt that she realised what Field Trial Competition was all about.

Next in line I would place the International Field Trial Champion Knockmore Red Molly. She was not trained by me but bought in after winning an Open Stake. She had the great blinding pace that one associated with her line, a very, very, precise nose, and was able to find birds a long way off. In her day she was practically unbeatable. I will always recall the day that she won the Irish Championship as giving the nearest performance I have ever seen to what one might call perfection. She was a bitch of excitable temperament and was better on a one-day Trial than on a circuit of Trials on which she was inclined to warm up too much and perhaps lose her head. Moanruad Thistledown, another Irish Setter bitch by the great Portown Romeo out of Moanruad Sheila, won an Open Stake here in Ireland before being sold to France and became top Setter or Pointer in France at Grand Quete Trials in 1965, a position no Irish Setter has ever occupied.

The little bitch Moanruad Chilly Breeze was probably the best puppy I have ever owned. She became a Field Trial Champion as a puppy and was certainly the fastest dog I have ever owned. Great nose, great backer, very wide goer and easily handled, she was exported to Italy at an early age and made a big impression in Field Trials. The Pointer bitch International Champion Queen of Glengar was also a milestone of her breed. A very pre-potent dam, it is now impossible to get a Pointer in Ireland and some parts of the British Isles without one or two lines to Queen of Glengar. In her day she was practically unbeatable but on reflection she lacked the real courage of the top ones. She certainly was not as good as her dam, Butterfly Queen, but she did have a better brain. In all she combined all one would ever wish for in Pointers.

Next in line one must place Moanruad Sprite, an old-fashioned looking bitch with a box-like head. For real courage it would be hard to beat her. At an early age she broke the femur bone in her thigh yet she continued to run and win Trials with a steel pin in the bone. She had a very high head, great style on point, and a very, very long nose. Her real *forte* was roding out a tricky old cock. She became a Field Trial Champion in Ireland at an early age and looks like being a great producer, as her first litter all show great promise to Chess of Maytown.

There were many others but the author confines me to speaking about the great ones and we will leave it at that. *John Nash, Oola, Co. Limerick, Eire.*

SOME GREAT LABRADORS

Nearly 20 years ago, I received an issue of the *Kennel Gazette,* the official organ of the Kennel Club, which carried a report on the Kennel Club's Non Winner Retriever Stake. The Stake was won by a 21-month-old puppy called Galleywood Shot and a photograph of this dog portrayed him as a brilliantly alert looking individual. The judges' report described him as 'A dog with a brilliant future'. Whoever wrote these words must have either been in possession of a crystal ball, or an uncanny ability to appraise a young Retriever accurately as these words did indeed come true. Shot was born in February 1954 and was sired by F.T.C. Staindrop Murton Marksman out of Hiwood Peggy and on his dam's side, was a grandson of Dual Champion Staindrop Saighdear.

Shot, although undoubtedly a brilliant dog in his own right, had the good fortune throughout his working career to have a trainer and handler of outstanding merit, one who I would personally rate as one of the top two men in the country. Quite simply, Shot's trainer liked him, the dog reciprocated this affection and always gave his formidable best.

Shot's first Open Stake win was at the Herts., Beds. and Bucks. Retriever Society's meeting in 1956, very quickly gaining his title thereafter by winning the International Gundog League's Open Stake. In 1957 he came second in this event, after winning the Midland Counties Open. His crowning triumph that season was the winning of the Retriever Championship. One of the judges afterwards remarked that Shot did not go quite as hard as he could but kept bringing his bacon home when others failed, finally clinching matters by disappearing into a wood and returning with a waterlogged bird, always a most difficult retrieve as the bird rides low in the water and gives off little scent. This Championship followed a period of very heavy rains and many of the covert bottoms were under water.

This particular Championship also saw the come-back, out of retirement, of the great veteran, F.T.C. Grouseadee, who at about eight years of age, took Reserve prize in this event, his son F.T.C. Peteradee, winning third prize. Peter, himself, won the Championship at a later date.

Shot did not have a brilliant season in 1958, winning only three Certificates of Merit and a third in the Kennel Club Open Stakes but finishing the season by successfully defending his title and winning the Championship again, under appalling scenting conditions. In his first Championship, he demonstrated how he could get out, unsighted from his handler, make good his ground and find his game under his own initiative. In his second big event, he proved just how accurately he could be handled out on to virtually scentless birds, when good hunting dogs were coming unstuck.

Shot was used very extensively at stud and sired a satisfactory proportion of top winning stock. Truly, as an Irish friend would say, 'One of the milestones of the breed'.

From the same kennels as Shot came F.T.C. Hiwood Dipper. Dipper was born in January 1956, by Championship winner F.T.C. Greatford Teal, out of a half-sister to Shot, F.T.C. Hiwood Gypsy. Dipper was an incredibly stylish, forceful retriever, not afraid of the rough stuff and had a most unusual career, inasmuch as he matured fairly early but carried on winning for six seasons, finally winning a Certificate of Merit when close on his eighth birthday. As a youngster, he did little in Non Winner Stakes, was placed second at the Gamekeepers' National Association's Trials, then went straight into Open Stakes, winning the International Gundog League's Open Stake and placed second in the Herts., Beds. and Bucks., finishing a successful first season by gaining a Diploma in the Championship.

It is a comfortable feeling for a handler to have the first leg of a title under his or her belt at the end of a puppy's first season. That second Stake then never seems quite so far away.

Dipper soon rectified this in 1958, winning the Midland Counties Trial and confirming his title by winning the Gamekeepers' Association shortly afterwards. A dog, of course, only requires two Open Stakes to become a Field Trial Champion but it is always satisfactory to win a third Stake. It tends to prove that the first two were not flukes.

In 1959, Dipper successfully defended his cups at the Midland Counties Meeting by winning this Trial for the second year running, finishing the season with a Diploma in the Championship.

In 1960, he won the Midland Counties Trial for the third year running and later that year won the Championship at Sutton Scotney. This estate must be the most southerly venue for the Retriever Championship and it is interesting to record that, on this occasion, second place was won by the most northerly contender, F.T.C. Ruro Snipe.

Dipper did not do much thereafter. He defended his title in 1961 and was awarded a Diploma and ran again in 1962, winning a couple of thirds and a Certificate.

Scotland has produced some excellent Labradors, consistently over the years. Mrs. Esther Thomson, widow of the late Colin Thomson, won the Retriever Championship several years ago with her F.T.C. Rivington Braeroy Swift and this dog's gamekeeper handler gave the lie to the theory that Trial dogs are not used for ordinary shooting purposes by describing him as 'Part of my shooting day equipment'.

But of all the Scottish kennels of post-war years, the name Glenfarg stands out like a beacon. This kennel produced many Field Trial Champions and won the Retriever Championship at least twice but it would appear that Glenfarg Skid, born January 1957, by F.T.C. Glenhead Zuider out of Ballyduff Eastwalton Sloe, must rank as one of the most consistent Glenfarg dogs.

As a puppy, Skid won the North Western Counties Novice Stake, held in the Longtown area of the Border country. I was at this Trial myself and saw Skid perform extremely well. He was a big, forceful masculine looking dog. He won a second in an Open Stake in Scotland that season and won his first Open Stake at the Labrador Club of Scotland's Trials at Cromlix in 1962, taking a diploma in the Championship that year. He was made up in 1963 by winning the Strathmore Working Gundog Club's Trials and concluded the season by winning the

Retriever Championship, defending his title in 1964 and being placed Reserve. A fine specimen from a kennel which, I believe at one point in time, had seven living Field Trial Champions under its roof.

SOME GREAT COCKERS

I have already dealt in detail with several great Cockers in *The Complete Book of Gundogs in Britain*, edited by Tony Jackson (Barrie & Jenkins), so as I dislike going over the same ground twice, I will skim briefly over this topic and deal with some great Cockers collectively.

The first great Cocker I saw was F.T.C. Jordieland Bunty, a very small, very clever blue roan bitch who won, the Cocker Championship at Grimsthorpe Park in Lincolnshire in January 1957.

Running second to her on this occasion was F.T.C. Carswell Solomon, a big Springer-like dog of vast experience handled to perfection by the late John MacIntyre. Solomon won several Cocker Stakes and also had the distinction of winning two Any Variety Stakes in competition with English Springers. He also ran second the following season to F.T.C. Buoy of Elan in the Cocker Championship held at Presaddfed, Anglesey, who on the Grimsthorpe occasion, finished Reserve under the expert handling of the late John Forbes.

Buoy himself must go down in history as one of the greatest Cockers of all time. Hard going, calm, clever and kind, Buoy represented all that was best in his breed, winning the Championships in 1955 and 1958. He must surely be one of the most potent stud forces in the Cocker world, as not only did he sire several Field Trial Champions but many good Cockers go back to him on three or four lines, which is the acid test of a stud dog's soundness. Some sires can sire good enough stock but should one line breed to them, peculiarities can arise in the resultant progeny, which points to a degree of unsoundness in the background of the dog.

Another of John Forbes' great Field Trial Champions was Simon of Elan, who won the Championships in 1960 and 1961. Simon really could move with a true Cocker action but he was a hot one and John did extremely well, at such an advanced age, to stay with Simon at all.

By F.T.C. Merlin Micky but going back to Buoy on his

dam's side, was the late Lady Auckland's F.T.C. Wilfred of Cromlix. Wilfred was another hot dog who could take the law into his own hands when the opportunity presented itself but finding his unshot game in positive fashion and retrieving with precision. He won the Championship at Woburn in 1967, was a class dog who could go as hard as any Springer, and came back to take Reserve in 1970.

No Cocker of any great note came to the top for some years after Wilfred won in 1967. F.T.C. Templebar Blackie and F.T.C. Monnow Mayfly ran consistently during this period but both were rather unfortunate in the Championships they competed in.

Then, like a miniature Hales Smut, Speckle of Ardoon burst like a bomb on the Cocker stage. Speckle, known to some as 'the Sele of the Cockers' and 'The Polecat' to us at home, was sired by an old Irish show dog out of an Elan bitch who never seemed inclined to do much work. But Speckle is a freak of nature. In temperament and drive, she is closer to the Springer, Sele, than any Springer I have ever handled since Sele. As a youngster in training, she had an almost berserk quality and was so hot that had she not possessed an exception- ally stable underlying temperament, it would have been quite impossible to train her. As it was, I had to pull out everything that a succession of determined Springers had taught me in order to get through to her and channel this fantastic ability.

She is a most exciting bitch to handle and shoot over but is basically extraordinarily honest. There is nothing crafty or underhanded about her and any time she has overstepped the mark it has been due to sheer exuberance. Fortunately such happenings have been rare and have occurred when I have been shooting over her, giving me the opportunity to convince her that in spite of advancing middle age I can still cover the terrain in her direction at a reasonable speed.

Speckle has stimulated as much interest as Hales Smut but has attracted less criticism. In fact she is not a controversial creature at all and only one lady handler of my acquaintance has ever suggested she is less than brilliant, basing her comments on one isolated Trial in Speckle's first season, when, after a period of consistent winning, she had an 'off' day, going ragged, missing game and refusing to handle on a blind retrieve. She has restored a certain measure of dignity to the Cocker as a breed at a period of time when the Cocker was at a rather low ebb and the critics were issuing the maximum amount of damaging publicity.

At one time I imagined Speckle was the best Cocker since the war but in the light of continued success, it does not cause me the slightest embarrassment to state that I believe she is the best Cocker of all time. She has won nine Open Stakes and three consecutive Championships, an all-time record and in addition she won the Game Fair Spaniel Tests in 1972, which although only a Test, proved her versatility as the majority of Cockers refuse to perform at Tests and the few that do cannot normally hold a candle to the Springers.

Speckle is not yet five years of age and belongs to the present as well as the past. She is in her kennel, alert and dangerous still and as my book is now finished, I will go and feed her.

Index

223